Appalachia's Path
to Dependency

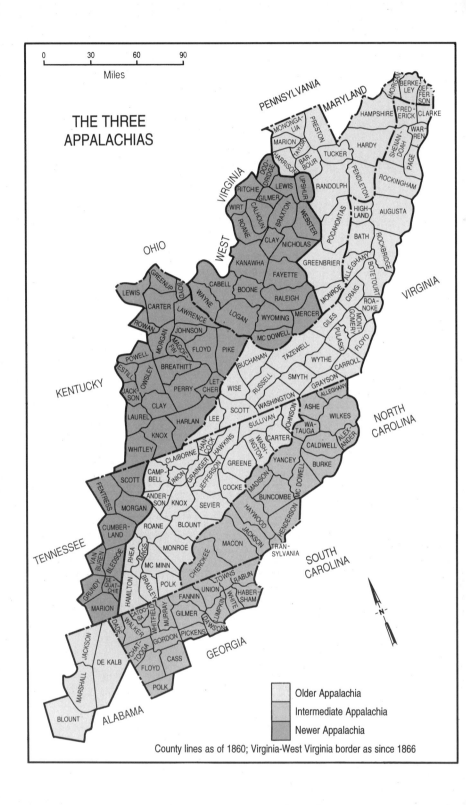

THE THREE
APPALACHIAS

County lines as of 1860; Virginia-West Virginia border as since 1866

Older Appalachia
Intermediate Appalachia
Newer Appalachia

APPALACHIA'S PATH TO DEPENDENCY

Rethinking a Region's Economic History 1730–1940

PAUL SALSTROM

THE UNIVERSITY PRESS OF KENTUCKY

Publication of this volume was made possible in part by a grant
from the National Endowment for the Humanities.

Editorial and Sales Offices: The University Press of Kentucky,
663 South Limestone, Lexington, Kentucky 40508-4008

Frontispiece: Map from Robert D. Mitchell, ed., *Appalachian Frontiers:
Settlement, Society, and Development in the Preindustrial Era*
(Lexington: University Press of Kentucky, 1991)

Library of Congress Cataloging-in-Publication Data

Salstrom, Paul
    Appalachia's path to dependency : rethinking a region's economic
history, 1730-1940 / Paul Salstrom.
        p. cm.
    Includes bibliographical references and index.
    ISBN 0-8131-1860-3 (cloth : alk. paper)—ISBN 0-8131-0868-3 (pbk :
alk. paper)
    1. Appalachian Region, Southern—Economic conditions.
2. Appalachian Region, Southern—Social conditions. 3. Poor—
Appalachian Region, Southern—History. I. Title.
HC107.A127S24   1994
330.974—dc20   93-39818

Contents

Tables and Figure

Preface

In 1972 I moved to a county in rural Appalachia, bought land there, and read Harry Caudill's book *Night Comes to the Cumberlands*. At that time I knew scores of other young people doing the same thing. It is now known that *thousands* of others did that, including reading Harry Caudill's book, which by then was already nine years old but to us seemed very new. Some of the "homesteaders" of that day, including my younger brother and his wife, have stayed on the land. Most, however, have resumed mainstream behavior. My own desire to expound the joys of homesteading helped draw me away quite soon. In 1975 an elderly friend named Mildred Loomis, director of a back-to-the-land group called the School of Living, asked me to edit that group's monthly magazine *Green Revolution*. To produce the magazine, I began working at a labor-history press in Huntington, West Virginia, called Appalachian Movement Press. In 1978, as that marginal operation itself became history, I took the further step "back in" of returning to school. After receiving a work-experience B.A. from Marshall University in Huntington, and then starting graduate work at Southern Illinois University, my wife suggested we sell our goats and move to a big city. That landed us at Brandeis University near Boston, where this book was first drafted with no little nostalgia for the hills. Like many other books, it tries to continue what Harry Caudill started, piecing together the puzzle of how Appalachia became the way it is.

Meanwhile however, during the 1980s, Appalachia changed (again). In a 1990 interview, John Gaventa of the Highlander Research and Education Center said:

I think it's a whole new period for Appalachia. I think much of our work over the last 20 years has been around trying to get a fairer share of the pie. Now we find that the shape of the pie is changing altogether. It's a whole new ball game, and it poses whole new questions about what economic development ought to be.

You see the crisis now not just in what industries are leaving. You see it in what new jobs are coming in. Because people are so desperate, those jobs are lower paying. There's fewer unions, worse benefits than were there before. The region's moving backwards economically. (John Gaventa, quoted in Woodside, "Creating the Path as You Go," 20.)

This final version of what started as a dissertation will try to reinterpret the history of Appalachia in the light of what Gaventa calls "new questions about what economic development ought to be." It will ponder Appalachia's history, especially its changing relations with other U.S. regions and with the national economy. It will look at Appalachia's past in light of challenges that the region now faces and in light of today's *national* economic challenges—such as our uncompetitive industries, adverse trade balances, and growing deficits.

This book is an extended argument covering the entire course of Appalachia's economic history since white settlement began. The fulcrum of its argument is Appalachia's increasing vulnerability to capitalist development during the second half of the nineteenth century. To understand Appalachia's vulnerability to capitalism we must understand how ill matched the values of most rural Appalachian people were with the industrial transformation that occurred in their midst. Appalachia's early settlers understood entrepreneurship—often they manifested it dramatically—but they usually did so within the context of what I will call their local subsistence-barter-and-borrow networks. In the absence of very much money, and so long as available land continued to be plentiful, their local subsistence-barter-and-borrow systems were successful expedients. Later, however, and although their low-money systems continued to help support them, they began to hire out much of their labor to an industrialization that depended on outside financing and outside decision making. Gradually, for many of them, even their traditional subsistence life-style grew dependent on the extra income they were earning from wage work.

In other words, while their subsistence life-style was helping to subsidize, and to maximize, Appalachia's industrialization, that industrialization was in turn helping to subsidize and maximize subsistence activities in Appalachia. Although the amount of subsistence farming per family decreased, the total amount of subsistence farming in the region grew through a population explosion. Thus the region's dependence on outside-financed industry grew.

This book discusses a particular kind of dependency: economic. It does not broach questions concerning cultural or psychological dependency.

In and of itself, economic dependency does not automatically make people poor. A much-quoted definition comes from Theotonio Dos Santos:

> By dependency we mean a situation in which the economy of certain countries is conditioned by the development and expansion of another economy to which the former is subjected. The relation of interdependence between two or more economies, and between these and world trade, assumes the form of dependency when some countries (the dominant ones) can expand and be self-sustaining, while other countries (the dependent ones) can do this only as a reflection of that expansion, which can have either a positive or negative effect on their immediate development. (Theotonio Dos Santos, quoted in Richard White, *The Roots of Dependency,* xvii.)

The insight behind dependency theory is that economic development can be hampered not only by local obstacles but also by obstacles that are external to a region or country. Wherever development has been impeded mainly by local obstacles, a path toward development can be illuminated by modernization theory, which emphasizes the importing of outside values, outside institutions, technology, and capital. But in regions or countries in which the main obstacles to development have been *external,* dependency theory can aid understanding better than can modernization theory.

Economic dependency does not necessarily prevent all forms of development. It prevents *independent* development. Meanwhile it can actively foster dependent development in some economic sectors—such as in Appalachia's extractive sector. In other sectors it can foster *un*development—such as in Appalachia's agriculture, manufacturing, and finance. Appalachia's extractive industries were (and still are) almost entirely dependent on outside capital. This has fostered dependent development, with attendant alliances between outside capitalists and a major proportion of the region's own elite. But, by contrast, in parts of Appalachia that are simply *un*developed, depletion has outweighed *any* form of development (even dependent development) as earlier local enterprises have found themselves unable to compete with external enterprises, and as most of those areas' remaining assets have then been used to maintain mere subsistence.

Thinking about Appalachia in this way raises more questions than a single book can address. The debate over the source of Appalachia's economic problems has been going strong since *Night Comes to the Cumberlands* appeared in 1963, and now even more questions are "on the table." The keys to this book are (1) its new three-part subregional division of Appalachia, which reflects the sequence that settlement followed inside the region; (2) its fusion of behavior with grassroots economic conditions to illuminate mentality; and (3) its comparative approach, drawing on comparisons and examining economic relationships between Appalachia and other parts of the United States and the world.

The Appalachia examined in this book is southern Appalachia, extending from Virginia and West Virginia south to the northern fringes of Georgia and Alabama. (See frontispiece map.) This boundary encompasses 190 counties in 7 states and has provided a much-used definition of the region since the publication (in 1962) of *The Southern Appalachian Region: A Survey,* edited by Thomas R. Ford. I will divide the counties into three subregions—Older Appalachia, Intermediate Appalachia, and Newer Appalachia—reflecting the sequence in which the various parts of the region became well settled and passed beyond their initial frontier conditions.

Many mountain people, archivists, librarians, friends, and others have furthered this study. It is a pleasure to thank my Brandeis University advisor Stephen A. Schuker (now of the University of Virginia) and his two colleagues on the dissertation committee, Donald Worster (now of the University of Kansas) and the late Frank Freidel. Others at and around Brandeis who advised me include Rudolph Binion, James Matthew Gallman and Thomas Pegram (both now at Loyola College in Baltimore), John S. Hill (now at Ohio State), June Namias (now at the University of Alaska in Anchorage), John E. Schrecker, and Alan Taylor (now at Boston University). My typing at Brandeis was efficiently handled by Elaine Herrmann, and my typing in West Virginia by David Imhoff.

Among Appalachian specialists, Robert D. Mitchell and Altina L. Waller have helped me more than I can ever hope to reciprocate. Many other Appalachian specialists have also sustained this project with their interest and advice, particularly Dwight B. Billings, H. Tyler Blethen,

Martin Crawford, Rodger Cunningham, Ronald D Eller, Steve Fisher, Lucy K. Gump, John C. Inscoe, Loyal Jones, Anne Mayhew, Gordon B. McKinney, James E. Murphy, Mary Beth Pudup, Barbara Ellen Smith, Jeff Todd Titon, John Craft Taylor, Paul J. Weingartner, John Alexander Williams, and Curtis W. Wood.

In Lincoln County, West Virginia, I wish to thank Odell Adkins; Dorothy Black; Jim and Connie Chojnacki; Ray Elkins; Boyd and Ruth Hogbin; Flossie Lawson; Ken and Norris Lucas; Ric McDowell; Woodrow and Beatrice Mosley; Charles Ott; Charles and Phyllis Pack; the Spooner family; Jim and Donna Stone; John, Jan, Seoka, and Matt Salstrom; and Home Place, Inc. Others who helped me there have passed on: Henry and Anna Baker, Ray Gene Black, Raymond and Freeda Black, Hallie and Edith Edwards, Mabel Elkins, Almond and Glena Lewis, Rev. Buster Lovejoy, Spec and Virginia McComas, and Nancy Murphy. They practiced voluntary reciprocity and explained it to me.

I appreciate help and ideas from my former colleagues at Appalachian Movement Press, especially Charles Berry, Thomas W. Gibbs, Miriam Ralston and the staff of *MAW Magazine,* and Tom Woodruff (now of the National Hospital Workers Union).

At Marshall University I was helped by Alan B. Gould, Barbara R. James, Gina Kates, Karen Li Simpkins, and David R. Woodward.

At West Virginia University I received valuable assistance not only from the Appalachian gold mine Ronald L. Lewis but also from his fellow historians James Cook, Jeff Cook, Ken Fones-Wolf, John C. Hennen, Wilbert Jenkins (now of Temple University), Emory L. Kemp, John Allen Maxwell, John R. McKivigan, Billy Joe Peyton, Paul Rakes, Barbara Rasmussen, Thomas Robertson, Phil Ross, John C. Super, and Michael E. Workman. At West Virginia University's College of Agriculture and Forestry, I was aided by Randy Childs, Dale Colyer, Keith Dix, Jerald J. Fletcher, Stacy A. Gartin, Walter Labys, Layle D. Lawrence, John Lozier, Edna McBreen, Virgil J. Norton, Kerry S. Odell, Dennis K. Smith, Thomas F. Torries, and Steve Zaricki. There too the computer specialist Amy Van Zant moved things along.

Among librarians, especially helpful were Richard Crawford at the National Archives, Kim Iconis at Antioch College Library, Cora Teel and Leslie Brown at Marshall University Library, Jo. B. Brown at West Virginia University Library, and the staff librarians at WVU's remark able West Virginia and Regional History archive collection: David Bartlett, John Cuthbert, Harold Forbes, Randall Gooden, Martha Neville, Christy Venham, David Ware, and Daniel Williams. Scholarship is a communal enterprise.

During the rewriting stage, grants from the West Virginia Humanities Council and the Appalachian Studies fund of Berea College proved invaluable.

And finally, I wish to thank my present colleagues at the Mountaineer Policy Institute, especially Linda Cunningham, Richard diPretoro, Andrew Maier, Tom and Judy Rodd, Steven Schrom, and Joan Sims.

The result is dedicated to my parents and daughter.

Introduction: The Issue

> The issue is not whether analysis of regional differences . . . . should remain value free, but whose values and what values underlie the statement that one region suffers from regional disparity in comparison with another.
>
> —Ralph Matthews, *The Creation of Regional Dependency*

As of 1840, southern Appalachia figured as one of the most self-sufficient regions of the United States. By 1940 it had become one of the country's *least* self-sufficient regions.

Between 1880 and 1930 the southern mountains experienced a rapid transition toward industrialization. During that half century, the region's self-sufficiently in food production waned. Later, when Appalachia's industries faltered in the 1930s, the federal government provided relief on a massive scale. Relief became so extensive that it brought many mountaineers more economic stability than they had known for generations—since, or even before, industrialization had begun—but in the process it also made many of Appalachia's full-time farm families more dependent on regular money income than they had ever been. Since the Depression, federal welfare programs have been revived and maintained, constituting today a major component of the Appalachian region's income. In 1990 in West Virginia, for instance, 23.54 percent of total personal income consisted of transfer payments of some kind, whereas the overall U.S. average was only 14.98 percent.[1]

This book first surveys the origins of Appalachia's economic dependency within American market relations.[2] Then it examines the exacerbation of that dependency through federal political acts. Next it discusses why the region's dependency was further increased by industrialization and, finally, why its dependency was not reduced by the New Deal of the 1930s.

Along the way, economic relationships are explored and comparisons are broached. For almost a generation now, Appalachian scholars have suggested similarities between the economic history of the mountains and the economic history of colonial states in the Third World. Politically, of course, Appalachia has never been a colony in a formal sense. The region's disadvantaged position is largely a result of market forces—albeit those market forces were partly shaped by political acts that discriminated against Appalachia and other financially "peripheral" regions of the United States.

So rather than *colonial*, the adjective *peripheral* best describes Appalachia's economic position. Although it is not on the fringe of the international economy but within a "center" capitalist country, Appalachia since the middle of the nineteenth century has increasingly been relegated to the periphery of America's market economy.

Today scholars generally accept the designation of Appalachia as an economic periphery. But with this adoption of the "center-periphery" model, the call for a "decolonization" of Appalachia has by no means grown irrelevant. In particular, the 1970s' model of "internal colonialism" has contributed to our understanding.[3] But now we should probe further. It is time to search for the economic logic behind Appalachia's situation. Keeping in mind the center-periphery model, I think we should delve into Appalachia's past and ask questions about the day-to-day logic of people's economic choices. There are conundrums facing Appalachia today that such historical dredging can help us understand. Asking about the extent of economic enterprise, economic security, and family commitment in the past—and asking whether these things were mutually compatible—can help us understand what is happening in the region today. Trying to reconstruct the economic logic that underlaid people's earlier choices might help alert us to unheralded options available today.

Trying to reconstruct earlier generations' economic mentality need not be a highly theoretical exercise. We wish access, after all, to the thinking of ordinary people. We'd like to see their situation through their eyes. In Appalachia's preindustrial era—roughly before 1880—one obvious fact about farming was that it had to almost entirely provide the subsistence of the families who were farming. No contradiction existed between market farming and this necessary subsistence farming, for Appalachia's most important farm products were livestock and grains, which were just as suitable for supplying outside markets as they were for home consumption.[4]

Appalachia's preindustrial era was not monolithic, however. Two distinct stages can be identified—an *earlier* (frontier) and a *later* (postfrontier) stage. Frontier preindustrial conditions were quite unlike postfrontier conditions that were still preindustrial. Appalachia's earlier, frontier forests and clearings provided a very easy subsistence and relatively easy sources of extra income through hunting, gathering, and the raising of marketable livestock. Thus Appalachia's frontier settlers could afford to be speculative and entrepreneurial without risking their underlying subsistence—whereas under later, postfrontier conditions, speculation and enterprise became luxuries that only an emerging elite of better-off mountaineers could afford. So an increasing dichotomy between the wealth and mentality of emerging "upper" and "lower" classes marked the later preindustrial stage. Despite no major industrialization, a preindustrial transformation had occurred. It resulted from four main causes: (1) expansion of the population, (2) depletion of the resource base, (3) destruction caused by the Civil War, and (4) federal homesteading and banking legislation enacted during the Civil War.

The earlier and later preindustrial stages are defined primarily by conditions, not by dates. The earlier stage began when Appalachia's white settlement first began, about 1730, but its termination cannot be tidily dated. It ended when and as frontier conditions ended in the region's various districts. In the Shenandoah Valley, for instance, which was where Appalachia's white settlement first began, the frontier stage was already over by 1776.[5] But in the region's last-settled section—the hilly Appalachian Plateau west of the mountains proper—the frontier stage did not end until the 1880s. Thus the later preindustrial stage was beginning in the Shenandoah Valley by the time of the revolutionary war, but it did not reach across the entire Appalachian Plateau until after the Civil War.

Some strands of Appalachia's dependency reach back to the market relations that existed even during the beginnings of white settlement in the region's wide and fertile valleys. As settlement covered the Great Appalachian Valley and frontier conditions steadily receded, and as settlement then turned southeastward into the Carolina and Georgia mountains and finally turned northwestward into the even less hospitable Plateau country, a demographic story flowed smoothly until all of Appalachia's frontiers were in use. Then the demographic story became one of congestion. Following the Civil War, a veritable population explosion on the Plateau precipitated Appalachia's own regional "closing of the frontier"—the closing of a frontier that long since had grown surrounded by thicker settlement. This closing threatened the Plateau subregion economically when its population growth barely slowed

Table 1. Population Growth in Appalachia's Subregions and in the
Midwest (the Old Northwest), 1790s–1940s

Decade	Older Appalachia (%)	Intermediate Appalachia (%)	Newer Appalachia (%)	Ohio, Indiana, Illinois, Michigan, & Wisconsin (%)
1790s	57.7	58.5	ca. 482.6	n.a.
1800s	21.1	39.0	78.7	433.9
1810s	23.6	ca. 28.4	108.4	191.1
1820s	30.1	ca. 65.0	58.0	85.4
1830s	13.0	ca. 60.0	39.0	99.0
1840s	27.4	64.0	62.3	54.7
1850s	13.2	30.5	48.6	53.1
1860s	6.8	9.6	17.7	31.7
1870s	34.1	34.7	46.2	22.8
1880s	20.1	22.3	32.7	20.3
1890s	19.2	16.1	24.2	18.6
1900s	15.0	6.4	32.8	14.2
1910s	12.4	7.1	26.5	17.7
1920s	11.7	17.5	19.7	17.8
1930s	10.7	16.7	17.4	5.3
1940s	13.8	8.8	4.1	14.2

NOTE: Early figures often approximate due to slight boundary variations.

SOURCE: United States Censuses of Population, 1790–1950.

despite signs of an approaching Malthusian crisis. Because of this, the *heart* of Appalachia's dependency as it has grown to major proportions since the Civil War is rooted in the economic life of Appalachia's Plateau subregion.

During the earlier, flowing part of the demographic story, ample outlets existed for surplus population. As late as the 1920s, in fact, the earlier-settled Valley subregion was still sending many migrants into the Plateau subregion.[6] What is loosely called the Great Appalachian

Valley (including its parallel valleys) will thus be labeled here Older Appalachia, the subregion settled first (see map).[7] In this Older Appalachia, a combination of out-migration and reduced family size drastically slowed the rate of population growth by the turn of the twentieth century. By the time World War I finally brought a significant level of industrialization to Older Appalachia, a demographic equilibrium had been achieved. (See table 1 for decennial population growth rates.)

The contrast with the Appalachian Plateau, which I will call Newer Appalachia (see map), could not have been greater. The Plateau was Appalachia's least accessible and last-settled part. No demographic equilibrium was even in sight by the time the Plateau's industrialization began. Admittedly, industrialization grew extensive here several decades earlier (in the 1880s) than it did in the Older subregion (the 1910s), but the Plateau's living-standard indicators had begun plummeting downward *prior* to any major industrialization. Plateau Appalachia can illustrate Richard Wilkinson's thesis in his book *Poverty and Progress* that a "population's increasingly exploitable situation . . . provides the basis for the growth of capitalist institutions."[8]

What *else* did it take to get industrialization under way in Appalachia's Plateau subregion? Besides the fall that occurred there in many people's living standards, that subregion held magnificent virgin forests and plentiful bituminous coal, much of the coal of high quality by steel-making standards. Beyond such resources, industrialization on the Plateau also required a capitalist mentality among some at least of the local population. The post-1880 era would see capitalist relations of production grow wherever industrialization took hold, and it would see capitalist attitudes spread among many local people who had some capital (or, more commonly, who had major land holdings) that they could invest in development.

Meanwhile, among the bulk of the population, which had little more than its labor to invest in development, and which thus tended to pursue development by labor-intensive means, the growth of capitalist relations did not inspire much adoption of capitalist values. Indeed, for most of Appalachia's people, the industrialization era may well have intensified both the practice and the attitude of voluntary reciprocity within their own "family groups." Capitalist relations and local mentality were related, of course, but often in Appalachia they were related antithetically. As we go on, therefore, the question of mentality will be examined in its own separate chapter (chapter 3), which treats mentality separately from the transformation of economic relations.

Chapter 1 discusses Appalachia's economic situation up to 1860. The inauguration of the federal agricultural census in 1840 allows calculations from then on of Appalachia's agricultural wealth and production per capita. During the 1840–1860 period, considerable decline occurred (per capita) in Appalachia's farm wealth and production—particularly on the Appalachian Plateau (Newer Appalachia).

Chapter 2, on the 1860–1880 period, finds that Appalachia's per capita farm production continued to plummet. Agricultural competition from the Midwest, which experienced per capita increases in farm output during the same period, lowered the ability of Appalachia to sell its farm produce. Cheap midwestern food redounded adversely on Appalachia, and that effect was accelerated by the post-1862 federal policy of dispensing free western homestead and railroad lands beyond the Mississippi River. Appalachia's growing commercial disadvantage was further aggravated by the post-1865 federal policy of inhibiting the creation of currency. Appalachia's farmers increasingly found their options narrowed to labor-intensive subsistence farming, which required them to continue raising large families at a time when most of America's farm families were turning toward more capital-intensive farming that allowed smaller families. Subsistence farming can gain no access to capital, of course, because its products are not sold. Even mere crop loans could never be repaid. So uncompetitive did Appalachia become in marketing farm produce that well before 1900, the region's nonfarm population was being provisioned in large measure from the Midwest. Toward the end of chapter 2, I will interpret this agricultural decline within W. Arthur Lewis's theory of why capital-poor countries (or in our case, regions) often grow economically dependent.

Chapter 3, as mentioned, discusses mentality. My argument here applies not only to Appalachia but also to North America generally. When the region's (and the continent's) resources were still abundant and its population still sparse, a spirit of enterprise was widely diffused. This manifested in entrepreneurial labor investments as well as entrepreneurial capital investments. But then followed a "regression" (in terms of our usual one-way model)[9] in which growing scarcity forced most people to become less enterprising and to concentrate instead on achieving their basic subsistence. These two distinct stages—the earlier characterized by an enterprising mentality, the later by rising subsistence problems—correspond to the earlier and later stages into which I divide Appalachia's overall preindustrial (pre-1880) era.

Appalachia's two preindustrial suberas began and ended at different times in different areas. The area settled first, the Shenandoah Valley, was opened about 1730 when the thirteen colonies were on the verge of unprecedented population growth. By 1776, frontier seekers were moving to adjacent valleys, to central North Carolina, to eastern Tennessee, and to central Kentucky,[10] then to western North Carolina, northeastern Alabama, northern Georgia, and, finally, to Appalachia's Plateau subregion of western West Virginia, eastern Kentucky, and east-central Tennessee. As each of those areas saw its frontier stage end it also saw entrepreneurial enthusiasm shrink because most people's subsistence needs kept growing harder to meet. Trying to understand these people and the choices they made is fascinating work.

Recently our understanding of preindustrial America has been advanced by a strategy of research and interpretation called the "new rural history." Several writers have applied new-rural-history methods to the study of Appalachia. One book-length case study concerns the Shenandoah Valley,[11] another nibbles at Appalachia's southern edge in Georgia,[12] and yet a third applies new-rural-history methods to understanding the Hatfield-McCoy feud that troubled the heart of Plateau Appalachia in the Tug Fork Valley where West Virginia meets Kentucky.[13]

The new-rural-history methods can help us share empathetically in the mentality of Appalachia's early people. That does not mean, however, that old-fashioned political economy can now be cast aside. When it comes to political economy, in fact, Appalachian scholarship is still surprisingly incomplete—overlooking, for instance, the effect of banking regulations on the region's development. In the mid-1810s, the mid-1830s, and throughout the 1850s, capital was accessible to a larger proportion of America's people than it was during the intervening periods. An authority on public-land sales notes that in the mid-1830s, "even squatters along the frontier participated" in the "speculative conflagration" going on there. "All expected to profit," he adds.[14] In the years 1837–1840, what was called a "free banking movement" appeared in the United States, and, partly as a result, credit was unusually easy to obtain in most of the country by the early 1850s. Also during the 1850s, the use of capital in frontier areas tended to be apportioned more efficiently than it previously had been.[15] Finally in 1865, however, Congress abolished the locally regulated creation of banknotes by imposing a prohibitive 10 percent federal tax (effective 1 July 1866) on the dispersal by any bank of banknotes issued by a non-nationally regulated bank.

This restriction of currency-issuing power made the financing of development in regions like Appalachia increasingly beholden to centers that, thanks to their earlier capital accumulation, were now authorized to create a greater percentage of new banknotes. And remember that Plateau Appalachia still consisted largely of frontier areas in 1865. Thereafter the Plateau (and to a lesser extent even the earliest-settled part of Appalachia, the Valley subregion) became increasingly dependent on outside sources for development capital. The Plateau's large coal operators, even indigenous ones, depended for capital largely on northern investors. Relatively little coal money was controlled within Plateau Appalachia except what was distributed as wages. And, at that, many miners were paid in company scrip for exclusive use in company stores. Thus the self-creation of capital for self-determined development was largely denied to Plateau Appalachia by older areas that had insisted on it for themselves in their own early years but were now federally granted a preponderant right to issue money for (and reap interest and profits from) the rest of the country.

Although capital for industrialization came mainly from outside Appalachia, the labor for it came primarily from the region's poorer farmers, supplemented by large newcomer minorities of southern blacks and European immigrants. After the Civil War, Appalachia's growing number of hard-pressed farmers deviated from the course of action that such farmers tended to follow elsewhere in the United States. Elsewhere, most hard-pressed farmers were producing fewer products for their own subsistence needs and were producing more to sell—or else were abandoning farming altogether and migrating to wage jobs in the nation's cities. In Appalachia, by contrast, wage jobs came to farmers in the countryside. Many of the region's farmers accepted low-paying jobs offered them near home by timber and coal operators, and then, to supplement this income, they continued subsistence farming. From their own perspective, they probably saw themselves as starting wage work in order to supplement their farm income. In any case, their strategy of economic development emphasized labor investment rather than emphasizing the capital investment for which capitalism reserves its largest rewards. Within their own local subsistence-barter-and-borrow systems, by contrast, the most beneficial form of economic investment had been (and remained) labor investment rather than capital investment.[16]

When I speak of Appalachia's low-paid labor in this book, bear also in mind that most of Appalachia's people were embedded in localized economic systems propelled by subsistence agriculture and reciprocity. Thus *they* at least valued labor highly. When they brought their labor into the new coal mines—literally into the bowels of capitalist enterprise—mountain farmers were bringing something they valued more highly than did their employers. Gradually they realized this, and their initial loyalty to their employers melted away. They came to work merely for the wages that work brought. Class antagonism then took root in Appalachia—though it often exhibited peculiarities as the region's two economic systems with their respective value systems coexisted, sometimes in a state of mutual incomprehension.

Not all of the incomprehension has been dispelled. Daniel Vickers recently commented that "our knowledge of economic behavior and social structure in early America has far outdistanced our understanding of the values that infused them."[17] In the 1990s our growing awareness of problems caused by the industrial revolution has prompted us to ponder why industrialization occurred in the first place. Our own personal commitment to "limits to growth" or, alternately, to "entrepreneurship" may well influence our personal evaluation of the industrial revolution. But today's hindsight does not necessarily give us any insight into the values held by early Americans themselves—even by those early Americans who immersed themselves in commerce or who initiated America's industrialization. Daniel Vickers points out that an "obsession with competency troubled early Americans far more than worries about the legitimacy of commerce." (A "competency" was defined as a resource base adequate to support one's self or one's family.) And Vickers adds that although a competency was a "superficially benign ideal," it "was, in fact, the source of deep social tensions that . . . people managed only with difficulty to control."[18]

Similarly, David F. Weiman speaks of a "fundamental tension among rural households between their bourgeois ethic of private accumulation and the kin and communal relations that structured their private economic activities."[19] That is why, to rethink Appalachia's economic history, I am separating questions about mentality from descriptions of behavior. How Appalachia became an arena for capitalism can only be explained by describing behavior. Changes in mentality accompanied the behavioral changes, but they did not cause them. For instance, within a subsistence-barter-and-borrow economic environment, entrepreneurs tended to invest labor rather than capital. The reasons capital investment nonetheless became more profitable in Appalachia than labor investment have little to do with values, with mentality. The reasons concern behavior.

Appalachia was filled with people whose values—values such as voluntary reciprocity—kept their subsistence-barter-and-borrow systems going. Let me hasten to emphasize, however, that Appalachia's local subsistence-barter-and-borrow systems did not deprive people of rewards for enterprise. Auspicious conditions could make those people just as entrepreneurial as John D. Rockefeller. I plan to show in chapter 2 that Devil Anse Hatfield, of feuding fame, was highly entrepreneurial although he never handled more than a pittance of money.

In that case, you may ask, what causes subsistence-barter-and-borrow systems to pervade certain areas (such as early Appalachia) instead of the capitalist system? The cause is simply a paucity of money in those areas. We could call subsistence-barter-and-borrow systems mere expedients—if we understand that capitalism too is merely an expedient. And within capitalism, just as within the low-money systems, objective conditions can inspire a preoccupation with providing subsistence and family security. When that is what people need—when survival strategies demand priority—capitalists lose their enterprising spirit as fast as Primitive Baptists do. Within the capitalist system, capital can be merely a means to acquire one's subsistence, just as (contrariwise) within a subsistence-barter-and-borrow system labor can be used to maximize one's profits.[20] It remains nonetheless important that far less wealth can be amassed within the low-money systems than within capitalism.

In brief, then, a defining characteristic of a subsistence-barter-and-borrow system is its paucity of money. And the economic mentality within such a system will not necessarily be "subsistence-oriented" but will respond to objective conditions. What has happened over time in

Appalachia is a shift from an initial splurge of enterprise to a later pre-occupation (at least among most people) with merely maintaining sub-sistence. But concurrently, although this may sound contradictory, Appalachia's people have increasingly abandoned their subsistence-barter-and-borrow systems and increasingly adopted the capitalist sys-tem. In other words, despite the shift toward a subsistence-oriented mentality, the region at the same time has used increasing quantities of money and thereby has undergone a transformation to capitalism. Meanwhile (to add another nuance), the federal banknote-issuing tax that was legislated in 1865 inhibited *local* control over the region's cap-italist transformation and favored its control by outsiders.

Michael Merrill has estimated that as of 1800, only about one-quarter of America's economic exchanges, as measured by value, oc-curred in commercial markets.[21] In Appalachia that level may not have been reached even by the time of the Civil War. Furthermore, much or most of that commercial one-quarter of the region's total exchanges was conducted through barter, without money changing hands. And this pattern was reinforced by the 1865 termination of state-bank curren-cies. So when the region's industrialization began to reach major pro-portions in the 1880s, locally issued money could finance only a small part of the new production and marketing investments that then occurred.

Thus it is hardly surprising that Appalachia's transformation toward capitalism depended on outside capital. Many studies of the region end their analysis in the 1920s when its capitalist transformation peaked. This book does not stop there but moves on to look at the New Deal's effects. A new era began in the 1930s, marked by major changes in the region's industrial conditions. There was the unionization of labor, prompting unionized industries to mechanize more, and thereby per-petuating the massive unemployment that had begun when the Depres-sion struck. Beyond those industrial changes, the 1930s also brought less-noticed changes in Appalachia's agricultural life.

The Depression's effects differed in different regions of the United States, and its effects in Appalachia differed considerably from its ef-fects in most of the rest of the country. Its effects, in fact, were not the same everywhere *within* Appalachia. Because many of Appalachia's full-time farm families were subsistence farmers producing most of their own consumption items, or else bartering for locally produced consumption goods, those families needed little money to maintain their living standards. Not only as minimal buyers but also as minimal sellers, such full-time subsistence farmers were only minimally affected by market conditions and thus by the Depression.[22] Some of Appalachia's full-time subsistence farmers found the great drought of 1930–1931 a worse ordeal than they found the Depression.[23]

At the other extreme within the region (not geographically but economically) stood full-time wage earners. Many of these people worked in raw-material industries, especially in bituminous coal mining. By contrast with Appalachia's full-time subsistence farmers, the region's full-time miners were among those Americans hardest hit by the Depression. Most Appalachian miners did a little supplemental farming on the side, and this helped them cushion what they suffered from partial or total unemployment, but coal mining was one of the industries most adversely affected by the Depression—partly because coal was intimately tied to two of the country's hardest-hit economic sectors, producer goods and construction materials, and also because mining entailed high fixed costs that continued even when the mines were inactive. Full-time coal miners who lacked jobs needed all the money relief they received and often could have used more.

As for the New Deal's effects on the region, they mixed benefits with harm. Briefly, New Deal programs committed four types of harm. First, because Appalachia's wage workers frequently supplemented their wage income with subsistence farming and bartering, they did not need as *much* wage income as most workers elsewhere in the United States. Therefore the wage (and price) *supports* mandated by the National Recovery Administration (NRA) harmed the competitive position of Appalachia's industries. Second, the acreage limitations and subsidy payments established by the Agricultural Adjustment Administration (AAA) helped capital-intensive farmers at the expense of labor-intensive farmers, thus helping regions like the Midwest at the expense of Appalachia. Third, the Works Progress Administration (WPA) reinforced Appalachia's growing exclusion from production for markets by paying wages higher than many of the region's private producers could afford to pay. And finally, the money influx into Appalachia's farming areas that was financed by the WPA and other relief programs put some of the transactions that had formerly used barter on a cash basis, especially among the region's full-time subsistence farmers. This change to cash transactions diminished the amount of industrial labor power that was subsidized by Appalachia's subsistence agriculture, further weakening the region's ability to compete in America's market economy. As Marjorie Griffin Cohen points out, "The existence of subsistence production serves a variety of functions, but its primary importance for the capitalist sector is in supplying and maintaining a labour force at prices which permit capital accumulation in this sector."[24]

This suggests only part of what followed from New Deal intervention. The New Deal did provide some benefits for Appalachia, because another part of the story is that many of the region's coal and textile operators had not been *able* to pay their workers a fully family-supporting wage. The great expansion of those industries in the late-nineteenth and early twentieth centuries had been possible only because many of their workers maintained ties to agriculture, particularly to subsistence agriculture.[25] And partly because of this, the agricultural demands that were made on mountain and Piedmont land had grown extremely destructive by the 1920s. Erosion and soil depletion were threatening to denude many farmed hillsides beyond the point at which they could support even the reforestation they desperately needed.[26] Thus the New Deal did confer benefits on Appalachia over and above simply feeding people. The New Deal's money injections, though they harmed the region's textile and coal industries, helped to save its land by making many people less dependent on farming their land. So a trade-off was involved.

This does not mean that if industries had stayed away from Appalachia the land would have received exemplary treatment. A self-defeating agriculture had been practiced since white settlers first started arriving. It had begun with the mismarriage of colonial American farming customs to the region's unusually hilly topography, and it was compounded by the tradition of bequeathing land through partible inheritance (i.e., division among all the heirs, or at least among all male heirs). And yet, although pressure on the land's productive capacity often yielded diminishing returns, most mountaineers resisted migration. They stayed put, eventually enduring impoverishment and injuring the land. They remained primarily because they valued proximity to their parents and siblings more than they valued individual economic advancement. Although most mountaineers lived in nuclear-family households, their basic economic unit was the multigenerational family.

Their family orientation was not comparable to a fully communitarian life-style—as exemplified, say, by the traditional village communes of Russia. Rural Appalachia's basic socioeconomic group was much smaller, composed, as one eastern Kentucky study has found, of "two, three, or more family-households that were particularly solidary and bonded together by strong ties of mutual friendship, and frequent visiting exchanges, as well as by ties of kinship. These were primarily groups of siblings' families or of siblings and their parental families." Beyond these family groups, the same study found, there was "little cooperation in common tasks for the good of the whole neighborhood. Few interfamily economic relationships, such as borrowing farm implements or exchanging labor, existed."[27] A similarly pronounced "familism," accompanied by a comparable lack of community cooperation, has likewise been discovered by West Virginia case studies[28] and by a North Carolina case study.[29]

According to the Depression-era union organizer Jim Garland—whose family went back five generations in southeastern Kentucky—a decline of wider community solidarity had begun quite early. Garland writes that "when there remained no more unclaimed farmland to take up, . . . two classes of people emerged. . . . Thus, even before the coal operators came into the region, mountain society had begun to disintegrate."[30]

In the late nineteenth century, as the living standard of many mountain families fell, members of those families often went to work for wages that were lower than the wages paid for comparable jobs elsewhere in the United States. Had the region's agriculture not already been strained—had impoverishment not already threatened some farm families—wages could not have been scaled low, and in that case much less industrialization would have been feasible in Appalachia. The mountain products, primarily timber and coal, were very heavy. Transporting them to markets, usually markets in the North, was expensive. But because these resource-extraction jobs kept most Appalachian workers in rural areas where they could continue farming as a sideline (supplementing their meager pay with home production), Appalachia's coal was generally able to undersell northern coal until 1933, when the National Recovery Administration (NRA) sponsored wage-and-price supports that destroyed the region's advantage.

Admittedly, Appalachia's coal-mining areas would have needed

Depression-time relief payments even without the NRA's policies. The coal areas had already become heavily money-dependent before the Depression began, and what they desperately needed during the Depression was money. Consequently, major welfare provision was the only humane federal policy possible for Appalachia's coal areas in 1933 (and earlier, for that matter, despite the delay until 1933).

As for those quite different Appalachian areas where little or no coal was mined and where the predominant occupation was still subsistence farming, my findings suggest that federal relief (including the work relief furnished under the WPA) produced a result there that was less clearly beneficial. There the 1930s' influx of relief money tended to undermine local subsistence-barter-and-borrow networks by making the possession of money a precondition for an increased proportion of local transactions.

Meanwhile, a change was occurring during the New Deal era not only in the scale but also in the rationale of government intervention. The creation of consumer purchasing power became a major motive for providing relief (welfare) payments. Genuine human concern characterized the New Deal, but that cannot be the sole criterion for assaying a historical evaluation of its long-term effects on Appalachia.

Indeed (this may as well be explicit), *today's* theories are inevitably the criteria by which the cogency of yesterday's theories and the consequences of yesterday's practices must be gauged. This study's use of theory is eclectic, drawing on both neoclassical and neo-Marxist ideas. Without theory of some sort, sense cannot be made. Now in the 1990s, the nation is growing less and less willing to maintain Appalachia in a state of dependence on transfer payments indefinitely. My hope is that a rethinking of Appalachia's past, including a reexamination of the conscious choices that helped to shape its past, can help us envision a future that is within our power of choice today.

Admittedly the New Deal itself had come out of a rethinking process. Neoclassical economists had failed to predict the Depression and could prescribe no cure for it, so seemingly the Depression had refuted neoclassical economics. In fact it had not, but it did inspire new departures in neoclassical theory, including in 1946 the first full formulation of the center-periphery model by the Argentine economist Raúl Prebisch.[31] (Prior to Prebisch, the terms *center, periphery,* and *dependency* had been used by Werner Sombart in the 1920s, but only in passing.)[32]

Argentina, whose central bank Prebisch spent the 1930s organizing and directing, presented a classic case of economic dependency. During World War I, however, and again during the 1930s Depression, a policy of import substitution was forced on Argentina and its dependency shrank. Prebisch's figures told him that his country thereby thrived.

Unlike Argentina, unfortunately, Appalachia cannot legally establish its own central bank, but it can benefit from what Raúl Prebisch learned while starting Argentina's. By 1937 Prebisch was questioning the classical assumption that export-led growth was required in order to develop an undeveloped country. Prebisch had seen Argentina's greatest industrial strides occur when its exports were at their lowest—first during World War I and then again during the Depression. During both periods, self-sufficiency through a process of import substitution had been forced on Argentina. In hindsight, great benefits from import substitution became clear to Prebisch.

By the late 1940s, Prebisch was attacking the classical axiom that an international "comparative advantage" necessarily follows for any country that achieves lower production costs. What actually happens, said Prebisch, is that the economically "center" countries can afford to finance technological innovations (thus increasing their productivity per worker) without causing any fall in prices, and this allows those center countries to increase wages as they increase what economists call the average product, or average output, of labor. They can do this, says Prebisch, because they control virtually all of the world's capital. But by contrast, at the periphery, where far less capital is controlled, a new technology often *does* pull prices down, for labor at the periphery is too job hungry and unorganized to gain a share of technology's benefits. The difference between the periphery's low labor costs and the center's high labor costs confers an absolute advantage in favor of the center, despite the periphery's comparative advantage in trade competition. Prebisch admitted that world economic upswings tended to raise prices and wages at the periphery as well as at the center; but when downswings came, he said, the resistance to any lowering of incomes was more effective at the center, because labor unions were stronger there and more money was available for wages.[33] To this explanation, others have added that because the center's products tend to be more differentiable than are the products of the periphery, the center's products can command relatively monopolistic prices from the periphery.[34]

Prebisch's 1950 United Nations report contains figures showing that between the 1870s and 1938, the relative value of the primary products (raw materials) that Great Britain imported from the rest of the world fell so far that by 1938 "an average of 58.6 per cent more primary products was needed to buy the same amount of finished [British] manufactures."[35] Producers at the periphery had to buy manufactured goods at whatever price they could get them, and yet their own raw products almost invariably seemed to fall in price whenever a new technology (or a good harvest, or any other cause) made their products cheaper to produce.[36]

Such were the origins of dependency theory. It was an application of neoclassical principles to questions that had gone unasked until world economic relations came under scrutiny from vantage points in the Third World. Since the 1960s, debate about dependency has been dominated by neo-Marxists, but some crucial insights have also been contributed by a neoclassical West Indian economist, W. Arthur Lewis. While working for the United Nations, Lewis began realizing that terms of trade between countries result primarily from the potential each country possesses to produce necessities that both it and its trading partners share in consuming. Lewis points out that all countries share in consuming food, and he asks how *much* food (per capita) any given poor country can produce *for its own consumption.* Lewis asks, in other words, how much productivity per capita exists in the subsistence agriculture of a capital-poor country, and how much productivity per capita exists in such a country's *other* domestic food production (that is, in its food production for its internal markets). If a country has few capital resources, says Lewis—and in addition its non-export (domestic) agriculture limps along with low productivity—then *whatever* that country exports will tend to be sold for relatively low prices, even if it exports manufactured goods and even if it achieves high productivity in turning out its exports, whether they be agricultural or manufactured.[37] (The Philippines furnish a manufacturing illustration of this that is still glaring in the 1990s.)

Like Prebisch, Lewis studied economic relations between separate countries, not between regions within the same country. Nevertheless, his insights cast light on relations between the northern United States and Appalachia. Lewis is explicit that less-developed countries (and here I read "regions," thinking of Appalachia's coal) "cannot escape . . .

unfavorable terms of trade by increasing productivity in the commodities they export, since this will simply reduce the prices of such commodities." The surest way for a less-developed country (or region) to achieve trade parity with a developed country (region) is to equal its per capita production of food for local consumption. As Lewis puts it, "The factoral terms of trade [that is, terms of trade per "factor," including per worker] can be improved only by raising . . . productivity in the common commodity, domestic foodstuffs."[38]

What Lewis is saying here becomes clearer if we place his insights within the hypothetical "stages of economic growth" postulated by Walt W. Rostow. Rostow defined five stages of growth: (1) the traditional society, (2) the preconditions for take-off, (3) the take-off, (4) the drive to maturity, and (5) the age of mass-consumption.

In Rostow's schema, an economy generally achieves the preconditions for take-off by importing capital investments.[39] Here, however, dependency often soars. Historically, foreign capital investments have usually been made for the purpose of growing food to export or extracting raw materials to export. In addition, foreign investment has often financed construction of the infrastructure (such as railroads, roads, ports, telegraph lines, etc.) that is required to grow, extract, and transport those export products. As Rostow asserted concerning his stage of preconditions for take-off, when "investment increases [it is] notably in transport, communications, and in raw materials in which other nations may have an economic interest."[40]

In thinking about Appalachia, of course, we have to think of its relations with other U.S. regions, not with other countries. The point is that investment decisions are made by the investors. Most major investment in Appalachia comes from outside the region. A great many locally desirable investments have never been made simply because they would have returned no profit to outsiders. A case of this sort was highlighted in the 1970s when U.S. Steel Company ended seven decades of coal mining in southern West Virginia's McDowell County. The county seat of several thousand people, the town of Welch, had spent its U.S. Steel—dominated decades as one of the largest U.S. cities to lack treatment for its raw sewage—which still today in fact flows raw into the Tug Fork River. In 1990 the county's officials agreed to allow massive garbage imports into McDowell County in exchange for the treatment of Welch's sewage by a waste management firm based in

Philadelphia.[41] Citizens have organized against the garbage imports, but as of 1993 a final decision has not been reached.

McDowell County's dilemma may be worse than most, but, at best, an economy in Rostow's preconditions stage—investing its labor wherever outsiders are willing to invest capital—will grow dependent on outside investors. So what will propel a preconditions-stage economy to the take-off stage—what will propel it to self-sustaining growth?

Rostow hypothesized that a take-off can be defined by "the rate of effective investment and savings" *within* a society. When effective investment and savings within a society exceed 10 percent of the "national income" (here, for our analysis, we should think of Appalachia's internal regional income), Rostow considered a take-off virtually assured. He pointed out, however, that certain modernizing attitudes are necessary before a society's investment rate *can* rise to 10 percent of its income. And historically those modernizing attitudes have arisen not so much because of economic goals as because of political goals. In Rostow's words, "The building of an effective centralized national state . . . was a decisive aspect of the preconditions period; and it was, almost universally, a necessary condition for take-off."[42]

Where does this leave a preconditions-stage region that lies within the same nation-state as the mature-stage region that controls most of its investment decisions? Appalachia has no legal grounds for defending its economy from control by the economy of the North. But in Rostovian terms, Appalachia has been stuck in its preconditions stage for over a century now, its take-off still apparently as remote as it was more than one hundred years ago when its major industrialization began.[43]

Let's look again at agriculture. In W. Arthur Lewis's schema, agriculture is crucial. It is also prominent in Rostow's preconditions for take-off. Rostow said that "in the first instance, comparative advantage lay in agriculture and the production of food-stuffs and raw materials for export." The way forward, he said, lay in finding "an economic setting in which a shift from agriculture and trade to manufacturing was possible."[44] Such a shift does not consist of agriculture and trade discontinuing, of course, but of manufacturing joining them. As manufacturing is added and the take-off proceeds, said Rostow, "agriculture is commercialized."[45]

Here W. Arthur Lewis would doubtless interject that much Third World agriculture has been commercialized prior to any signs of a take-off, and, indeed, without a take-off following afterwards. But Lewis would agree with Rostow's dictum that "revolutionary changes in agricultural productivity are an essential condition for successful take-off."[46] For Lewis, however, it is specifically agricultural productivity for *domestic* consumption that, in the absence of financial wealth, is fundamental to prosperity. Lewis finds that agricultural productivity for export can easily become self-defeating.

One important success story Rostow had trouble fitting into his schema was that of Japan since the 1860s. Japan's economic success makes better sense if analyzed in Lewis's terms, for Japan's agricultural productivity gains have been considerable since at least the 1880s,[47] and those gains have not served export markets. Rostow called Japan's economy mature by 1940, but he nonetheless wondered if one really *should* "rate as mature an economy with so labour-intensive an agricultural sector. The answer is affirmative," he went on, "only if one is prepared to take as given—outside the definition of maturity—a society's decision about its population size." Japanese agriculture, Rostow decided, with its "extraordinary refinement in the use of both water and chemical fertilizers, does indeed reflect a high form of modern technological achievement, even if modern farm machinery, designed to save labour, is capable of only limited use."[48]

This makes sense, but Rostow missed an important nuance here when he supposed that "a high form of modern technological achievement" in agriculture allowed Japan's economy to reach maturity *despite* labor-intensive farming methods. In the light of the progress Japan has continued achieving since Rostow wrote (1961), it may well be that a long-term advantage has accrued to Japan's economy specifically *because* a large proportion of its population remained so long in agriculture. Japan managed, for much longer than Appalachia managed, to keep subsidizing its industry with pervasive subsistence agriculture. The result in both cases was low-paid industrial labor—but it continued much longer in Japan than in Appalachia. An additional difference is that Japan's low-wage labor was exploited within a national development plan.[49] During the Meiji period (1868–1912), "Japan's main asset seemed to be its abundant reserves of cheap labor"—so industrialization expert Tom Kemp tells us.[50] And well past the Meiji period Japanese agriculture continued on a self-sustaining basis.

Thus the role played by Japan's agriculture in supplying its industrial sector with subsidized labor was not frittered away, as it was in Appalachia's case.

In Appalachia, by contrast, the agricultural sector was only temporarily able to contribute very many workers who needed only low wages. During Appalachia's industrializing era (1880–1930), the region's subsistence reproduction of labor power dwindled per capita as a result of land-destroying farming and timbering practices. Then, during the New Deal, many of Appalachia's full-time subsistence farmers began to depend on money that they received from the federal government, particularly for working on projects of the Works Progress Administration (WPA). This added up to a considerable reduction of low-paid labor, and at that time it was generally considered progress. Indeed, subsistence farming itself was considered a drag on the economy by the school of thought that dominated New Deal economic policy making. In the 1920s, subsistence farms had held half of the U.S. farm population. Liberal economists lamented subsistence agriculture's small *money* contribution to the industrial sector (its low level of purchases) while ignoring subsistence agriculture's massive contribution of low-paid labor to the industrial sector.[51]

Japan's longer-lasting subsistence sector is only one of several ways in which Japan's path to economic independence diverged from Appalachia's path to dependency. The era when Japan was closed to Westerners (1641–1854) prepared that country well, ironically, for economic success under Western-style capitalism. On the eve of its industrialization, Japan was equipped very differently from Appalachia for what was coming. The demographic contrast could hardly have been greater. Japan had achieved virtually zero population growth. After multiplying two and a half times from 1600 to 1720, Japan's population leveled off and grew hardly at all from 1720 to 1868—at which point the Meiji restoration opened the way for industrialization. This near-zero population growth was achieved despite labor-intensive Japanese farming. Most of Japan's farm families were relatively small, and they endured grueling workloads.

That same century and a half (1720–1868) also formed the prelude to Appalachia's industrialization, but, in Appalachia's case, large families continued to predominate. Like most Appalachians, most Japanese were subsistence farmers at that time, but unlike Appalachia's farm families, Japanese farm families found that they could increase their per capita income by raising *fewer* children.[52]

The significance of rural Japan's low population growth was that families could make ends meet, generation after generation, without having access to new land (as Appalachians did have access while their frontier lasted) and without excessively eroding and depleting their resource base[53] (as Appalachians tended to do after their new land ran out). Thus Japan's agricultural sector could continue almost indefinitely to hold a large proportion of Japan's overall population—and as a result it could continue almost indefinitely to perform the subsistence reproduction of labor power that helped keep industrial wages low.

How did Japan's success in this regard come about? During the mid-nineteenth century, the average Japanese farm household was self-sufficient in grain and grew a surplus of grain for the market. Furthermore, 20 to 25 percent of Japan's farmers carried on a supplemental occupation of one sort or another, generally a small business.[54] This gave them economic flexibility.

Two decades later, in 1872, almost 75 percent of Japan's working population was still in the agricultural sector.[55] Many of these people still practiced trades or ran small businesses on the side. Soon a growing number of them would become *wage* workers to supplement their farm income—but they would not be pressured into wage labor by the specter of impoverishment (as many of Appalachia's families were). The standard of living on Japan's farms remained high enough to indirectly cause frequent labor shortages in industries such as silk reeling, cotton spinning, and coal mining. Skilled labor for Japan's heavy industry continued to be inadequate as late as the 1930s. Thus although Japanese agriculture retained "excess labor" while industry went short of help, most "excess" farm people manifestly considered themselves better off by maintaining at least roots where they were—better off than they envisioned themselves becoming if they left agriculture completely for full-time wage work.

Japan's industries kept raising pay and improving conditions to pry workers loose from the farms, yet a pattern of "dual employment" entrenched itself. By 1920 a full 63.3 percent of Japan's farmers, lumberjacks, and fishermen were also practicing a secondary occupation.[56] This continued giving them economic flexibility. As of 1975, 62.2 percent of Japan's farm families were deriving more than half their income

from off-the-farm sources, and the viability of farm families' dual-
employment practices made their disposable income 13.1 percent
higher than the disposable income of nonfarm Japanese families.[57]

Walt W. Rostow, as we have seen, wondered in 1961 whether we
should really "rate as mature an economy with so labour-intensive an
agricultural sector" as Japan's. Rostow did grudgingly rate Japan's
economy as mature by 1940. But he did not realize that a large agricultural sector—assuming that it is self-sufficient—forms an economic
asset. Over thirty years have passed since Rostow wrote. Knowing the
competitive position of Japan today in world trade, it seems timely to
compare Japan's and Appalachia's rural economies. Among major non-
socialist industrial countries, Japan as of 1970 still retained the largest
percentage of its work force in agriculture—close to 20 percent,
whereas only 3.8 percent of U.S. workers then remained in
agriculture.[58]

Of course, a large percentage of a population cannot stay in agriculture if the land is abused as it was in much of Appalachia. Indeed,
where the rural population is rapidly growing, as it was in Newer Appalachia, soil conservation is difficult to practice. Even with the help of
a land ethic like Japan's, the Japanese countryside doubtlessly would
have deteriorated if its population growth had resembled Newer Appalachia's. Fortunately for Japan, its population growth remained virtually nil until industrialization began creating new economic sectors that
could support additional population.[59]

Whatever the reason, the fact remains that while Japan conserved
and replenished its hillside topsoil, Appalachia let much of its topsoil
wash away. Finally the 1930s' New Deal agencies intervened by initiating financial incentives for soil conservation, but some of the best
methods of hill farming are still being overlooked in Appalachia. Appalachia, in this regard, is yet to grow "richer by Asia."[60] (In chapters
6 and 7, I will discuss forest-type "tree crops" that the New Deal rejected and that Appalachia's farm experts are still ignoring.)

At a subtler level, Japan's subsistence labor reproduction was sustained by an appreciative attitude toward labor that was very different
from how labor has been regarded in most of the United States since the
Civil War. Each case has harbored its own logic. Japan's restricted land
base and scarce resources cried out for highly proficient labor—whereas
America's frontier conditions and abundant resources barely penalized

wasteful and skill-less work habits. On Appalachia's subsistence farms, however, where labor was sustained largely by its own direct products (rather than by money-bought products) and where money scarcity prompted a flourishing system of moneyless labor exchanges, labor *was* generally valued above capital, and in fact labor was considered the fundament of low-money economic development. Unfortunately, the advantages derived from Appalachia's subsistence labor reproduction were not *kept* within Appalachia—they were diffused outward into the entire American economy, and there Appalachia's valuable contribution of low-cost labor was valued very low, if not indeed denigrated. Nineteenth- and twentieth-century America has increasingly ignored labor's contribution to development while extolling capital's role.

I'd like to stress this last point, because once we see some of the reasons America's capital became highly valued and its labor came to be taken for granted, we will also be able to distinguish today's still-dominant capital centricity from our own considered choice of values— from our own *personal* choice of values. We can realize then that the dispersement of labor and capital under contract obligations is not basic to all economic life but only to one type of economic system. And we will not thereby be renouncing the spirit of enterprise, which is as inseparable from what is good as from what is bad about America. Enterprise can take as many forms as there are economic systems.

With that said, all the propositions needed to construct a general theory of Appalachia's path to economic dependency have been broached. It is time to apply them.

1

Early Settlement and
Self-Sufficiency, 1730–1860

Precapitalist economies have an internal logic and solidity which should not be underestimated. . . . So long as the direct producers retained direct access to their means of [economic] reproduction, they would not voluntarily turn to specialization, unless there *previously* had been massive improvements in the security of the food supply. . . . [But on the other hand, direct producers] could, relatively easily, find themselves without access to the land required for their reproduction simply as a result of the demographic growth and parcelization of holdings which were the unintended outcomes of previous generations of peasants pursuing their individually rational patterns of reproduction and inheritance.
—Robert Brenner, "The Social Basis of Economic Development"

The settlement of North America, including the settlement of Appalachia, occasioned major examples of what Robert Brenner calls "massive improvements in the security of the food supply." Between 1714 and 1775, for example, thousands of rent-racked flax and linen producers abandoned their tiny leaseholds in Northern Ireland and flooded across the Atlantic to America, where many or most of them "lit out for the territories" of that day. Their venturesome settlement of Older Appalachia multiplied their direct access to their means of economic reproduction.

But why, then, did their descendants eventually find themselves economically dependent on other American regions? Here the four main causes already mentioned in the Introduction bear repeating: (1) the expansion of population, (2) the depletion of resources, (3) the destruction attendant on the Civil War, and (4) federal homestead and banking legislation enacted during the Civil War.

How these four causes affected the various areas within Appalachia was determined largely by each area's position in the sequence of the region's settlement. And the sequence of settlement, in turn, was determined mainly by geography. As Frederick Jackson Turner once put it, early American settlers poured "their plastic pioneer life into geographic moulds."[1]

Appalachia's permanent white settlement began in the late 1720s in the Shenandoah Valley and continued rapidly southwestward with little topographic obstruction, soon spilling over into the rest of the Valley of Virginia—into what is called the upper valley—and continuing with it in the same southwesterly direction. Those two fertile troughs, the Shenandoah and the rest of the Valley of Virginia, together extend for several hundred miles and at points they widen to sixty miles—encompassing a vast amount of land. But both valleys, underlain by limestone, proved so favorable for colonial agriculture that their first settlement wave peopled their vastness in little more than a single generation, by 1776.[2] This scale of settlement was only possible because natural increase and transatlantic migration raised population in the thirteen colonies more than threefold during that generation, from about 630,000 in 1730 to about 2,150,000 in 1770.[3]

Even so, that first wave of Appalachian settlement filled only the northern half of the Great Appalachian Valley—which continues southwestward as the Valley of East Tennessee, and then extends far into northeastern Alabama. By the time of the American Revolution, white settlement was well under way in East Tennessee, although not in northeastern Alabama.

Broadly defined (as it will be defined in this study), the Great Appalachian Valley includes not only the seldom-obstructed six-hundred-mile southwesterly course of its major trough but also the many similarly long and wide valleys that run parallel to it, mostly to its west. Land seekers soon spilled over into those parallel valleys—turning northwestward out of the Valley of Virginia, for instance, to enter the fertile valleys of the New River and its tributary the Greenbrier. Here, in the area that would later become southeastern West Virginia, the Big Levels of the Greenbrier Valley became an early center for cattle raising.[4]

Colonial Virginia applied stringent land-settlement laws, yet, even so, many of the official land titles issued by Virginia became targets for conflicting claims. Land-ownership questions grew particularly vexed in the Shenandoah Valley.[5] Such manmade obstacles influenced the settlement pattern far less, however, than geography. In Kentucky, too, land titles often faced conflicting claims, yet many land seekers took their chances by passing northwestward to Kentucky through the Cumberland Gap, located where Virginia joins Tennessee. When the Revolution ended in 1783, Kentucky contained only twelve thousand settlers, but by the first national census seven years later, their number had grown to about seventy thousand.

Meanwhile, other land seekers were not entering the Great Appalachian Valley at all but were bypassing its northern mouth (which is the Shenandoah Valley's northern ingress) and traveling farther up the Potomac River. There they found rich land along the Potomac's two headwater branches, especially along its south branch in what would later become part of northeastern West Virginia. Like the Big Levels of the Greenbrier Valley, the South Branch of the Potomac soon became a cattle-raising center.

By 1820 Appalachia contained almost half a million inhabitants—four-fifths of them in the benign valleys just described. Western North Carolina could also boast of some wide and fertile valleys, but these were harder of access and higher in altitude. North Carolina's mountain section was settled both from the Carolina Piedmont to its east and from the Valley of East Tennessee to its west. In far southwestern North Carolina, some white pioneers appropriated fields that had previously been cultivated by Cherokees, and this occurred also in northern Georgia.[6] Nonetheless, from 1800 through to the Civil War, Appalachian North Carolina contained only a third as many inhabitants as the better-endowed East Tennessee.

In Kentucky, migration at first left little residue in that state's eastern mountain area, which acted mainly as an obstacle to settlement in the rest of state. By 1830 eastern Kentucky could not yet claim fifty thousand inhabitants. As for northern Georgia, little white settlement was allowed there until 1832—five years after gold was discovered in the area. White settlement was then allowed concurrently with the ousting of Georgia's Cherokees.[7]

Those were still fringe areas, however. As of 1830, three-fifths of Appalachia's population remained huddled together in Old Virginia's long, fertile valleys and in the Valley of East Tennessee. As of the 1830 census, East Tennessee's population overtook that of Appalachian Old Virginia, but West Virginia (counted here as though it were already a separate state) accounted for another one-fifth of the region's total population, and West Virginia's residence pattern was then still heavily weighted toward what would later (during the Civil War) become its border with its mother state. Thus as of 1830, about four-fifths of the region's population was still concentrated in the Great Appalachian Valley, broadly defined.[8]

Early New England has recently been subjected to scores of case studies by practitioners of the "new rural history," but that is not true of early Appalachia. Of the book-length new rural histories, only Robert D. Mitchell's *Commercialism and Frontier* deals extensively with the very earliest period of settlement in an Appalachian area. It considers the Shenandoah Valley and finds that its first generation of settlers typically managed to sell less than one-tenth of their total production (hunting items included) but that "commercial tendencies were present from the beginnings of permanent settlement." As the Shenandoah Valley's population became "larger, more occupationally varied and credit-dependent . . . the proportion of goods for sale increased typically from one-third to one-half or more of total output." Mitchell concludes that commercial tendencies were "the most dynamic element in the emerging pioneer economy."[9]

This judgment is consistent with information about the area that later became West Virginia. Guns, for instance, were typical of the investments pioneers made not merely to provision their families but to acquire extra income by selling animal pelts. As of 1822, when pelts were still being traded at stores in the relatively rugged northwestern corner of Older Appalachia, rabbit skins sold for two cents each, raccoon skins sold for twenty cents, fox skins for fifty cents, deer skins for fourteen cents a pound, bear skins for $1.25, and otter skins for $3.00. That trade in peltry virtually disappeared there by 1830, however, as fur-bearing animals grew scarce.[10]

Some of Appalachia's earliest whites were looking not so much for game as for ginseng, the medicinal root coveted by Americans who traded with China. Many early pioneers discovered such plentiful ginseng that its high exchange value could finance most of their store purchases. One merchant family in the Greenbrier Valley of Virginia (now of West Virginia) made only 2 percent of its sales in 1784 on a cash basis. Of its £906 ($4,403) worth of sales that year, 70 percent were paid for by ginseng root—at the rate of 2s. 6d. ($0.625) worth of store goods in exchange for each pound of the customers' ginseng.[11] Thus this merchant family acquired almost two and a half tons of ginseng in 1784.

Although ginseng often grew scarce,[12] the forests and the early clearings continued to provide settlers with a very easy subsistence and extra income through livestock raising. By 1754 the Shenandoah Valley had become well known for its cattle.[13] And prior to the revolutionary war, the practice of fattening cattle on corn had become common on the Big Levels along the Greenbrier River (near today's Lewisburg, West Virginia) and also along the South Branch of the Potomac River. By the time of the Revolution, lean cattle were already being bought up by leading South Branch cattlemen so they could fatten them and drive them to market. As early as 1761, a herd of stall-fed cattle were driven from this vicinity to Pittsburgh and sold there to provision British troops.[14]

The herds of individual owners were not large by today's standards. Partial surveys of western Virginia's cattle holdings in the early 1770s reveal that the average herd contained about seventeen head and the average weight per animal was probably only about 375 pounds. Nonetheless, in the valley of the Potomac River's south branch (in today's Hampshire, Hardy, Grant, and Pendleton counties of northeastern West Virginia), cattle raising became more than merely a temporary pioneer expedient of extensive farming. Later it would be supplemented, but not replaced, by more intensive farming. The valley itself *was* intensively farmed for corn (maize), but the uplands also were relatively fertile and they offered such ideal grazing conditions that stock raisers were able to use the valley's corn not only to carry cattle through the winters but also to fatten them for market. Furthermore, by 1785 progressive breeders on the South Branch were improving the quality of breeding stock there with cattle imported from Britain. This selective breeding, combined with better feeding, soon increased the average weight of South Branch cattle.

In the late 1790s, several South Branch cattlemen moved west, driving choice cattle with them and settling near present-day Chillicothe in the Scioto Valley of south-central Ohio. These cattlemen maintained contact with friends and relatives on the South Branch who initially provided a way station for cattle that were market bound eastward from the Scioto Valley.[15] The first recorded cattle drive directly from that part of Ohio to eastern markets occurred in 1805.[16]

Meanwhile, a large absentee landowner reported in 1804 that *most* of the cattle then reaching the markets of Washington, Alexandria, and Baltimore originated in the valleys of the Monongahela River and its tributary the Cheat River (which included parts of today's West Virginia counties of Preston, Tucker, Randolph, Barbour, Taylor, Harrison, Marion, and Monongalia). Later the Kanawha River valley (now in west-central West Virginia) became a major thoroughfare for stock drives eastward. According to a woman writing in 1823, the road along the Kanawha River was then "alive from morning till night, with people, horses, cattle, but principally hogs: myriads of hogs are driven this way annually, to the east. They commence driving in September, and from that [month] till Christmas, you can look out no time in the day without seeing a line of hogs."[17] In 1826, sixty thousand hogs went east to market along this Kanawha Turnpike, twenty-six thousand of them within the space of two autumn months.[18]

Robert D. Mitchell's judgment that in the early Shenandoah Valley, commercial tendencies were "the most dynamic element in the emerging pioneer economy" is consistent with all of this continued commercialization westward, and also with evidence from an early period in the settlement of upcountry Carolina and Georgia. Thriving commercial activity during the eighteenth century in North Carolina's Piedmont has recently been reconstructed in detail by Daniel B. Thorp, using the account book that a rural store-and-tavern-keeping family maintained from 1755 to 1775. The account book reveals few money transactions and yet mentions frequent export-import trips to Charleston, South Carolina—a five-hundred-mile round trip.[19]

Another newly studied ledger is one that was kept from 1782 to 1794 by a merchant in northeastern Tennessee's present-day Hawkins County. Studying that ledger, Lucy K. Gump has found that "about 68 percent of the credit total was paid [to the merchant] in traditional barter items. Cash was named in only 7 percent of all payments; however, about 19 percent may have had a cash component."[20] Most of that merchant's customers paid him in skins, furs, iron, cattle, horses, or salt.

Lewis Atherton, after examining many country-store account books from the 1800–1860 period, wrote of highland farmers in the Carolinas and Georgia that "the barter record of their efforts in the field of production offers little evidence to sustain the popular impression that inhabitants of the Piedmont and mountainous regions of the South were shiftless and degenerate."[21]

Thorp, Gump, and Atherton all describe a rural life in which cash was scarce and yet considerable quantities of produce were marketed. Country merchants established stores farther and farther upcountry in order to intercept Piedmont or mountain farmers who were bringing down wagonloads of produce for marketing. North Carolina farmers brought down wheat, corn, oats, flax and flaxseed, meat and skins, lard, feathers, beeswax, brandy, whiskey, and other products. In exchange they sought salt, molasses, and other subsistence needs, but they also sought trinkets and miscellaneous luxuries, and in addition they often wished to go home with money in their pockets.[22] They needed a little money to pay their taxes. Beyond that, money could be important for people who hoped to acquire land or slaves.

Neither Thorp nor Atherton dwell on the early livestock trade of the Carolina mountains, but other scholars do. By the 1760s cattle were being driven from eastern North Carolina to northern market centers such as Philadelphia. An average holding of cattle in North Carolina at this time was six to sixteen head, but a typical drive northward would include much larger numbers.[23] In 1794 a drive of two hundred cattle proceeded from Wilkes County, in the Appalachian section of North Carolina, north to Washington or beyond.[24]

Not cattle but hogs, however, dominated livestock holdings in the Carolina mountains. Whereas a single cow required fully fifteen acres of pine forest to survive during the winter months, a hog could survive on much less pine forest.[25] In the records of Haywood County (west of the Asheville area), nineteen wills and inventories survive from the period around 1810. In these, the average holding of hogs numbers twenty-two. Cattle holdings average only eight head, although three holdings list more than twenty cattle. Half of the lists include sheep, but their numbers are smaller. And judging from the presence of plows on sixteen of the nineteen lists, animal husbandry was not practiced to the exclusion of cultivation. By far the largest cultivated crop was corn, followed by oats, wheat, and barley in that order.[26]

The year 1827 marked a breakthrough in the commercial life of western North Carolina. In that year the Buncombe Turnpike, largely following the French Broad River, reached completion from Greeneville, Tennessee through to Greenville, South Carolina. This new turnpike greatly facilitated livestock drives out of the mountains toward the coastal plain of South Carolina. Each autumn an estimated 150,000 to 175,000 hogs traveled the Buncombe Turnpike south toward South Carolina. With the exception of whiskey distilling, the most profitable uses for corn were to either sell it as hog feed or else feed it directly to hogs and then sell the hogs. Starting in the 1830s, hotels that were originally built to house drovers during the autumn animal drives began to acquire a second function as summer resorts for wealthy people escaping the humid, pestilential lowland summers.[27]

By selling in coastal or at least in urban markets, mountaineers increased their access to money. When they sold their animals and produce to *country* merchants, by contrast, they were paid mainly in merchandise, which in turn the country merchants had generally acquired from northern wholesalers on credit.[28] Receiving money payments for their products could be of crucial importance for farmers who were intent on major purchases, such as of land or slaves.

Not that slaves were required for successful farming. During the late antebellum period in East Tennessee, so one study has found, "it was not the owning of slaves which made [a yeoman] more prosperous," but rather, "he was able to buy a few slaves because he was a bit more prosperous," and, in fact, many yeomen did desire "to invest their surplus in that type of property."[29] A look at the U.S. census reveals that the aggregate number of slaves in East Tennessee inched upward until the time of the Civil War—but it also reveals that slaves as a *proportion* of East Tennessee's total population reached their highest number quite early, about 1810. Indeed, in Appalachia's first-settled area, the Shenandoah Valley, the proportion of slaves had already passed its peak during the 1780s. In the case of western North Carolina, which was settled considerably later, slavery proved profitable for most slaveholders right up to the Civil War[30]—and yet the proportion of slaves in western North Carolina's population peaked thirty years before the war, about 1830. In Appalachia as a whole, slaves as a proportion of the total population passed their apogee around the early 1820s. At that time slaves constituted about 13 percent of Appalachia's population. The 1820s were also, and perhaps for related reasons, the decade that saw Appalachia's overall population expand at its fastest, growing more than 40 percent.[31]

What this indicates is that the average Appalachian white family was probably not growing richer during the last generation before the Civil War, and may well have been growing poorer. Certainly it was not abolitionism, but cost, that deterred the vast majority of white mountaineers from owning slaves. After abolitionism became a lively issue in the North in the 1830s, it rapidly became a dead issue throughout the South, including the Appalachian South, and even in the border states abolitionist sentiment shrank to a remnant.[32]

The declining proportion of slaves in Appalachia's total population is only one of several indicators that important elements of the region's per capita real wealth were already in decline by the antebellum period. Other indicators, as we have noted, are agricultural. The Deep South received much of its livestock from Appalachia and the border states. Hogs, cattle, and mules were driven out of the mountains in large numbers to be sold in the cotton areas of the Deep South, where boom periods found many plantations maximizing their cotton profits by minimizing the acreage they devoted to such cotton-culture inputs as the breeding of plow animals and food animals. By 1840 to 1860, however, the cotton South's demand for animals had begun to outstrip Appalachia's supply. By then livestock was sometimes so scarce in Tennessee that Deep South purchasers had to continue north into Kentucky, or even into Ohio, to acquire their herds. Along the main droving routes southward, hotèls and boarding houses eagerly sought the patronage of drovers. Farmers along the way sold feed for the animals or opened their fields for a price.

According to a report at the time, 1859 set a record for livestock prices and for the amount of livestock driven on foot out of East Tennessee.[33] It is significant, however, that although the work-animal count of East Tennessee (and of Appalachia in general) continued to grow during the antebellum years in absolute numbers, the count of food-providing animals (hogs, sheep, and cattle) was already declining in absolute numbers in the earlier-settled parts of Appalachia, including East Tennessee. The total bushels of grain produced did continue to increase until the Civil War, even in those older parts of the region—but the all-important fact was that the human population was growing faster than virtually every category of agricultural production—faster even than the supply of work animals, which, along with food animals, could generate cash by sale in the cotton lands.[34]

Thus Appalachia's per capita agricultural production was in decline by the time the Civil War dealt it an exogenous blow. At the beginnings of white settlement, agriculture in the region had enjoyed more than ample resources, but the course of time had brought steadily narrowing options that the population had answered with a succession of expedients—cultivating first the best land in the widest valleys but steadily working through to the worst land in the narrowest hollows, and then up onto the steep hillsides. [35]

In our customary image, we visualize pioneer families toppling trees and uprooting stumps to create arable land, but most Appalachian pioneers made greater use of an Indian method: they burnt the underbrush and killed larger trees in situ by girdling their trunks. Corn and other crops were then planted between the dead but standing trees. After several growing seasons, such "fields" were generally abandoned—or, rather, turned over to stock grazing and firewood gathering—and a new section of forest was burnt, girdled, and planted. Most Indians had confined these practices to flat bottomlands, but white settlers, as their density increased, pushed such slash-and-burn agriculture up onto the region's hillsides. [36]

Both the pace and the geographical pattern of settlement are crucial in understanding Appalachia's past. In its culture and mentality, Appalachia was a homogenous unit, but economically there emerged three Appalachias, three *sub*regions (as we shall continue calling them). The three subregions were cleaved from one another not by different practices but by the fact that farming practices did *not* change when Appalachia's people ran out of new land on which to apply their customary practices. Underlying the resultant economic differences between Appalachia's subregions were their major geographical differences. In terms of Frederick Jackson Turner's "moulds," Appalachia's pioneers poured the same lifeways into three quite different "moulds"—the Valley, the southeastern Blue Ridge, and the Plateau—and they did so mainly in that sequence.

In each of the three subregions, the earliest frontier settlers achieved surpluses far over and above what they needed for self-sufficiency. Prior to the Civil War, the South as a whole was basically self-sufficient in food. [37] Indeed, its degree of self-sufficiency was probably increasing. [38] After the Civil War, however, as of 1870, the states of the Deep South (South Carolina, Georgia, Alabama, Mississippi, and Louisiana) were producing only about half as much food per capita as they had produced in 1860—and the Deep South's subsequent rebound in per capita food production proved only slight.[39]

Appalachia had only 10.4 percent of its population in slavery as of 1860,[40] and thus the mountain region did not undergo the same degree of economic dislocation as emancipation occasioned in the Deep South. Nonetheless, during the third quarter of the nineteenth century, food production per capita fell drastically throughout Appalachia, particularly in the Plateau subregion (see table 2). This decline may not have completely obliterated Appalachia's food self-sufficiency as a region before the 1880s (when industrialization began its dramatic surge on the Plateau), but clearly it did reduce living standards for many of the region's people, softening them up, as it turned out, for later industrial exploitation.

That the specter of impoverishment can goad people toward change is not a new idea. In his *Poverty and Progress*, Richard Wilkinson analyzes much of ancient as well as modern history from that perspective. And what Wilkinson concludes about the first factory workers—that they "only accepted the rigours of early urban industrial life in the hope of improving their subsistence situation"[41]—was surely no less true of most of the people who went down to toil in Appalachia's first underground coal mines. Yet, curiously, this has not been the conventional wisdom among Appalachian specialists. The dean of Appalachian historians, Ronald Eller, tells us in his *Miners, Millhands, and Mountaineers* that "Appalachia on the eve of industrialization was a land of scattered, loosely-integrated, and self-sufficient island communities." Eller explicitly specifies that "the small, marginal farm usually associated with the stereotyped picture of [preindustrial] Appalachia was in fact a product of modernization."[42]

It is no secret that vast contrasts have existed throughout Appalachia's past, and especially in the long, narrow subregion I call Older Appalachia. Yet I cannot believe that "self-sufficient" accurately describes most of the mountain families who turned toward wage labor in the decades following the Civil War. Most of them, I suspect, were prodded into the mines by subsistence needs. Some of Appalachia's earliest miners were admittedly recruited from outside the region, and others had originally been recruited from elsewhere to help build the region's first railroads, but most early Appalachian miners entered the mines directly from farms within the region.[43]

Some of these farmers no doubt entered the mines in an enterprising spirit—intending to use their labor in the mines (as it could be used on the land) to accumulate a degree of surplus wealth. But the data of the U.S. Agricultural Census suggests that most farmers who turned toward wage work did so after, not before, their farms began to grow marginally by their own standards. The new outside-financed industrial development provided many mountaineers with their only alternative to long-distance migration. The new local timbering and mining jobs helped many of them continue to be—as they wished—landowning proprietors of family farms. Plateau Appalachia's per capita farm production had been plummeting for at least thirty years before significant industrialization began—which rules out the possibility that industrialization initiated the region's decline in self-sufficiency. Taking wage jobs did, however, reduce many farmers' agricultural activities to part time, and many of them then allowed the size of their farms to shrink faster than ever—down to sizes that destroyed any hope of regaining landed self-sufficiency if their wage jobs vanished.[44]

This is the basic difference between Appalachia and Japan, and it forms the basis of the Appalachia-Japan comparison in the Introduction. With its population size virtually static, rural Japan faced no crisis of subsistence. Japan embarked on industrialization for political reasons, whereas Appalachia could only be opened to rapid large-scale development because an agricultural subsistence crisis threatened part of the population in its Plateau subregion. No such specter of economic necessity prodded the Japanese. Prior to industrialization, Japan's population had hardly increased for 150 years.[45] Perhaps Japan's farmers were gradually *nudged* toward wage labor by subsistence needs, but they were not *prodded* by such needs, as some Appalachian farmers clearly were.

In natural-resource endowments, Appalachia was better off than Japan, but in the crucial areas of self-sufficiency and self-financing, Appalachia was worse off.[46] Japan's first thirty years of industrialization were achieved without importing significant amounts of investment money.[47] From 1868 to 1898, when Plateau Appalachia's industrialization depended almost entirely on outside investments, Japan found its own farmers able to supply funds on a grand scale for investment in schools, factories, roads, harbors, railroads, and the like. Many investments were placed by the government, and one scholar notes that Japan's "land tax accounted for 78 percent of ordinary [government] revenues (the bulk of total revenues) from 1868 to 1881, and, although the figure tended to fall after that, it still stood at 50 percent in 1891."[48] Major investment money could be contributed by Japan's farmers, this scholar implies, only because "most peasant families supplied all or nearly all of their own food" and also partly because "commercial values did not penetrate a very large area of [rural] economic relations, which remained embedded in custom-bound social groups."[49] The scholar adds that, "had [Japan's] rural population been moving away from tradition as rapidly as some other elements of the population, it is at least doubtful that so large a rate of investment or so fast a rate of modernization could have been sustained."[50]

The relative liabilities that faced Appalachia by the time its industrialization got underway form a contrast with the initial self-sufficiency of Appalachia's agriculture, and with its people's earlier capacity to produce a marketable surplus of farm products to fill their other needs. Already before the Civil War a rapid fall of food production per capita was taking place throughout Appalachia—particularly in the Newer subregion but also in the Older and the Intermediate subregions. (For the per capita figures, see table 2.)

Although in Older Appalachia (the Valley) population growth had drastically slowed, that had not happened in Newer Appalachia (the Plateau). There population grew roughly 62 percent in the 1840s, 49 percent in the 1850s, and 18 percent in the 1860s. The next leap—of 46 percent in the 1870s—must be considered the brink of a "frontier closing" as far as Appalachia was concerned. (See table 1 for the decennial population growth rates.)

Table 2 indicates that in the 1850s, farm livestock holdings per capita began falling much faster in Newer Appalachia than in Older Appalachia. And as farm meat output thus fell per capita, farm grain production per capita did not increase to compensate. Instead, as with livestock, so with grain: the yields per capita fell. And again they fell faster in Newer than in Older Appalachia.

Farm potato output per capita did hold steady in the Newer subregion during the 1850s. Meanwhile, however, in the Older subregion, it was advancing slightly. Finally, judging from butter and cheese figures,

Table 2. Farm Livestock, Commodities, and Acreage Per Capita of Total Population, with Average Farm Size, 1840–1880

	Hogs	Sheep	Total Cattle (incl. Dairy Cows & Work Oxen)	Dairy Cows	Horses, Mules, Asses	Work Oxen	Total Live-stock Value	Farm-killed Live-stock Value	Total Grain (bu.)	Corn (bu.)	Other Grains (bu.)	Pota-toes (bu.)	Farm-made Butter & Cheese (lbs.)	To-bacco (lbs.)	Aver-age Farm Size (acres)	Farm Acres Per Capita
							Older Appalachia									
1840	2.58	1.36	1.07	n.a.	0.40	n.a.	n.a.	n.a.	61.3	36.6	24.7	2.75	n.a.	4.11	n.a.	n.a.
1850	1.92	1.11	0.94	0.29	0.30	0.04	$29.85	$5.73	52.3	33.9	18.5	1.96	11.3	1.39	280	20.2
1860	1.51	0.84	0.81	0.27	0.29	0.05	$41.95	$9.06	48.1	32.4	15.7	2.24	12.0	6.69	n.a.	n.a.
1870	0.85	0.76	0.66	0.23	0.23	0.04	$37.80	n.a.	34.6	19.7	14.9	1.32	10.1	2.00	226	18.5
1880	0.94	0.65	0.65	0.22	0.23	0.02	$26.17	n.a.	38.0	25.8	12.2	1.45	12.4	3.85	166	16.2
							Intermediate Appalachia									
1840	2.72	0.79	1.16	n.a.	0.27	n.a.	n.a.	n.a.	46.0	37.5	8.5	2.83	n.a.	1.07	n.a.	n.a.
1850	2.33	0.89	0.92	0.29	0.22	0.06	$23.37	$5.83	41.7	33.2	8.4	3.95	7.4	0.93	303.3	23.1
1860	1.98	0.71	0.73	0.24	0.23	0.07	$33.26	$8.80	41.8	33.2	8.6	3.85	7.3	3.40	n.a.	n.a.
1870	1.09	0.71	0.61	0.23	0.17	0.07	$25.49	n.a.	28.0	20.1	7.8	1.99	7.9	1.58	182.4	18.9
1880	1.11	0.54	0.54	0.21	0.17	0.04	$21.10	n.a.	31.8	24.5	7.3	1.65	9.5	4.29	145.4	17.1

	Hogs	Sheep	Total Cattle (incl. Dairy Cows & Work Oxen)	Dairy Cows	Horses, Mules, Asses	Work Oxen	Total Live-stock Value	Farm-killed Live-stock Value	Total Grain (bu.)	Corn (bu.)	Other Grains (bu.)	Pota-toes (bu.)	Farm-made Butter & Cheese (lbs.)	To-bacco (lbs.)	Aver-age Farm Size (acres)	Farm Acres Per Capita
Newer Appalachia																
1840	2.73	0.99	1.23	n.a.	0.36	n.a.	n.a.	n.a.	54.0	42.8	11.2	1.80	n.a.	1.18	n.a.	n.a.
1850	2.68	1.22	1.02	0.32	0.26	0.09	$21.32	$5.24	47.0	39.9	7.1	2.63	9.6	1.05	350	34.2
1860	1.70	0.97	0.86	0.24	0.22	0.11	$32.01	$7.12	41.6	35.0	6.6	2.65	11.2	5.29	n.a.	n.a.
1870	1.22	1.04	0.71	0.25	0.21	0.09	$33.54	n.a.	32.5	26.2	6.3	2.54	10.3	4.35	229	26.8
1880	1.29	0.72	0.69	0.23	0.21	0.05	$25.01	n.a.	37.0	31.2	5.8	2.19	12.4	5.33	173	21.3
The Midwest (Ohio, Indiana, Illinois, Michigan, and Wisconsin)																
1840	1.90	1.10	0.92	n.a.	0.31	n.a.	n.a.	n.a.	49.1	29.8	19.4	4.06	n.a.	2.85	n.a.	n.a.
1850	1.44	1.51	0.76	0.28	0.26	0.06	$22.93	$4.69	56.4	39.2	17.2	3.09	15.6	2.73	136	11.0
1860	1.24	1.00	0.76	0.28	0.30	0.06	$34.11	$6.79	60.9	40.5	20.4	4.06	21.8	5.80	124	10.5
1870	0.79	1.24	0.59	0.25	0.28	0.02	$49.20	n.a.	55.1	30.4	24.7	4.95	18.5	3.76	115	9.6
1880	1.21	0.94	0.68	0.27	0.29	0.01	$36.54	n.a.	80.9	52.6	28.3	4.42	21.2	5.20	107	9.4

n.a.: not available

SOURCE: U.S. Censuses of Population and Agriculture, 1840, 1850, 1860, 1870, and 1880.

milk production advanced slightly per capita in both subregions during the 1850s, but by no means did it advance enough to compensate in protein or calories for the amount of meat lost.[51]

Significant here are not only the absolute ratios of livestock and grain to total human population but also the *rapid rate of decline* that is revealed in these decennial ratios. Gone now were the days when ginseng covered the hills and bought many of its diggers most of their store purchases. Gone also were the decades (roughly the first one-third of the nineteenth century) when the Plateau in particular had offered an easy livelihood for livestock raisers. One authority estimates that during the early decades of the nineteenth century, "the per capita holdings of swine in the Cumberland Plateau outranked all other [southern] farming regions."[52] But by 1840 an agricultural decline per capita had begun throughout Appalachia, and by the Civil War a rapid decline was underway—in Newer Appalachia particularly but also in Older and Intermediate Appalachia.

Hogs did the best. As late as midcentury, in the region as a whole, as many farm hogs were counted as all other farm livestock combined, excluding poultry. The overwhelming majority of these hogs ran loose, some turning wild as they foraged through the wooded hills carrying brands or clipped ears to designate their owners. An old-timer in Clay County, in West Virginia's Plateau section, recalled his father's legally registered livestock mark as "a crop and two splits off the right [ear] and a hole in the left." As late as the 1890s in that county, many people had to hunt down their hogs with dogs and guns. Yet under normal conditions hog thieves were uncommon.[53]

Table 2 demonstrates that by 1860, Newer Appalachia had lost its overall advantage, for its farm livestock numbers per capita were now virtually as low as Older Appalachia's. Note also, however, that Older Appalachia's 1860 level had come about through a slow and steady decline over the previous twenty years—whereas Newer Appalachia had virtually sustained its level in the 1840s but then in the 1850s suffered a precipitous fall. Comparing the same set of indicators for the Georgia and North Carolina mountains shows that per capita agricultural decline proceeded faster there than in Older Appalachia but slower than in Newer Appalachia. That is why I label the Appalachian sections of those two states as Intermediate Appalachia.

The picture of faster economic decline in Newer Appalachia is confirmed when we glance at farm livestock values as recorded in dollars in the latter two of the three antebellum agricultural censuses. (In 1840 no dollar values had been recorded for livestock except for poultry.) Although by 1860 the farm livestock numerical count was roughly equal per capita in Older and Newer Appalachia, note on table 2 that in dollars the Newer subregion's farm livestock was worth only $32.01 per resident, whereas the Older subregion's was valued at $41.95. Some of this higher valuation in the Valley subregion was probably attributable to better breeding and feeding there. The rest presumably resulted from the Valley's easier access to markets. Lest we suppose, however, that the dollar-value variance resulted from a higher proportion of stock raised *for* the market in Older Appalachia, it is noteworthy that a comparable gap separated the dollar values of livestock *slaughtered* on farms in the two subregions. Newer Appalachia reported only $7.12 worth of farm livestock slaughtered per person in 1860, whereas Older Appalachia reported $9.06 worth.[54]

As for the possibility that in Older Appalachia a large number of animals might have been slaughtered locally but then sent elsewhere for consumption, a circumstance that would invalidate using slaughter figures to draw any conclusions about the standard of living, little such business existed. Refrigerated transport was still in the future. A small amount of meat packing in barrels for distant markets was carried on in East Tennessee, but the overwhelming majority of marketed livestock was driven on foot to the cotton-growing lands or port cities.[55] So every indication supports the conclusion that by 1860 Newer Appalachia's supply of livestock was as depleted as that of Older Appalachia, and in terms of money was worth considerably less.

Of course, meat is not all that people eat, but a comparison of the three antebellum censuses also reveals a large and continuing fall in Appalachia's grain output per person. And between the two subregions, the Plateau's larger per capita loss in farm livestock was accompanied by a faster fall in per capita grain production. In 1840 the Plateau's farms produced 54 bushels of grain (including corn) per Plateau resident, but by 1860 its farms were producing only 41.6 bushels per resident. The Valley's farms fared better, beginning in 1840 with 61.3 bushels per Valley resident and merely declining by 1860 to 48.1 bushels.

Corn (maize) accounted for most of Appalachia's grain production, particularly on the Plateau. But from 42.8 bushels of farm corn per person in the 1840 census, Newer Appalachia declined by the 1860 census to a mere 35 bushels per person. And most of this drop was concentrated in the 1850s, thus coinciding with the Plateau's precipitate fall in farm livestock per person during that decade. Corn was the grain generally fed to livestock, and clearly, during the 1850s, Newer Appalachia's production of grain for on-farm use underwent a menacing decline. As for the Valley subregion (Older Appalachia), there the per capita decline of farm corn production was more gradual and not so great—falling only from 36.6 bushels in 1840 to 32.4 bushels in 1860. All other farm grain production, considered together, fell by over one-third per capita in both the Older and the Newer subregions.[56]

This picture of falling per capita grain output is reinforced by the census data on farm work animals. Because the work *oxen* on farms were not distinguished in 1840 from other cattle, a full work animal count was not made until 1850, when Older Appalachia held 0.34 work animals per person and Newer Appalachia held 0.35 work animals per person. Ten years later in 1860, the count in Older Appalachia still revealed 0.34 work animals per person, whereas the count in Newer Appalachia had fallen to 0.33 work animals per person. Thus in 1850 the Plateau had been the subregion better endowed with farm work animals, but by 1860 it had become the subregion worse endowed.[57] And remember that Appalachia's work animals were not only used for work but also raised and sold to acquire money, as were food animals.

And indeed, all of the Plateau's livestock figures per capita would have been significantly lower if a livestock boom had not prevailed throughout the antebellum period in the leg of the Plateau that extends down into east-central Tennessee. The boom there presumably serviced the livestock needs of plantations west of the mountains. By contrast, over on the east side of the mountains during the antebellum decades, the Piedmont foothills of the Blue Ridge were relatively livestock poor. It is safe to assume that as the Civil War approached, the Piedmont's worn-out plantations were no longer creating much demand for livestock.

Meanwhile, for home consumption, less-desired foods drew new attention. Farm potato production, for instance, maintained its per capita level during the 1850s in Newer Appalachia despite the population expansion there, and in Older Appalachia the bushels of potatoes harvested per capita (counting both Irish and sweet potatoes) even increased slightly.[58] The only recorded line of agriculture that expanded its per capita production during the 1850s in both Older and Newer Appalachia was dairying. Unfortunately, county-by-county census figures did not distinguish milk cows from other cattle until the 1860 census. (As of 1860, 35 percent of Appalachia's nonworking farm cattle were dairy cows.) The census did, however, begin reporting farm butter and cheese production ten years earlier, in 1850. During the intervening decade of the 1850s, farm butter and cheese production rose, even when calculated per capita. It rose 6.2 percent per capita in Older Appalachia and 16.7 percent per capita in Newer Appalachia. Overall milk production presumably rose at about these same rates. A portion of the increase perhaps resulted from increased milk yields per dairy cow, but an increase could also have followed from the milking of more cows.[59]

The picture that emerges from all of these figures, considered together, is not one of complete impoverishment but of belt tightening. Appalachia's people did have resources to fall back on. As meat became less available, more of the grain crop became available for direct human consumption. And although people's average meat protein intake clearly fell, milk with its protein evidently continued to be plentiful. Meanwhile, potatoes were obviously a continuing starch-providing staple.

Appalachia's outlook as of 1860, although perhaps worrisome, was not alarming. But then the Civil War struck.

2

Accelerated Agricultural Decline and Adverse Federal Policy, 1860–1880

> Human ingenuity would have had difficulty contriving a more perfect engine for class and sectional exploitation [than the National Banking System]: creditors finally obtaining the upper hand as opposed to debtors, and the developed East holding the whip over the undeveloped West and South. This tipping of the class and sectional balance of power was, in my opinion, *the* momentous change over the twenty-three-year period, 1850–1873. Of course, not all of this shift in the economic balance of power can be attributed to changes in the institutional structure of banking, but it is significant that the structure of the system greatly affected the final result.
>
> —Robert P. Sharkey, "Commercial Banking"

The Civil War hurt agriculture far more in the Great Appalachian Valley (Older Appalachia) than on the Appalachian Plateau (Newer Appalachia). Table 2 makes this evident. Despite minimal population growth during the 1860s in the Older subregion—about 6.8 percent as compared to about 17.7 percent in the Newer subregion—the number of farm hogs per person in Older Appalachia was nonetheless cut almost in half. In Newer Appalachia, by contrast, farm hogs per person fell by less than a third in the war-torn 1860s.

Paralleling these hog numbers was the supply of feed for fattening hogs: farm corn production per capita was down by almost half in the Older subregion but by less than a third in the Newer subregion. Even the money value of livestock fell per capita in Older Appalachia, despite major inflation of the dollar during the 1860s. Further, per capita potato production was down by more than two-fifths in the Older subregion, whereas it held steady in Newer Appalachia.[1]

Figures on the size of farms, however, clearly indicate that agriculture still retained greater *potential* in Older Appalachia. During the years between 1850 and 1880, the average farm in Older Appalachia fell from 280 acres to 166 acres, but that subregion's population increase of 60 percent was significantly cushioned by a 28 percent increase in the total amount of land *in* farms. Thus, although 1850 saw 20.2 farm acres per capita in Older Appalachia, this had only fallen after thirty years to 16.2 farm acres per capita. And the "improved" acreage (that is, cultivated acres, cleared pastures, orchards, and the like) per capita remained unchanged at 6.5 acres.[2]

On the Plateau, a less benign picture emerges. Between 1850 and 1880, the Plateau's population grew a phenomenal 156 percent. This was still before a major level of industry appeared. In 1880 only about four thousand Plateau residents, well under 1 percent of the population, as yet mined coal at any given time.[3] The burgeoning population's demands on agriculture are evident in the Plateau's declining number of farm acres per capita—driven from 34.2 acres in 1850 to only 21.3 acres in 1880. Whereas in 1850 the Plateau's average farm had contained 350 acres (much larger than the Valley's average), by 1880 that size had fallen by more than half to 173 acres. Thus the average farm among the narrow hollows and steep hillsides of the Plateau was by 1880 a scant seven acres larger than the average farm in the wide, limestone-based valleys and on the graded uplands of Older Appalachia. On the Plateau, improved acreage had to be increased from 4.3 acres per capita in 1850 to 5.3 acres per capita in 1880.[4] This increase of improved acreage meant more work for farm families, but it did not imply that they were consequently better off. Investigating a place fictitiously called "Beech Creek" in eastern Kentucky (part of the Plateau subregion), Paul J. Weingartner finds that from 1850 to 1880 the value of the average farm fell 25 percent—although by 1880 a higher percentage of land per farm was improved. This decrease in farm values, combined with the increase in the percentage of improved land, suggests to Weingartner that the productive value of the land was probably decreasing from 1850 to 1880.[5]

The Civil War's assault upon southern livestock had not spared dairy cows, but the Plateau's relative immunity from Civil War depredations made possible the milking of more cows per Plateau resident in 1870 than in 1860.[6] Judging from butter and cheese figures, however, by 1870 each cow was giving less milk (see table 2).[7] Perhaps that is partly why interest in livestock breeding increased after the war,[8] but small farmers hesitated to breed cattle solely for their milk-producing poten-

tial. Among blooded cattle, small farmers generally preferred breeds
that would prove good for beef as well as for milk—such as Herefords
and Shorthorns—although their milk yields could rarely equal those of
the best milkers, such as Guernseys, Holsteins, and Jerseys.[9] A Short-
horn cow had versatility. It could be milked, butchered, or sold for either purpose.

The mountainous island of frontier land within the eastern United
States was clearly, by this time, a frontier in its final phase of closing.
Yet the large labor demands of its subsistence agriculture continued to
inspire large families, and the custom of partible inheritance continued
to subdivide farm holdings. More and more of Appalachia's people were
thus beginning to find themselves in a lower class, wedged between the
proverbial rock and a hard place. Thus pinioned, and despite their preponderant Civil War loyalty to the Union, they now received an exogenous blow through federal homestead legislation and other federal
grants of western land. As far back as 1846 a federal homestead bill had
come before Congress. In 1852, as new midwestern railroads prolifer-
ated, a federal homestead bill passed in the House of Representatives,
but easterners managed to defeat that bill in the Senate. Some easterners had correctly perceived that agricultural surpluses from the West
would work to hold down food prices and thus make profitable farming
harder to achieve in the East.[10]

In the House of Representatives, the 1852 Homestead Bill had
passed with 107 votes in favor and 56 votes against. Appalachia's fifteen
congressmen split evenly on the bill, seven voting for it, seven against,
and one abstaining. Those Appalachian congressmen who represented,
on balance, Older Appalachia tended to vote in favor of providing western homestead land, whereas those who predominantly represented
Newer Appalachia tended to vote on the negative side. Congressmen
from Intermediate Appalachia (the Georgia and North Carolina mountains) also tended to oppose the 1852 Homestead Bill.[11]

The threat was genuine. During the 1850s, railroad milage in the
states of Ohio, Indiana, Illinois, Michigan, and Wisconsin would increase from 1,275 to 9,616 miles. Agriculture would boom in those
states, and by 1860, an estimated three-fifths by value of their major
agricultural products were being shipped east—where food prices, although they did not begin to drop, nonetheless ceased to rise in measure
with the rapid rate of urbanization then underway in the East.[12]

Notwithstanding this threat to eastern agriculture, eastern trade and manufacturing interests persisted in supporting free western homestead grants, allying on this issue with westerners.[13] Early in 1860 a weak homestead bill managed to pass both houses of Congress, but President James Buchanan, a Pennsylvanian, vetoed it. Later in 1860, however, an Illinoisan was elected president.

Recall that the decline of per capita food output during the 1850s had been particularly adverse in Newer Appalachia, the Plateau. But in the five midwestern states at that time, exactly the opposite was happening. Despite the Midwest's far faster urbanization, its per capita food output was expanding in the 1850s.[14] Its farm grain production grew 4.5 bushels per capita (an 8 percent rise). The number of farm work animals (horses, mules, asses, and work oxen) increased 12.2 percent per capita. Farm cattle (and also dairy cows within that category) held even, but butter and cheese production grew 39.6 percent per capita (see table 2).[15]

American agriculture clearly crossed a watershed, if not with the 1862 Homestead Act per se, then with its application to lands ever farther west. In the 1870s, U.S. land in farms increased 31 percent and farm output jumped a full 53 percent. During that decade, the U.S. population increased less than half as fast as farm output.[16] As a result, the 1870s became a decade of severe distress for farmers, and the 1880s brought little improvement. Federal land grants to railroads were suspended in 1871, but their effects continued. At some point in the 1870s or 1880s, as larger and larger agricultural surpluses glutted the American market, it should have become obvious that the well-being of *all* American farmers, even of new immigrants, depended on also suspending the operation of the Homestead Act before the High Plains were invaded by farmers whose produce would jeopardize returns for everyone already farming.[17] And, in fact, by the late nineteenth century, almost the entire East would become uncompetitive in producing the main crops that the Midwest and Plains produced for market. One major exception to this was that Virginia's section of the Great Appalachian Valley still managed to supply grains and meat to neighboring cities as cheaply as those could be supplied from the Midwest and Plains.[18] West Virginia's market agriculture, however, faced a crisis when it could not compete with midwestern products after 1873.[19] Concurrently, industrial developments that paid low wages began proliferating in West Virginia. And even in fertile East Tennessee, grain imports from the Midwest were making locally grown grain hard to market in Knoxville by the 1890s.[20] Soon low-wage industrialization would spring up there too in the form of textile mills.

The Homestead Act and the railroad land grants thus helped to hasten Appalachia's economic dependency by artificially (politically) lowering the cost of producing market staples on the Plains. Visualize the typical midwestern farmer and consider how much he already differed, by 1860, from the typical Appalachian farmer. They admittedly shared some similarities. Both still maintained a high measure of self-sufficiency.[21] Both, furthermore, were generally independent producers who owned their own land and their own means of production. Each was thus a free agent. But their economic outlooks were already diverging drastically. The midwestern farmer, with his expanse of prairie loam, was perfectly situated to exploit new fruits of technology such as the mechanical reaper and the thresher. The thresher sold for as little as thirty to forty dollars, and as early as 1840 its use had become widespread even in states with a rolling topography, such as Tennessee— with the significant exception in that state of *East* Tennessee.[22] For most Appalachian farmers, the thresher was simply not worth its price, for it could not increase the average mountain farmer's money income as much as it would cost him in money outlay.

Appalachia's farmers thus mechanized at a far slower rate than most farmers elsewhere in the United States. In the Midwest by 1850 the average farm held $82.53 worth of farming implements, and in non-Appalachian Kentucky the average farm held $75.18 worth, whereas the average on eastern Kentucky's farms was only $27.75 worth.[23] And then during the next thirty years, while the average value of farm implements on midwestern farms rose to $121.60, the average value on non-Appalachian Kentucky farms fell to $67.02, and that on Appalachian Kentucky's farms fell to $23.71.[24]

The midwestern farmer, with his land's prime fertility and easy workability, and with his access via railroads to national and world markets, was becoming an excellent object for investment by eastern capitalists. Most midwestern farmers possessed plentiful land for market farming and merely faced the question of whether to work it labor intensively or capital intensively. The suitability of their land for machine farming increasingly pushed them toward capital-intensive methods.

Meanwhile, the opening of the Plains on westward through land give-aways and cheap transportation—combined with the new labor-saving farm machines—relegated Appalachia's farm families all the more decisively toward subsistence farming alone. And subsistence agriculture, as already mentioned, was denied capital investment because it produced no cash income from which interest could be paid or capital could be repaid.

Prior to the Civil War, eastern capital had helped to finance the export from Appalachia of its agricultural surpluses.[25] After the Civil War, when little or no net farm surplus remained to export from the region, eastern investment was by no means withheld from Appalachia. Rather, outside investment began to take new forms, such as timbering and mining, and under those new forms the mountaineer found himself no longer an independent producer but a wage-earning employee.[26]

By 1880 the poorest strata of the Plateau's people were finding that they must use new economic options if they wished to remain in place. Somewhat more than four thousand Appalachians were mining coal at some point in the course of that year—although only about four thousand at any given time.[27] Also by 1880, several thousand Plateau residents were cutting timber for wages on a seasonal or occasional basis.

This is not to say that expedients within agriculture were completely exhausted. The postbellum years saw continuing use of slash-and-burn methods to clear hillsides that were then cultivated in grain for a few years until returned, via a pasture phase, to woodland. But now population pressure was such that abandoned fields had to be reused sooner. Less time was allowed them to recover to woodland before their turn came for reslashing and reburning. Such overuse of slash-and-burn techniques could trigger severe soil erosion.[28]

Livestock raising continued vital for both subsistence and marketing, but after the Civil War the "open range" tradition came under increasing attack by large landowners. As early as the 1790s almost two hundred landowners on the South Branch of the Potomac (now in northeastern West Virginia) had petitioned the Virginia General Assembly to forbid hogs from running at large. That request from landowners had been refused.[29] Small holders and landless people fiercely defended the open range, upon which their livelihood often depended. Not until the 1830s, forty years later, did Virginia begin to evolve state legislation that allowed local option laws that in turn would permit the fencing of more than just crops. South Carolina, indeed, *protected* the open range (by positive legislation) until well after the Civil War. And, similarly, not until late in the nineteenth century did Tennessee permit the fencing of more than crop land.[30] Alabama had a local-option law from 1866 onward and Georgia from 1872 onward, but it was 1890 or later before the fencing in of livestock was required in any substantial part of the Alabama or Georgia mountains.[31] Similarly in West Virginia, as of the 1890s, livestock owners could register their distinctive ear markings with the clerk of their County Court, and those ear markings constituted legal proof of ownership even if livestock wandered across county lines.[32]

The imposition of fencing constituted a major setback for small farmers, depriving their livestock of many acres of "mast" (mainly acorns and chestnuts), which still at that time fell in abundance from Appalachia's forests. An indication of how plentifully the Plateau's virgin hardwood forests produced mast has been preserved by an early 1890s tree count on 12,263 acres in West Virginia's Wayne and Mingo counties (see table 3). The count revealed an average of six large oak trees per acre, each measuring at least a foot and a half in diameter at four feet above the ground. Ominously, this count was not made to estimate mast production but to identify profitable timber. Besides the six large oak trees, an average of five and a half other marketable trees were found per acre.[33]

Although the destruction of such forests merely awaited the arrival of railway spur lines amidst their fastness, the timber industry did not seriously inhibit livestock production in most of Appalachia until after the turn of the century. Less timber was cut in Appalachia before 1900 than would later be cut during the four years of World War I.[34] One old-time timber surveyor in Clay County in the Plateau section of West Virginia recalled that "during and immediately after the [First] World War, a lot of people tried to get into the lumber business. There were small mills scattered all over the country."[35] In the South overall between 1880 and 1924, the volume of standing timber was reduced by an estimated 90 percent.[36]

Congress in 1911 passed the Weeks Act authorizing the establishment of federal forest reserves in the states. (Until then federal forest reserves had been established only in U.S. territories.) This made possible Appalachian timber preservation—although a 1922 "exchange

Table 3. Tree Count in Virgin Hardwood Forest, Wayne and Mingo
Counties, West Virginia, Early 1890s

Count of Hardwoods		Count of Softwoods	
White Oaks	24,760	Tulip-Poplars	12,450
Chestnut Oaks	38,848	Pines	3,472
Black Oaks	8,525	Lindens	2,325
Red Oaks	943	Cucumbers	240
Hickories	21,298	Buckeyes	28
Chestnuts	7,681	Ashes	271
Locusts	1,996	Hemlocks	903
White Maples	1,588	Total Count of	
Sugar Maples	450	Softwood Trees	19,689
Birches	1,344		
Gums	1,044		
Black Walnuts	393		
Sycamores	13		
Total Count of			
Hardwood Trees	108,878		

NOTE: The count was confined to trees measuring at least 18 inches in diameter at 4 feet
above the ground—with the exception of hickories, locusts, and black walnuts, which were
included if their diameter at that height measured at least 10 inches. The count was made
on 12,263 acres (almost 20 square miles) in Wayne and Mingo counties, West Virginia, in
the watershed of the West Fork of Twelve Pole Creek. The altitude ranged from 650 to
1,000 feet above sea level.

SOURCE: Summers, *The Mountain State*, 30–32.

law" allowed the Interior Department to provide lumber companies
with good timber lands in exchange for cut-over lands.[37]

Because Appalachia's wholesale deforestation for commercial timber
was thus an early twentieth-century phenomenon, it cannot be blamed
for the region's nineteenth-century agricultural decline. The dairy
products increase that accompanied overall livestock decline in the
1850s (see table 2) shows that fully fifty years before the region's virgin
forests were devastated, a plentitude of meat protein could no longer be
taken for granted by Appalachia's people. Ideally, that 1850s turn toward dairy protein would have involved providing better (even if less)

grazing land for milk cows, as well as feeding them more grain. But increased milk production could also be gained by milking more cows from a herd or, as a last resort, by milking each cow longer after each of its calvings.

As for other agricultural options, an increase of grain production promised farmers greater economic flexibility than did the production of crops like tobacco or cotton, which offered little use at home and which could only be marketed as plant products. A crib of corn, by contrast, could either be sold as such or distilled into whiskey and then sold. Or it could be consumed by the farm family or fed to livestock. If fed to livestock, the animals could then in turn be milked, eaten, or sold. In the postbellum South, the value of livestock tended to fluctuate with the market value of cotton,[38] but nonetheless, the diverse uses of grain and livestock fostered less dependence than did purely cash crops such as tobacco and cotton. Cash crops that lacked home uses maximized a farm family's reliance on conditions beyond its control. Similarly, whenever a grain or livestock farmer turned to wage labor (timbering, coal mining, etc.) he likewise tended to increase his dependence on conditions beyond his own control.

Steven Hahn has shown that postbellum farmers in the Georgia Piedmont increased their production of cotton in tandem with their increasing need for merchandise advances from local storekeepers.[39] Hahn shows that the farmers involved in this situation were primarily trying to meet their families' subsistence needs rather than trying to maximize their financial return.[40] In the process, these Georgia Piedmont farmers increased their dependence on outside market forces beyond their own control.

In the cotton belt, the role of merchandise "advances" provided by local storekeepers was heightened by the 1865 congressional act that terminated state bank notes.[41] Without that law, the direct provision of crop loans by banking institutions would have spread far more widely in the cotton South—and the high-interest merchandise advances of storekeepers would have been that much less. But the 1865 law stymied southern banking from "atomizing" in tandem with the post-Civil War atomization of southern farming units. Merchandise provided by thousands of local storekeepers became the main source of crop loans to southern farmers. As one economist puts it, "Deposits and checks had not been widely used in the South in antebellum times. With state bank notes taxed out of existence and few national banks in the territory of the South circulating their own promissory notes [i.e., banknotes], this primitive and usury-laden system of barter prospered."[42]

After the creation of local banknotes was curtailed in 1865, an increased proportion of locally used capital was imported. Imported capital was less likely than local capital to finance local markets, and particularly to finance local markets that were supplied by local production. Local production with outside financial backing tended to be export oriented. Hardest hit by this trend were areas with a high capacity for production but a low level of accumulated wealth with which to back the issuing of banknotes and loans—areas that, in short, were still rapidly developing frontiers. Frontier areas, such as much of Plateau Appalachia remained in 1865, offered greater productive capacity per capita than did older areas, but frontier areas were also less endowed with the accumulated financial reserves that after 1865 were required as backing for banknotes.[43]

Until West Virginia was created in 1863, no single state was predominantly Appalachian, and this doubtlessly helped to restrict the region's independent financial resources. Within Virginia's state politics prior to the Civil War, for instance, banking discrimination was one of the main grievances of western Virginians. By 1810 western Virginia contained more than one hundred thousand people, and yet not a single bank was allowed to open there. When unchartered "private banks" stepped into this breech by accepting deposits and issuing banknotes, the Virginia legislature in Richmond levied heavy fines that squelched them. Finally, under western pressure, a Wheeling bank was chartered in 1817 and was authorized to establish branches at Morgantown, Clarksburg, and Wellsburg. Another western Virginia bank was not allowed, however, until 1834.[44]

An equally typical alignment occurred in early Tennessee when the 1819 financial panic inspired pressure from the Nashville basin and western Tennessee for the establishment of an easy-money bank to relieve debtors, but the proposal was defeated by opposition from Tennessee's then most developed section, East Tennessee.[45]

By the time the next great panic struck in 1837, the Nashville basin's development had surged ahead of East Tennessee's. When East Tennessee pressed in 1838 for an easy-money state bank to finance internal improvements, western Tennessee joined that cause. But this new bank plan was opposed in the state legislature by representatives from the Nashville basin, which by then had grown well developed.[46]

The federal crackdown on state-regulated banknotes came in 1865. How significant was it? In the received wisdom, its significance was vitiated by a change in the method of issuing loans—by no longer issuing most loans in the form of newly created banknotes but in the form of bank deposits that could then be drawn out by writing checks.[47] Unfortunately, such new bank-deposit loans circumvented the 1865 crackdown much more exclusively for the benefit of individuals who actually received those loans than the pre-1865 cash loans had operated. Before 1865 just as afterwards, the relatively rich (or at least the enterprising) received most of the loans made. But loans made in cash had directly benefited nonborrowers (the general population) because cash changed hands not only in large transactions, like checks, but changed hands at all levels of economic exchange. The beauty of plentiful cash had been that some of it had trickled down to almost everyone in its vicinity. Checks changed hands only between the relatively rich, whereas cash had changed hands between virtually everyone.

When state-chartered banks were effectively prohibited from issuing banknotes, many of them, if sufficiently large, then acquired charters as national banks in order to regain this right. But Congress had set a limit on the overall amount of banknotes that national banks as a body could issue. This limit of $300 million was quickly approached by eastern banks alone (generally the first to be chartered), and banks in other regions, if and when they too eventually received national charters, were left with the dregs of the banknote quota.

It would be difficult to exaggerate the significance of money-creating rights in the decades following the Civil War. From 1869 to 1899, the U.S. population nearly doubled, farm production more than doubled, and the value of manufactures (calculated in constant prices) grew six times.[48] Despite all this growth, circulating cash failed even to double during those thirty years. Calculated per capita, circulating cash fell about 10 percent in the United States from 1865 to 1890.[49] Two very important changes were involved here. One was that now loans by state banks could no longer take the form of newly issued banknotes, for state banks were now permitted to create new money only in the form of deposits against which their borrowers could then write checks. And the other important change was that Congress failed to authorize national banks to accept real estate in any form as collateral for loans—a de facto prohibition against national-bank mortgages that stayed in effect until 1914. Because the assets of Appalachia's local people were primarily real estate assets (mainly land, minerals, and timber), Appalachians qualified for relatively little credit from the only banks that could issue banknotes, national banks.

But how about greenbacks? By 1865 about $450 million in U.S. government greenbacks were circulating, and by 1879 this had dropped only to about $350 million. Nonetheless—and despite the growth of gold and silver specie that had begun with the California gold rush—cash growth soon fell far behind America's rapid overall financial growth. When the Civil War ended, the United States held only $1.50 in deposits for every dollar of cash; but by 1914 deposits would rise to $9 for every cash dollar.[50] Even national banks, although they were allowed to issue loans in cash, could reap more profit by issuing loans in the form of checking deposits. Behind national bank notes the government required 111 percent U.S. bond ownership, but the government required no significant reserves behind deposits in national banks.[51] This encouraged even national banks to expand checking-deposit loans more readily than banknote loans.

What this all added up to was a new financial system in the United States. Marking the break with the pre-Civil War system was the fact that whereas all forms of cash were interchangeable, bank checks were *not* automatically changeable into cash. A check-issuing bank would convert its own checks into cash, but other banks would generally accept checks only on deposit. Thus checks were an inconvenience for people without their own bank accounts in which to deposit them. Easy money still existed in the form of bank accounts, but no longer in the form of banknotes. This amounted to easy money for the rich but not for the poor. Before the Civil War there had been no such trend. From 1834 to 1860 the circulating cash had, in fact, grown faster than all forms of bank deposits, rising 251 percent while bank deposits had risen only 204 percent.[52]

The postbellum cash drought and concurrent deposit boom affected people's lives. Altina Waller's 1988 book *Feud* furnishes a detailed account of one preindustrial mountain entrepreneur—Devil Anse Hatfield—who was hobbled by the postbellum cash drought and whose assets were eventually bought up by people who had plenty of money at their disposal. Devil Anse Hatfield held several thousand acres of timberland through most of the 1870s and 1880s, but he lacked any good way to capitalize either his holdings or his crew's labor, and he was forced out of business.

This occurred in the heart of Plateau Appalachia on the West Virginia side of the Tug Fork River, which separates West Virginia from Kentucky. When first starting his timber business in 1869, Hatfield lacked any significant money to invest in it. He operated on credit in the form of store merchandise, promising in 1872, for instance, to make a large delivery of poplar logs on the Tug Fork's spring 1873 floodwaters in exchange for advances of food and supplies from a storekeeper, John Smith. Devil Anse was unusual for his generation of Tug Fork Hatfields in that he did not inherit title to sufficient land to provide a comfortable subsistence for his family. So some personal belt tightening probably helped motivate him to embark on his timber business. But he was also clearly trying to make more profit than his family's subsistence required.[53]

Feud integrates the events of the Hatfield-McCoy feud with the twists and turns of Devil Anse Hatfield's timber business. By December 1887, his business had suffered many reverses and he could continue operations only by mortgaging much of his land to a Logan, West Virginia, merchant, thereby fending off other merchants who were suing him for nonpayment of previous debts. At that point a coalition of Kentucky McCoys—instigated by Devil Anse's former land rival Perry Cline—strategically chose to harass the Hatfields, culminating in the January 1888 Battle of Grapevine Creek. This trouble evidently prevented timber deliveries that would have enabled Devil Anse to liquidate his December 1887 mortgage, and he had to sell his timberlands to prevent their seizure for debt. Had these financial pressures not prompted him to sell out, he could have awaited a much higher price, because the Norfolk and Western Railway had announced a plan to place rails along either the Tug Fork or the Guyandotte River. (The Guyandotte flowed forty miles east of the Tug.) Later in 1888 the Norfolk and Western began surveying a Tug Fork route, and early in 1889 it announced its choice of that route.[54]

Devil Anse Hatfield's behavior was extremely market oriented, but what was he thinking? Was he entrepreneurial? *Did* he, as I claim, wish to make more profit than his family's subsistence required? The book

Feud tells us that Devil Anse's "shift in emphasis" from farming to timbering was demonstrated by his need to purchase corn in 1873. And "a list of personal items charged at Smith's store," it says, "reveals Anse's interest in what might in the mountains be considered luxury items— fancy bonnets and combs for his wife and daughters, gold watches, and 'fine' boots, frock coats, and hats for himself and his men." But the book immediately adds a not-merely-profit-minded interpretation of all this, because "this lavish expenditure for clothes and personal possessions indicated a concern with appearance that reflected [Devil Anse's] desire to enhance his status in the community."[55]

Evidence like this, however, shows that entrepreneurial thinking was not confined to only one "class" in Appalachia's history. In those Gilded Age years after the Civil War, what was increasingly limited to one class was entrepreneurial *success*. About the same time Devil Anse Hatfield had to sell out, three Wheeling capitalists bought about 2,000 acres in the Tug Fork area for less than $3,000. A mere three years later, in 1891, they were able to sell 1,568 standing poplar trees on that land for $7,840.[56] Such cases were typical. Wheeling had several national banks, and Wheelingites with large financial assets could use those assets as collateral to borrow more money, and then could invest that loan money in developing and marketing assets which themselves were inadmissible as national-bank collateral. Through such outside funds entering the Tug Fork Valley, general land values there rose more than 400 percent from 1890 to 1892.[57]

But why did Devil Anse Hatfield not borrow money from, at any rate, a state bank instead of acquiring merchandise on credit and borrowing money from merchants? He lived in what is now (since 1895) Mingo County. In Hatfield's day Mingo was still part of Logan County, and Logan County had no bank at all until 1893, five years after Devil Anse was forced out of business. His affairs had often taken him to the county seat, the town of Logan,[58] but Logan itself had no bank until 1900.[59]

As in the Deep South during the same period, banking failed to "atomize" in Appalachia after state-chartered banks lost the power to issue banknotes. Branch banks could usefully have provided some banking services in small towns, but federal law prohibited national banks to operate branches, and only two Appalachian states, Virginia and Georgia, allowed state banks to do so.[60]

At this same time, wage labor was proliferating in Plateau Appalachia. The shortage there of cash not only influenced the way low-money entrepreneurs such as Devil Anse Hatfield carried on their businesses but also influenced the lives of wage earners. Some wage workers were paid primarily or exclusively "in kind" (in goods), and most of the rest were issued company scrip that could command goods only at company stores. Coal operators' use of company scrip allowed company stores to charge artificially high prices, but such price gouging was just an auxiliary feature (which many companies did practice). The main reason coal companies began paying wages in company scrip was because neither they nor their banks possessed enough cash for payroll purposes.[61] About two-thirds of coal's market value consisted of wages at that time (see table 4). Coal companies sold their coal to railroads, manufacturers, and wholesalers who generally paid for it by check. After depositing those checks in their own banks, the coal companies could in turn write their own checks to their suppliers, including to the wholesalers who provisioned their company stores. Generally coal companies could not draw sufficient cash from their banks to pay wages in cash, for the banks generally lacked access to that much cash—enough to turn most of the region's gross coal income into cash. Nor could the coal companies generally pay their employees by issuing checks, for their banks lacked sufficient cash to redeem the checks. Company scrips served, in effect, as each company's private checks, each company store playing the part of an "in kind" redemption bank.

Company scrip, company store—such a system may not have sounded very enticing to a prospective employee. As the nineteenth century ended, however, many hard-pressed Appalachian farm families lacked any alternatives they considered more attractive, and they turned to such wage labor to supplement their farming. The context in which such farm families allotted their work was the living standard that they could have sustained had they continued only to farm. As compared with farm families' "stand pat" option and its declining living standard, even a low wage—whether it was paid in cash, in "kind," or in company scrip—could be attractive if it made possible merely a slight improvement in a farm family's living standard. As James C. Scott points out in *The Moral Economy of the Peasant,* "Because labor is often the only factor of production the peasant possesses in relative abundance, he may

Table 4. Bituminous Coal Value, Wages, and Number of Workers
1870–1902

	Value per ton ($)	Wages paid per ton ($)	Wages as % of coal value	Average number of employees at any time (est.)
Older Appalachia				
1870	1.45	0.95	65	796
1880	0.91	0.49	53	2,193
1890*	0.91	0.68	74	5,576
1902**	0.95	0.60	63	15,275
Newer Appalachia				
1870	2.15	1.36	63	846
1880	1.33	0.76	57	3,940
1890*	0.97	0.68	75	10,841
1902**	1.06	0.67	63	21,412
Ohio, Indiana, Illinois, Michigan, and Wisconsin				
1870	2.26	1.30	58	15,330
1880	1.38	0.93	68	38,104
1890	0.97	0.72	74	50,711
1902**	1.10	0.81	74	84,657

* Several counties with small production omitted by census (data incomplete).

** Counties below 200,000 tons omitted by census (maximum: 7% of Appalachian output).

SOURCE: 1870 Census, vol. 3; 1880 Census, vol. 15; 1890 Census, vol. 7; and 1902 Census Bureau Special Report on Mines and Quarries.

have to move into labor-absorbing activities with extremely low returns until subsistence demands are met."[62]

What table 4 sets forth is one consequence of this. In 1870, when less than 750,000 long tons of coal were mined in Appalachia, 65 percent of that coal's selling price was passed on to employees as wages in

Older Appalachia and, in Newer Appalachia, 63 percent was passed on as wages. By 1880, however, wage earners' share of coal proceeds had fallen to 53 percent in Older Appalachia and to 57 percent in Newer Appalachia.[63]

Table 4 also shows that the average price *commanded* by Appalachian coal likewise fell between 1870 and 1880. But the fact that wages (per ton) fell faster than coal's market value suggests that the origin of Appalachia's worsening position vis-à-vis the buyers of its coal lay in the willingness of many of its people to work cheaply. Put differently, had Appalachians held out for higher wages, less coal would have been mined in Appalachia, but it would have commanded a higher price when marketed.

Wage demands were low in Appalachia because the region's income from agriculture was low. In West Virginia, for instance, 1880 saw income from farming (including from farm labor) averaging only $144 per year, whereas income from non-agricultural work averaged $539 per year. By 1900, farming income averaged $150 while nonfarming income averaged $481—within which average West Virginia coal-mining income stood at $451 that year.[64]

W. Arthur Lewis cites similar examples from his studies of Third World development problems. In one example, Lewis compares Nigeria's underdevelopment with the successful development achieved by Australia. According to Lewis, "The market price gave the Nigerian for his peanuts a 700-lbs.-of-grain-per-acre level of living, and the Australian for his wool a 1600-lbs.-of-grain-per-acre level of living, not because of differences in competence, nor because of marginal utilities or productiveness in peanuts or wool, but because these were the respective amounts of food that their cousins could produce on the family farms." Lewis is explicit that "low productivity in food set the factoral terms of trade" (that is, the terms of trade per "factor," such as per worker) and he points out that not only peanuts and wool but also "minerals fall into this competing set. . . . Mineral-bearing lands were not infinitely elastic, but the labor force was."[65]

To see Lewis's principle at work on its positive side—in favor of the independent producer of a satisfying subsistence (whether actual or only potential)—we need not look all the way to Australia but merely back to the American Midwest in the 1850s. According to the 1860 U.S. Census, "At Cincinnati in 1848 and 1849, (which was the beginning of the greatest railroad enterprises,) the average price of hogs was $3 per hundred [pounds of dressed pork]. In 1860 and 1861 it was double that. . . . The cheap prices of the west have gradually approximated to the high prices of the east, and this solely in consequence of cheapening the cost of transportation, which inures to the benefit of the farmer."[66]

Why did these transportation benefits inure to the benefit of the farmer? Why did the price of food rise in the Midwest where it was being produced rather than falling where it was being consumed—in cities such as New York City and Philadelphia? Why did the Midwest, and particularly its farmers, reap most of the benefit from the plummeting cost of shipments to and from its region?

Over the entire period from 1816 to 1860, the average prices of Cincinnati's major exports rose dramatically in relation to the prices of Cincinnati's major imports. From 1816 to 1860, that midwestern city's terms of trade on its major exports and imports improved more than 200 percent.[67] In the Midwest overall by 1860, a given amount of farm produce could buy more than twice the amount of manufactured goods that it had been able to buy in 1816.[68] And it was mainly the individual farmer who reaped these profits. The antebellum prices paid for live hogs in Cincinnati amounted to about 80 percent of the eventual wholesale value of the packed pork and lard. Furthermore, the packers generally paid farmers or drovers in cash for their live hogs, not in any form of scrip.[69] Likewise in the Chicago market, farmers corralled the lion's share of proceeds. As of 1860, farmers received 84 percent of the wholesale value of Chicago's leading nine farm commodities.[70]

Why were the Midwest's falling transportation costs thus translated into higher income for midwestern farmers rather than causing lower prices for live hogs and for packed pork? Raúl Prebisch, whose ideas we glanced at in the Introduction, would have said that this occurred because midwestern agriculture had access to plentiful capital. Because plentiful capital was available (so Prebisch would have said), technological innovations could be made in the Midwest and productivity per worker could be increased there without triggering a fall in prices—allowing instead an income increase for midwestern farmers.

The W. Arthur Lewis answer would be somewhat different—not contradictory but describing the situation from a grassroots perspective. Lewis would say that the midwestern farmer would not have raised food for market unless he and his family could thereby live at a higher standard than they would have obtained by using their land to provide only their own subsistence. Lewis illustrates the economic principle at work here the principle that basically determines the terms of trade between countries or regions—by saying that "if tea had been a temperate rather than a tropical crop its price would have been perhaps five times as high as it was. And if wool had been a tropical rather than a temperate crop it would have been had for perhaps one-fifth of the ruling price."[71] In other words, whatever hinders a capital-poor country from adequately feeding itself will, by that very fact, reduce the price at which its people will likely be willing to sell their produce on the market. (And it will also reduce the price at which they'll tend to sell their labor, which by extension lowers the price of what they produce.) And here the hindrance under which farmers have labored in the tropics— the tropics' paucity of topsoil—is matched by certain self-defeating practices that characterized Appalachian agriculture, such as planting hillsides with soil-depleting, erosion-accelerating crops such as corn.

Thus Appalachia acquired disadvantageous terms of trade for the same sorts of reasons that many tropical countries did. Another illustration used by W. Arthur Lewis makes the similarity still clearer. In sugar cane production, says Lewis,

productivity is extremely high by any biological standard. . . . Output per acre has about trebled over the course of the last 75 years, a rate of growth of productivity which is unparalleled . . . by the wheat industry. Nevertheless workers in the sugar industry continue to walk barefooted and to live in shacks, while workers in wheat enjoy among the highest living standards in the world. . . . The subsistence sectors of tropical economies are able to release however many workers the sugar industry may want, at wages which are low, because tropical food production per head is low. However vastly productive the sugar industry may become, the benefit accrues chiefly to industrial purchasers in the form of lower prices for sugar. (The capitalists who invest in sugar do not come into the argument because their earnings are determined not by productivity in sugar but by the general rate of profit on capital . . .). . . . The prices of tropical commercial crops [for export] will always permit only subsistence wages until, for a change, capital and knowledge are put at the disposal of the subsistence producers to increase the productivity of tropical food production for home consumption. This analysis applies to all tropical commercial products [for export] of which an unlimited supply can be produced because unlimited natural resources exist—in relation to demand.[72]

How can Lewis's analysis of tropical export products help us see the position of Appalachia's export producers? As the option of wage work arose in Appalachia, Lewis would say, and as farmers increasingly availed themselves of export-oriented timbering and mining jobs, they were acting in the knowledge that greater poverty faced them if they continued merely to farm and did *not* accept the wage jobs. Wages of ten cents an hour exerted more attraction on a family that might go hungry without them than wages of twenty cents an hour exerted on a family doing quite well simply by farming. A dollar-a-day job might be more attractive in Appalachia than a two-dollar-a-day job in the Midwest. A midwestern farmer would have scrutinized a two-dollar-a-day offer, knowing that greater prosperity probably awaited him if he chose instead to operate as a free agent, farming for the market as an independent producer.[73] Even before the government began dispensing free land under the Homestead Act, the pay for a day's common labor in 1861 in southeastern Iowa was able to buy five bushels of corn or forty pounds of pork.[74] These high purchasing-power wages for common labor resulted from the strong market position of landowning farmers in the Midwest. Midwestern farm owners' strong market position enabled midwestern farm hands in turn to exact high-living-standard wages from those farmers. And the midwestern farm owner's strong market position was itself undergirded by the fact that if the market prices offered for his farm products dropped, he could still remain quite prosperous by resorting to subsistence farming alone. That was the basic foundation of the midwestern farmer's prosperity—the fact that if all else failed, subsistence farming alone would keep him prosperous. (And it helped that state laws were passed virtually everywhere to guarantee home places, and to guarantee enough land to maintain subsistence, against seizure to pay debts.)[75]

Reading this in the other direction—reading it upward from the midwestern farmer's attractive subsistence-farming option—we find not only that the prices of farm products rose in the Midwest during the 1850s (indeed, the California gold rush could have caused some of that price rise by pouring $320 million worth of specie into the U.S. economy by 1855)[76] but that later a rising share of the proceeds from midwestern coal mining went into the wages of midwestern miners. While Appalachia's miners were receiving a steadily smaller portion of the value of their coal output—11 percent less by 1880 than the portion they had gotten in 1870—exactly the opposite was happening in the Midwest. By 1880 midwestern miners were receiving a 17 percent larger portion of what their coal sold for than they had received in 1870 (see table 4).[77] The fact that the wages of midwestern miners per ton of coal fell slower than the price of midwestern coal indicates that those wages were in fact helping to hold up the coal price. As a result, it became advantageous for coal operators to mine coal elsewhere—in Appalachia, for instance, where weaker wage demands prevailed.

Why then did Appalachia's farmer-miners stay put? Why did they not move to the Midwest, where both farming and mining paid better, or indeed continue farther west and file a homestead claim? Some did avail themselves of those alternatives, but most people stayed in Appalachia despite the far lower income available there.[78] What motivated them to stay? Their behavior belied Frederick Jackson Turner's claim that "men would not accept inferior wages and a permanent position of social subordination when this promised [homestead] land . . . was theirs for the taking."[79]

To this question, Appalachian ethnographic studies have furnished a clear answer. Most of those who stayed in Appalachia harbored motives that were not dominated by individual economic aspirations. And later, when World War I created a spate of jobs outside the region, immigrants and blacks did emigrate out of the region in large numbers to fill those jobs,[80] whereas proportionally fewer of Appalachia's native whites did so. The mass migration of Appalachian whites began only when World War II created such extensive outside labor opportunities that nuclear families could migrate as parts of extended family units, as parts of what mountain sociologists call "family groups."[81] All this is meat for the next chapter, which concerns economic mentality.

But before even broaching the question of mentality, it is clear that many Appalachian wage earners initially could live at a higher material level by working for a pittance (while farming on the side) than they could by simply farming without taking a wage job. This insight is important.

3

Rural Appalachia's Subsistence-Barter-and-Borrow Systems

The "borrowing system" allowed scarce tools, labor, and products to circulate to the benefit of all and responded to the ongoing neighborhood need for exchange and mutual assistance. People utilized this neighborly network for most of the transactions necessary to the practice of farming. To have productive implements "and not be willing to share them in some sort with the whole community is an unpardonable crime," Caroline Kirkland warned prospective emigrants. "Your wheelbarrows, your shovels, your utensils of all sorts, belong, not to yourself, but to the public, who do not think it necessary even to *ask* a loan, but take it for granted." Outsiders, unversed in these customs, frequently misunderstood.

—John Mack Faragher, *Sugar Creek*

A scholar has remarked that the greatest success achieved by America's massive effort to export economic development to the Third World "was the attention it focussed on the transformation of our *own* early economy."[1] This may be so, but, contrariwise, one of the ideas that has hindered America's success in exporting development has also hindered scholarly understanding of early America. This is the idea that all development has to be measurable by the same yardstick.

The same economic goals have been pursued in different ways, and "development" has meant different things to people who have pursued similar goals in different ways. People have pursued similar goals by such different means that at times they have viewed each others' behavior with incomprehension. Thus I am less sanguine than the above scholar who implies that recent studies of America's early economy have increased our understanding of our own economic development. Admittedly, in the much-studied New England region, the thinking of early farm families has been reconstructed quite imaginatively by some scholars. Several New England case studies have scrutinized barter. One of them shows that central Massachusetts farm families, after bartering mainly among themselves for generations, began bartering more and more with storekeepers and thereby, like flies entering a spider's web, became entangled in the outside world's capitalist economy.[2]

In this book so far I have asked why so many descendants of the free-holding, prosperous farmers of early nineteenth-century Appalachia became coal miners, and also why they became poorer. Those two questions are connected, but how? Did the farmers become poorer before entering the mines, or did their living standard fall only after they became miners? This is the main question I have posed thus far, and, without denying the likelihood of many exceptions, I have concluded that Appalachian farmers who turned to wage labor generally did so because as full-time farmers they were growing poorer. This does not mean they were already impoverished but merely that their living standard was falling. They may not have sunk to a condition that they would have called "impoverishment," but perhaps they saw its specter in their future. Because the living standard they could sustain on their farms was falling, they felt constrained to accept wages that made possible—when combined with continued farming by other family members if not by themselves—a living standard perhaps only slightly higher.

This book is not attempting to make any assessment of an Appalachian character type. It is trying to identify economic opportunities (and constraints) as they evolved over the course of Appalachia's history. It is also looking for relationships and comparisons beyond Appalachia—for relationships that helped shape Appalachia's economic opportunities (and its constraints), and for comparisons that provide a means of measurement. Doing this requires evaluating economic opportunities and constraints through the eyes of those who experienced them.

Why were Appalachia's people willing to work for low wages? Primarily because of subsistence needs. Surely some of them, however, embraced wage work in an enterprising spirit. Appalachia's traditional subsistence-barter-and-borrow relations, based on voluntary, rather than contracted, reciprocity, encouraged many of the region's early wage workers to expect that they would receive *more* than merely their wages. Often they expected their loyal service to morally obligate their employers to meet whatever needs they had. Labor, after all, was then still the most pervasive form of investment in Appalachia's economy, and generally, after volunteering one's labor, one could confidently await return favors.

Of course, the new wage work was not actually volunteer work, but Appalachian wage workers often liked to feel that they were still volunteers. An early firebrick manufacturer reminiscing about eastern Kentucky wrote that "I cannot forget the loyal, able and efficient workers I found in this district. They were not only willing to render good service but they proved to be the best friends I ever had. . . . They were ready to come at any hour of the night or day and spurned the offer of pay. We will never forget the safety we felt among these mountaineers."[3]

In such an atmosphere, an enterprising spirit of investing labor may well have played a supplemental part in manning mines and logging operations—drawing some people into wage labor who were not driven to it. Once they *were* so employed, however, they probably began seeing their position from a new perspective. Many or most of them could not support their families solely on the wages timber or coal operators were paying. The more mature workers, especially those with families, usually had recourse to other means. Often they still held land, although probably over the years their land had undergone depletion and subdivision. Because Appalachia's timber and mining operations were rural, most of the region's wage earners (even nonlandowners) had little difficulty in practicing agriculture on some scale part time.

For such wage earners, as for full-time farmers, agriculture continued to be of the capital-poor, labor-intensive sort that benefited from large families. This was particularly so in Appalachia's Plateau subregion (Newer Appalachia). Demographic stabilization eluded the Plateau partly because of its industrialization. Plateau farmers could continue raising the large families still demanded by their continuing subsistence agriculture, and, thanks to rural industries, they could hope that their children, when grown, could acquire wage jobs and remain close by.

In the less-industrialized Older Appalachia, meanwhile, the availability of fewer wage jobs with which to supplement farm income meant that people who wished to continue living there rurally had to gravitate toward a more mechanized and capitalized agriculture. There a large family would more likely force a painful choice on the next generation—the choice either to migrate or to subdivide the land further. The point of mechanizing and capitalizing was to produce just as much output from a farm with fewer hands, and thus to need fewer children.

Such money investment demanded, however, a money return, so the agriculture of Older Appalachia perforce drew closer to the American norm than did the bifurcated economic life that by 1900 was commonplace on the Plateau.[4]

The Plateau's pattern of work allocation grew bifurcated to an exceptional degree, and this was not the Plateau's only economic abnormality. Another exceptional circumstance followed from the Plateau's role as the last large frontier area in the eastern United States. The exploitation of frontier economic opportunities (through land speculation, for instance) had required initiative, versatility, and often a supply of capital. Those pioneers who achieved a level of comfort and high status often stayed put. In numerous Appalachian areas, many of the very earliest pioneer families became leading citizens right where they had pioneered.[5] But less successful early pioneers, or their children, tended to move on to the next frontier to seek some new speculative bonanza. Meanwhile, later settlers with lower economic expectations arrived and expanded the enterprises already underway—people who realized that speculative gains were no longer likely but who were willing to accept a moderate subsistence in exchange for security.[6]

Such a process characterized the opening and settlement of many frontier regions, and in Appalachia there exists evidence of an ambitious and speculative mentality not only among many of the pioneers who pushed down the Great Appalachian Valley in the eighteenth century but also among many of those who scattered into the Plateau country during the first half of the nineteenth century.

Such pioneers could, at first, afford to be speculative. Nature's bounty provided them a relatively easy self-sufficiency. To be completely subsistence oriented would have been redundant. Even if their speculations failed, as often happened because markets were distant, they could easily maintain their underlying subsistence.

Those who directly followed the pioneers generally found less opportunity to acquire riches and status. Subsistence continued secure, however, for this second wave of settlers. The products they traded to acquire merchandise and money were products they drew from their surplus production. Eventually population expansion, resource depletion, Civil War destruction, and Civil War legislation combined to force living standards down for most Appalachians, but even then they did not totally abandon agriculture—like market-excluded farmers elsewhere were doing by migrating to city wage jobs. Rather, wage jobs came to

them, especially in the Plateau subregion (Newer Appalachia). This inaugurated Plateau Appalachia's exceptional incidence of part-time
farming, which by the 1920s would reach mass proportions.[7]

This also defined the point at which the region's *entrepreneurs* ceased
to replicate *their* previous pattern—their pattern of repeated migration
in search of new speculative bonanzas. The Plateau's population boom
in the 1870s, which by the 1880s was closing this "internal frontier" of
the eastern United States, came at a time when no easy new frontier
remained to be opened elsewhere, even in the West. Homestead land
was available, of course, but by the 1880s there remained only a remote
chance to acquire a fortune from scratch in the West. The average newcomer without capital stood little chance of acquiring wealth in the fin-
de-siècle West.

Yet even when all frontiers disappear, not everyone grows subsistence
oriented. As the Plateau frontier closed, some people stayed entrepreneurial. They stayed in place and continued speculating. Although
most of the investment capital for mining development came from the
northern United States, some of Appalachia's early coal operators, and
many of its land and mineral buyers, were drawn from among those local people who could afford entrepreneurial risks.[8] From earlier-settled
areas, those frontier entrepreneurs who remained unsatisfied with their
gains had generally moved on. But as the frontier disappeared, this option lost its allure. From the Appalachian Plateau—as likewise from the
Rocky Mountains and from the far Northwest—there remained no further beckoning destination. In these last three frontiers of the contiguous United States, trapped frontier entrepreneurs turned from
exploiting mainly resources (and their future potential) to exploiting
their fellows as well. As a consequence, each of these final frontiers soon
saw class war.[9]

Such, in outline, was the early Appalachian experience. What can it
tell us about mentality? Among the "new rural historians," a debate
about the mentality of early America's farmers has persisted since the
late 1970s, inspiring many case studies. James T. Lemon and others
have claimed that early American farmers were generally enterprise oriented, whereas James A. Henretta and others have contended that early
American farmers were generally subsistence and security oriented.[10]

Unfortunately this mentality debate has been rooted in ideology.
Louis Hartz's famous 1955 book *The Liberal Tradition in America*
claimed that from about 1800 onward, virtually everyone in America

had "the mentality of an independent entrepreneur."[11] Liberal scholars such as James T. Lemon have agreed and have sought evidence for an even earlier transformation of the average American to "economic man." And plenty of evidence has been found—not often of any transformation *to* "economic man," but evidence of economic men avidly pursuing wealth in seventeenth- and eighteenth-century America.

One scholar, for example, has discovered acquisitive entrepreneurship yielding striking success stories on the northwest Connecticut frontier in the mid-eighteenth century.[12] Probing back further, another scholar has found that *early* "eighteenth-century economic possibilities released ambition" among Connecticut farmers.[13] Still another scholar has found evidence, in the mid- to late seventeenth century, of an acquisitive and speculative spirit pervading newly settled parts of the Connecticut River Valley in central Massachusetts.[14] And a truly pioneering scholar has shown that profit-minded entrepreneurs even financed the founding of most of the earliest Massachusetts towns.[15]

Meanwhile, on the radical side of the argument—as ammunition against this "acquisitive" version of early American mentality—scholars have concentrated on showing that well into the nineteenth century, typical American farmers were preoccupied with their families' subsistence and security needs, and that thus they could only have given, at most, secondary attention to achieving speculative gains, because such gains (at least under nineteenth-century conditions in the East) would have required speculating dangerously with the land they needed for subsistence.[16]

This ideologically inspired controversy between "liberal" and "radical" new rural historians has thus debated the goals pursued by early American farmers. If the economic goal of most early American farmers was merely to subsist in comfort and amity—to maintain a "competency"—then those ordinary farmers would deserve none of the credit that liberals wish to bestow on them: the credit for spreading capitalism. But by the same token, they also would deserve none of the radicals' *blame* for spreading capitalism (blame that the radicals wish to place elsewhere). In dozens of case studies, members of the radical school have argued that almost all early American farmers were subsistence oriented. The products that they marketed, so the radicals correctly point out, were drawn mostly from surpluses of what they raised for their own subsistence. Only after American capitalism had grown highly developed, with an elaborate transportation and communication infrastructure, only then did most American farmers become market oriented and perhaps entrepreneurial—but then only because the market had grown so pervasive that it left them no other way to maintain their home subsistence.

This radical interpretation of rural American mentality has been challenged by the liberals, who claim that entrepreneurial attitudes predominated among American farmers from an early date—perhaps as early as the mid-1600s.[17]

But by thus focusing on the question of *when* a subsistence mentality gave way to a spirit of enterprise, the debate about mentality has uncritically been mingled with an older debate about how capitalism came about. Confusion has resulted. Self-sufficiency and enterprise can too uncritically be defined as opposite orientations. Anything can be called opposites in the realm of mentality. In the material world, however, self-sufficiency and enterprise make natural companions. A secure subsistence encourages enterprise. But on America's East Coast since at least the mid-eighteenth century, subsistence has been growing ever harder to achieve through agriculture. And that pattern has been replicated as each successive frontier has filled with people. In mentality, therefore, most American farmers have grown steadily less enterprising—increasingly more preoccupied with achieving their subsistence needs and maintaining their family security.

In Appalachia's early period, subsistence came easily and an entrepreneurial attitude was common. There were no major markets close by, and grain in particular was hard to export from the region, but by feeding grain to livestock, Appalachia's farmers managed to export large numbers of animals every autumn from the early 1800s until the Civil War. Secure in their subsistence, Appalachia's early farmers tended to be actively acquisitive.

After the Civil War, when a subsistence crisis began threatening the Plateau subregion, market relations continued to expand even there—but that expansion was driven less by acquisitiveness than by subsistence needs.

In early settled parts of the region—particularly in the Great Appalachian Valley, which stretches from northern Virginia to northern Alabama—population growth had drastically slowed by the postbellum period (see table 1), and most farms there remained large enough to satisfy farm families' rising money requirements through increased cash cropping. In the Plateau subregion, by contrast, population expanded 286 percent from 1840 to 1880, and from 1850 to 1880 the size of the average farm shrank by more than half.[18] Many Plateau farm families began facing a stark choice between wage work and migration—and they tended to choose wage work, meanwhile continuing to farm part time.

Throughout this sequence, basic economic goals tended gradually to shift from acquisition toward subsistence because opportunities for acquisition were growing less enticing and home subsistence needs more demanding. Goals changed in response to conditions. And conditions were deteriorating partly because farming practices remained *un*-changed. One farm specialist speaks accurately of "the Southern Appalachians where agriculture had changed little since pioneer times."[19] Such absence of behavioral change contributed to the region's problems.

To date, most of the new rural historians have studied New England or the mid-Atlantic region. But because Appalachia's capitalist era began much more recently than capitalism's rise in the East, perhaps examining Appalachia's economic data and probing its people's mentality might help to settle the new rural history debate. Weighing the commitment of rural people to long-term family security is difficult. James A. Henretta, a radical, admits that economic gain was important to farmers even though their dominant goal was usually to maintain subsistence and security.[20] Similarly, James T. Lemon, a liberal, does not deny that Pennsylvania's early farmers sought material success in order to benefit their families as well as benefiting themselves as individuals.[21] And another liberal, Stephen Innes, admits that a "market orientation did not connote a fully competitive, maximizing ethic. Free men and women in early America did 'accumulate,' but they did not 'maximize,' particularly at the expense of their neighbors."[22]

Thus, to study the strength of economic "familism" *versus* individual (or nuclear family) acquisitiveness will require studying situations in which family goals were incompatible with acquisitive goals—situations in which people had to choose between them. Such a choice has faced thousands of Appalachian people, and many or most have chosen family goals over individual (or nuclear family) economic gain. They have chosen to remain in the vicinity of their parents and siblings—thereby gaining economic security through their loyalty to their family. Only when economic opportunities outside the region became so massive that individuals and nuclear families could migrate as part of extended family units, only then (during World War II) did truly mass migration of native-born whites begin from twentieth-century Appalachia.[23]

The *mentalité* debate between liberals and radicals has thus far not proven very enlightening on its own terms. Something striking about the debate, however, is that the examples used to illustrate widespread enterprise or acquisitiveness usually date from the very early phase of a region's settlement, whereas the evidence presented to prove a subsistence or family-security orientation generally dates from later periods when settlement has grown relatively thick. This accords with a scenario in which an early profusion of entrepreneurial thinking was followed by a fall in the proportion of the population that could afford the luxury of entrepreneurial risks.

Chapter 1 documented widespread enterprise among early Appalachian pioneers whose subsistence base was plentiful. As the bulk of the region's people found themselves having to work harder and harder simply to maintain their basic subsistence, the spirit of enterprise grew increasingly restricted to the region's land-rich elite.

After the Civil War it was not so much enterprise as subsistence needs that brought poorer Appalachians into the timber camps and the mines. And the same applies to those mountaineers who migrated to Piedmont textile jobs (who, according to one source, numbered about 750,000 by 1922).[24] A 1927 study of Piedmont textile workers reports that "great droves of help from the mountains [were] brought down by the labor scouts from the mills during the temporary shortage of labor in the first decade of the twentieth century." Those textile-mill recruits were relatively enterprising, but the 1927 study found that they "were almost invariably doomed to discontent and homesickness. Many of them returned to the mountains."

In contrast to these enterprising recruits, says the 1927 study, were other mountaineers "on whose shoulders fortune had laid a heavy hand." Such hard-pressed mountaineers had "been steadily migrating since the early mills to the present [1927]." Unlike the eager workers who were actively recruited but who often returned home, these people who left the mountains through necessity left them "with mingled emotions," yet these hard-pressed mountaineers tended to stay permanently at the mills.[25] Evidently they possessed no adequate economic niche to which to return in the mountains.

I think this textile migration example can help sift substance from ideology in the *mentalité* debate. The liberals and the radicals have apparently fallen foul of each other through a shared misconception. Those who study the early history of a given region usually report an enterprising spirit among the general run of early settlers, whereas those who study conditions in the same region later usually find the mass of inhabitants *un*ambitious. Each camp can document its findings. Their disagreement seems to stem from a faulty model that both camps use to interpret their data. The students of early settlement apparently assume that any society that is already entrepreneurial by, say, 1680 will automatically become much more entrepreneurial by 1860—whereas those who actually conduct research about the same locality in 1860 evidently assume that the *subsistence* orientation that they find dominant in 1860 must consequently have been all the more pervasive earlier, especially way back in 1680.

An observer of this scholarly debate might wonder if dialectical thinking died out with Marx. Believing that most Americans now exhibit an enterprising mentality, which they do not, scholars have been probing the American past to determine when the American psyche metamorphosed and from what sort of cocoon today's presumed entrepreneurism emerged.

America has admittedly undergone a transition to capitalist economic relations since white settlement began, and especially since the Civil War. But does a transition to capitalism actually evoke more enterprise from most people? This seems unlikely if we define the capitalist transition as a process of land, tools, machinery, and other factors of production becoming the property of people who do not directly work them. Rather, the proportion of people who feel entrepreneurial would be more likely to *de*crease when a decreasing proportion of the population can use its own land, tools, and machinery to supply markets—and when an increasing proportion of the population must thus forego the profits of enterprise.

Those who saw a connection between self-ownership (or its future likeliness) and a spirit of enterprise included Abraham Lincoln. In 1861 Lincoln set forth an economic ideal of "men with their families—wives, sons, and daughters—work[ing] for themselves, on their farms, in their houses, and in their shops taking the whole product to themselves." Lincoln argued that "many independent men, everywhere in these States, a few years back in their lives, were hired laborers. The prudent, penniless beginner in the world labors for wages awhile, saves a surplus with which to buy tools or land for himself, then labors on his own account another while, and at length hires another new beginner to help him. This is the just and generous and prosperous system which opens the way to all—gives hope to all, and consequent energy and progress and improvement of condition to all."[26] Lincoln went so far as to imply that capital should be denied legal equality with labor. "Labor," he said, "is prior to, and independent of, capital. Capital is only the fruit of labor, and could never have existed if labor had not first existed. Labor is the superior of capital, and deserves much the higher consideration."[27]

An extreme instance of expanding self-ownership of land, tools, and profits occurred in the eighteenth century when tens of thousands of rent-racked flax-and-linen producers left tiny leaseholds in Northern Ireland, sailed for the middle colonies of British America, and poured down the spacious and bountiful Great Appalachian Valley. How so many heirs of those enterprising independent producers eventually grew entangled in a web of dependency while the heirs of other enterprising independent producers managed to escape that fate (as in the case of midwestern farmers) is a question this book is trying to answer.

In Appalachia's preindustrial era, enterprise was exerted more often within subsistence-barter-and-borrow economic systems than within the capitalist system. This distinction is crucial. Despite Appalachia's considerable market activity, not enough money circulated in the region for most of its economic transactions, or even most of its market transactions, to involve money. Instead, assets were generally held in less-liquid forms—in land primarily, in slaves to some extent, in productive durables such as tools, in consumption items stored for future use or barter, and in an ubiquitous money-of-account that reflected the economic status of every individual, household, and family group vis-à-vis every other individual, household, and family group with whom it exchanged labor or goods.[28]

Within such subsistence-barter-and-borrow systems no less than within the capitalist system, conditions were sometimes favorable for acquiring profits (albeit limited), and at other times, by contrast, condi-

tions threatened the basic components of subsistence. When a profit
seemed in the offing, enterprise tended to manifest, but any threat to
subsistence naturally demanded priority. Thus not everyone involved in
subsistence-barter-and-borrow systems was subsistence oriented, and,
contrariwise, not everyone involved in the capitalist system was enterprise oriented.

Between the two systems, values differed profoundly—for values are
evaluations of behavior. Enterprise could enhance profit and status
within either system, but enterprise required different behavior between
the two systems (as also did subsistence-aimed efforts), and thus the
mingling of the two systems entailed clashing evaluations of behavior.
The same goal could be pursued within either economic system, but the
means of pursuing it differed. Exchanges in which money was involved
often proved incompatible with transactions void of money. It was hard
to acquire very much money without violating some of the behavior
evaluations that perpetuated subsistence-barter-and-borrow systems.
As David F. Weiman puts it, "Market integration . . . required the replacement of kin and communal bonds with contractual relations based
solely on the exchange of private property. This transformation often
sparked intense social . . . struggles over . . . even the nature of the
obligations between parents and their children."[29] Such dilemmas have
troubled many a mountaineer.

Subsistence-barter-and-borrow systems perforce operated wherever
money was scarce. Within those systems, labor power (plus land on
which to use it) constituted the primary form of wealth. To acquire labor power, one propagated children, adopted children, or bought or
leased slaves. However, as agriculturally productive land grew scarcer,
and as money increasingly entered Appalachia from outside the region,
labor was bartered less and was increasingly hired. Labor continued
abundant, but because much of it was now paid for by outside money—
or by food and other merchandise imported to company stores—less of
the wealth that it produced stayed in the local area or in the region. Had
agriculturally productive land been as expandable as the labor supply,
wage labor need never have grown common in Appalachia. The increasing paucity of available land forced labor to leave self-employment and
enter the market. Because labor entered the market in abundance, it
could command only a low wage. Labor still produced wealth, but no
longer primarily for the laborer or his family.

In West Virginia's Kanawha County, many miners who farmed part time were still living quite well as of 1896. A touring organizer for the United Mine Workers reported that "there does not exist the hunger and suffering here that is found in [other coal fields]. . . . Every spot of ground seems to have received attention from the plow or spade, the houses resemble the homes of the market gardener. . . . This explains their comparatively comfortable position. They raise all the vegetables that they require and this assures them that the wolf shall be kept from the door."[30]

Employers could obtain the services of these part-time farmers cheaply because even a low wage enabled they and their families to live better than they would have lived without it. When we heed the economist W. Arthur Lewis, however, we also see that because the mountaineers who remained full-time farmers were generally growing poorer, those who became miners were likewise destined to grow poorer.[31] The level of wages for which they were willing to work was essentially established by the living standard that they could have sustained had they stayed on farms and not resorted to wage labor. That mental calculation on their part was what placed West Virginia's average miner's income at $451 a year in 1900, when that state's average income from farming was $150.[32]

As farmers entered the mines, they may or may not have reflected about their newly increased dependence on outside forces beyond their control. Many of them viewed mining as merely a temporary expedient—as a way station in their own progression (their "economic development," as they perhaps viewed it) toward a secure landed proprietorship that they would eventually be able to sustain without wage labor. As late as 1932, when Homer Morris interviewed 956 unemployed miners in Kentucky and West Virginia, 48 percent said they wanted to return to farming. Only 11 percent said that they wished to return to mining.[33]

Many such farmer-miners were calculating within different economic systems than the system of their employers—and eventually their employers' system prevailed. This resulted, however, not only because of a ruthlessness undeniably inherent in capitalism but also because a self-defeating factor lurked in Appalachia's subsistence-barter-and-borrow systems. Subsistence agriculture's inherent labor intensivity inspired the begetting of more children than ultimately there could be land for.

Land acquisitions by coal and timber companies admittedly hastened
the decline of Appalachia's internal economy, but basically the region
grew economically subsumed because there was not enough land to pro
vide subsistence for all the adults whose labor on the land had earlier
been useful when they were children—and who in turn parented more
children who could likewise help to work the land but to whom even
less land could later be provided when they in turn reached adulthood.[34] In Newer Appalachia the custom of partible inheritance, which
divided land among all heirs, continued a rapid subdivision of landholdings until about the turn of the twentieth century.

Meanwhile, however, many people in the 1880–1930 era still did
hold enough land to virtually ignore the money system. These full-time
subsistence farmers practiced systems of economic relations based inside
the region—based, indeed, in their own local neighborhoods—and
their systems could operate more or less autonomously so long as the
total landholdings among the participants continued to remain adequate to support competencies. Their systems were characterized by an
incessant borrowing and bartering of both objects and labor. To participate usually required a small amount of money, but the money requirement was not onerous. Lacking money raised only a minor obstacle
to participation in these systems, and that is what made them largely
autonomous vis-à-vis the outside world. As noted above, in eastern
Kentucky as of 1880, well before major industrialization began there,
the average farm held only $23.71 worth of farm implements or
machinery.[35] Even this scale of investment often proved unnecessary for
heirs. And afterward, just a few dollars annually could suffice for taxes
and for miscellaneous expenses that circumstances required in money
form. (Fig. 1 diagrams such a system and its relationship to the money
system.)

The only serious obstacle—serious especially for young people approaching adulthood—was that these subsistence-barter-and-borrow
systems required the use of enough land to support competencies. But
given adequate land (which grew more problematical for each new generation), Appalachian families practicing subsistence farming full time
could stay virtually autonomous vis-à-vis economic forces beyond their
localities.

Not that Appalachia's full-time subsistence farmers were self-
sufficient as separate family households. They rarely were. The typical

A Subsistence-Barter-and-Borrow Cycle and a Money Cycle

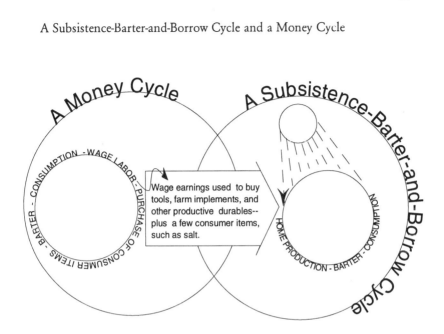

family household used more tools and equipment than it personally owned and had access to more animals and produce than it personally raised. It combined a degree of literal self-sufficiency with a prodigious amount of barter and borrowing of both objects and labor. The barter and borrowing did not occur with equal frequency between all residents of a locality but flourished instead primarily within what Appalachian sociologists call "family groups."

Folklore can tell us much about the nonmonetized economic exchanges of traditional Appalachia. The region's gossip networks are well known. The unspoken assumption is that everyone will offer the neighbors some account of his or her material life. An economic function lurking in this "snoopiness" (or friendliness) is revealed by the economic proposals that often follow on the heels of prying questions. If questioning reveals that a useful implement is lying idle, the questioner might ask to borrow it—and might also hint that help would be appreciated in using it. It is understood that the borrower will later lend something in return, or volunteer labor when it might prove useful, or perhaps contribute goods at some mutually convenient time. Whereas a mainly subsistence farm family might contribute mostly labor within these systems, a primarily commercial farm family might more readily lend out equipment.

In barter relations, no double standard of prices generally exists between "use value" and "exchange value." The fact that an object can be useful to one's neighbors does not generally lower the price for which one is likely to exchange it. When barter occurs between neighbors, prices are generally no lower than market prices. What does occur, however, is that the forms and the timespans of acceptable payment are stretched.

The workings of subsistence-barter-and-borrow systems are not obscure to the people who operate them, but they are hard to compare with money transactions. Money is clearly the most universal and most transportable asset to possess, but these attributes often hold limited appeal for people who plan to stay where they are and who share with their fellow "locals" a very specific environment worked with specific implements. Further, any generalizations about wealth or poverty based on annual per capita income—even if income "in kind" is included— reflect urban assumptions about what constitutes a standard of living. If comparisons are to be made, we need a formula that not only adds in a dollar figure for income acquired "in kind" (including home products) but also adds in the income that is *not* needed—because borrowing has performed its function. Pervasive borrowing not only reduces the need for money income but also reduces the need for home production and bartering. All other things being equal, frequent acts of borrowing tended to enhance a family's living standard.[36]

Within a subsistence-barter-and-borrow system, several or more households have access to every tool or implement possessed by any one of them. Consumption goods are borrowed and replaced as convenient, but larger savings can be achieved by borrowing productive goods such as tools and implements. Such productive goods are still borrowed and reborrowed (as well as being traded and retraded) throughout the Appalachian region.[37] Lending out a possession can be thought of as a form of leasing in exchange for a return favor, implied if not explicit. In money-system terms, we could call this a way of selling objects piecemeal to other people who, through their return favors, share in paying amortized attrition costs that otherwise might prove too expensive for the objects' nominal owners.

Of course, money too circulates at a certain rate, but this does not create advantages for subsistence farm families equal to what they gain from the circulation of useful objects. Money is not of direct use to a farmer (as farmer) while he or she holds it. A tool or a plow, besides its exchange value, has direct productive value. Appalachia's full-time subsistence farm families, having little need for an asset as liquid as money, have held productive goods that they have kept surprisingly liquid though frequent barter and borrowing.

But are Appalachia's subsistence-barter-and-borrow systems truly systems? They are not completely self-contained systems (as fig. 1 illustrates), but they can enjoy considerable autonomy. All known systems overlap with other systems in some way. The capitalist system managed to expand so successfully partly because it received low-wage labor, supplied to it far below cost by subsistence-barter-and-borrow systems.

And, conversely, in two crucial respects Appalachia's subsistence-barter-and-borrow systems depend on the market system. First of all, the barter aspect of Appalachia's internal systems depend on the market to provide price levels. As Karl Polanyi points out, "Unless [a market] pattern is present, at least in patches, the propensity to barter will find insufficient scope: it cannot produce prices. . . . The principle of barter depends for its effectiveness on the market pattern."[38] Secondly, Appalachia's subsistence-barter-and-borrow systems depend on the market for a relatively small but crucially important input of money itself— money with which storekeepers, if not subsistence farmers directly, can buy productive goods and consumer items that are locally used but are not locally produced.

Disappointingly, voluntary reciprocity in Appalachian life has not yet been studied from an economic perspective. One of Appalachia's best social histories, *Mountain Families in Transition,* does lucidly reveal the *social* implications of continuous barter and borrowing,[39] but in making economic calculations, that book, like others, merely supplements monetized income with the money equivalent of a farm's subsistence in-kind production.[40] The fact is, however, that money and money equivalents cannot accurately measure economic value in a money-poor but barter-and-borrowing-rich environment. Barter heightens liquidity, and borrowing reduces the amount of income needed in any form. Until a method is devised that will render subsistence-barter-and-borrow systems quantitatively comparable to the money system, we possess little ability to estimate the real income, even today, of a region like Appalachia.[41] Without a method of quantifying, we can make ethnographic comparisons aplenty, but we cannot make accurate economic comparisons between low-money systems and high-money systems. And therefore social scientists will perhaps continue puzzling over the supposedly "senseless"[42] (or to their partisans, "selfless") attributes of Appalachian behavior. And scholars will perhaps continue confusing ways of life with standards of living.

Today we might smile at a turn-of-the-century mining engineer's statement that Appalachian mountaineers were "supremely unconscious of their own misery."[43] But how would we evaluate the 1940 declaration by a socialist economist that "extreme poverty comparable to that of the poorest sharecropper, is all that the 'self-sufficing' farm can provide"?[44]

No less a thinker than Rupert Vance has confused ways of life with standards of living. Writing in 1962, Vance noted that the New Deal's "standards made at least half the population in certain Appalachian areas eligible for relief" and that this "introduced the people to the money economy and increased their wants. The depression, then," he went on, "actually served to raise standards for many families in the region who had lacked contact with the American standard of living." Vance hastened to add that the Depression "left the region with a high rate of relief and a low basis for economic security," but he let stand his equation of "the American standard of living" with a *raised* standard and not merely with "the money economy."[45]

Equally inadequate seems a more recent judgment by Jack Temple Kirby. By 1960, Kirby tells us, "millions of acres of [Appalachian] land were abandoned. The shabby remains of semisubsistence life on remote family farms were abandoned, too, or mercifully executed at last by the manifold outside forces of the commercial world, its demands of efficiency and specialization, and the cash nexus." Kirby does not tell us what should have replaced that "semisubsistence life on remote family farms." He questions the viability of an alternative that hundreds of thousands of mountaineers tried: "Tantalizing hopes of stable work in industries old and new were dimmed, if not dashed, by the vagaries of the world marketplace."[46] In view of this, it seems worthwhile to explore ways of reviving and upgrading "semisubsistence life on remote family farms."

Appalachia's economic problems have not basically been caused by the region's familism or by its subsistence-barter-and-borrow systems. These were rational expedients under the prevailing conditions, and they would have been as consistent with small families as they were with large families. Likewise, they would have been as consistent with constructive farming practices as they were with destructive ones. In and of themselves they did not cause Appalachia's economic problems.

The vast scale of money's penetration into Appalachian farming areas, during and since the New Deal, has weakened but not obliterated the region's subsistence-barter-and-borrow systems. Today many mountaineers look primarily to corporate employers or to the government for their sustenance. This has had many social and cultural consequences—and those kinds of consequences have already been delineated by others. Much insight has already been gained from social and cultural perspectives about the decline of traditional life.[47] My point in this chapter is that Appalachia's traditional life was perpetuated not so much by a "family system" or by a "community system" as it was by a certain type of economic system, and I have tried to set forth in economic terms the reasons for that system's decline. The decline of voluntary reciprocity in rural Appalachia can obviously be described in social and cultural terms as well as in economic terms, but only an economic analysis can explain *why* voluntary reciprocity has waned.

4

Labor-intensive Mining and the Subsistence Reproduction of Labor Power, 1880–1930

[Although] we are rich in energy, rich in industry, rich in perseverance, rich in stout hearts and brawny arms, we are poor in money.
—David P. Brown, quoted in Grace Palladino,
"The Poor Man's Fight"

During the eighteenth and nineteenth centuries, several colonial countries in various parts of the world experienced phenomenal population growth. One explanation now advanced for this is that an increased output was required from the inhabitants of those countries if they wished to maintain their previous living standards. Often, production for export was added to the already extant production for subsistence and internal trade—inspiring many local people to increase the size of their families to keep up with their enlarged workloads.

In rural eighteenth-century Northern Ireland, for example, children were set to spinning linen from flax as early as age four or five.[1] Similarly, in nineteenth-century Java (another scene, like Northern Ireland, of a population "explosion"), children could become net rice producers—producing more rice than they consumed—as early as age seven.[2] If a typical family could live better by having more children, need we look further to explain a population explosion?

During the industrialization of Plateau Appalachia a similar situation prevailed. The Plateau's rapid natural population increase between 1880 and 1930 shared common features with both Northern Ireland and Java. Part of the work of Plateau Appalachia's children occurred in export-oriented activities (like Northern Ireland's flax-spinning child labor). Appalachia's export-oriented child labor took place largely in and around its coal mines, and it flourished into the 1920s.[3] Mainly, however, Plateau Appalachia's children paid their way (thereby prompting their parents to raise more children) with work in the subsistence sector—like the work of Java's children. Crandall Shifflett mentions that "as early as five or six years of age, boys and girls began to help out" on Appalachia's farms.[4]

The analogy between Appalachia and Java has its limits. Java's Dutch-imposed nineteenth-century "culture system" required forced (unpaid) labor in that island's export sector as a percentage of all adult labor. Children were exempt from the labor-force calculations that determined each village's quota of export crops, so children came to represent a larger economic asset to their parents than purely market conditions would have made them. By contrast, the coal-mining industry of Appalachia, like the flax-and-linen business of Northern Ireland, required labor in amounts determined directly by market conditions. The point to note is that large families were not rendered economically obsolete in Appalachia by the onset of industrialization. Large families had helped to hasten the region's industrialization, but in turn industrialization helped to perpetuate large families.

The phrase "subsistence reproduction of labor power" refers to raising children on home-grown food and other supplies—a pattern that not only pervaded Appalachia's farm areas but also contributed to maintaining families in coal camps. Large gardens abounded, and livestock was pervasive not only where miners owned their own homesteads but also in many company towns. As late as 1924, by one conservative estimate, more than 50 percent of West Virginia's miners raised gardens as well as kept cows, hogs, or poultry. A better-researched 1923 report found that in West Virginia's Raleigh County, more than 70 percent of the miners planted gardens and kept livestock of some sort. Black and immigrant miners maintained agricultural activities as well as native white miners. Many coal companies presented annual cash or in-kind awards to the miners who were judged to have the most productive and attractive gardens. A northeastern West Virginia coal company reminded its miners in 1918 that in each of its coal towns "the first prize is three month's free house rent, the second prize is two month's free house rent, and the third prize is one month's free house rent."[5]

A pattern of development subsidized by subsistence labor reproduction was prefigured as early as the 1860s by at least one entrepreneur—a Kanawha County, West Virginia, developer who wrote:

During a series of topographical and geological surveys on the Elk and Coal Rivers, my attention was called to numerous spots that I conceived would make beautiful farms. Gentle slopes, flat-top ridges, and level dells were frequently met with. . . . Being interested in the resources of Kanawha, and having in view one of its fundamental principles of development—population—I determined to try an experiment. . . . I selected a spot. . . . As an inducement to my first pioneer tenant, I offered to let him have fifty acres, rent free, for five years, and after he had got his log-house built, fields enclosed, and road cut for a way out, he should have a lease for twenty-one years at thirty dollars a year rent. I soon found a tenant and thus far I can report the experiment eminently successful. . . . This small trial shows very conclusively that if immigration is judiciously encouraged, and land-owners induced to be more liberal in their concessions to the industrious laboring classes, thousands of acres of our back forest lands may be brought into a profitable state of cultivation, thus . . . increasing our population. . . .

Many persons will be inclined to remark: "This is all very well in theory, but in practice will it pay?" Now let us see. These lands, on an average, can be purchased for less than four dollars per acre . . . [6]

The writer proceeded to show that the plan would pay quite well, even if the entrepreneur had to borrow money to buy the land which would then be leased to settlers. There was also the consideration that because this was coal-bearing land, the new settlers would be fulfilling "one of its fundamental principles of development—population." Although this entrepreneur did not explicitly predict that tenant-settlers would be forced to supplement their farming with wage labor, nonetheless the small size of the first tract he leased out (fifty acres) virtually assured that the leaseholder would indeed be forced toward wage labor.

This forward-looking entrepreneur of the 1860s proved prescient. Combining subsistence agriculture with industrial wage labor made Appalachian Plateau enterprises boom for more than a generation— from 1880 to 1920—and benefits accrued to workers as well as to operators and owners. Nor was the government blind to the benefits derived from such dual employment. After 1914's Smith-Lever Act, the federal government began to encourage agriculture among miners. One authority records that in Plateau West Virginia, "Mingo county, almost entirely dependent on coal mining, was one of the early counties to raise local funds and request a county agent. . . . He and other agents who followed him in Mingo and other counties in the coal fields, helped increase production through better gardens, a few milk cows and goats, pigs, and chickens. . . . The county agents found the mine superintendents generally anxious and appreciative of their services."[7]

During and after World War 1, the average value of gardens was estimated in several of West Virginia's coal towns and ranged between 10 and 20 percent of the average miner's wages, even during the high-wage period of 1917–1920.[8] Livestock added further in-kind income. In 1918 a trade journal of the coal industry surmised that in northern West Virginia "the growing of gardens . . . probably helps to account for the rapid strides made by the region in the production department."[9]

Throughout the 1880–1920 period, the Plateau subregion not only attracted migrants but also maintained a high rate of population increase through large families. Such population growth *without* industrialization would have fostered "surplus population" in Malthus's sense, but, as long as boom conditions prevailed, all seemed well. It was only during the cutthroat coal competition of the 1920s that most miners and their families began facing poverty, and it was only after the Great Crash of 1929 that policy makers began viewing a large portion of Appalachia's population as "surplus." Plateau Appalachia, with its symbiosis of subsistence farming and rural industrialization, maintained into its post-1880 boom decades, and through them, a faster natural increase of population than any other section of the United States. As of 1920 the average American mother who was married to a miner had given birth to 4.3 children—an average higher than among mothers married to men in any other occupation. Mothers married to farmers followed second in the occupational scale with an average of 3.8 births.[10]

Counties that lay very few miles apart could be worlds apart demographically if they lay on opposite sides of the Allegheny Front that divides Valley Appalachia from Plateau Appalachia. Valley Appalachia's demographic stability is reflected, for example, in West Virginia's Monroe County—although it lies barely southeast of the Allegheny Front. Settlement began here about 1760. By 1800 Monroe County held 4,188 people, and by 1860 it held 10,757. From 1880 to 1930, the county's average farm size declined only from 192 acres to 122 acres. No industrialization occurred here, and the year 1920's population of 13,141 has not wavered much since.[11] A recent study by historian Barbara Rasmussen compares Monroe County with West Virginia's Clay County, which lies only fifty miles to the northwest but is located in the Plateau subregion (Newer Appalachia). Here recorded settlement did not begin until about 1809, and as late as 1860 Clay County's population had only reached 1,787. Then, however, it surged upward. Although coal mining remained insignificant in Clay County until the 1890s, the county's population grew 22.9 percent in the 1860s, 57.6 percent in the 1870s, and 34.6 percent in the 1880s, before climbing 77 percent in the 1890s. After that, population growth slowed but did not cease.[12]

Such a rapid increase of population before and during Plateau Appalachia's industrialization helps to explain why so many of that subregion's people must now either live on transfer payments or migrate elsewhere. With myriad subsistence farms, Plateau Appalachia in particular (and Valley Appalachia to a lesser degree) constituted an economic staging area that raised hundreds of thousands of future wage earners largely outside the money economy, and, in the same manner, supported hundreds of thousands of worn-out workers until they died.[13]

When we ask how Appalachia was economically transformed, we are asking how control of its resources was transferred from the nonindustrial economic sector to the industrial sector. In other words, we are asking how capital has been created within the region. A key means of this resource transfer, this capital accumulation, occurred through the movement of labor power from the nonindustrial to the industrial sector. And making possible this redirection of labor allocation was subsistence farming. In the already quoted words of a Canadian scholar, "On the periphery of capitalist development, [capital accumulation] is highly dependent on the existence of subsistence production in agriculture. The existence of subsistence production serves a variety of functions, but its primary importance for the capitalist sector is in supplying and maintaining a labour force at prices which permit capital accumulation in this sector."[14] Although Appalachian workers generally made their contribution to capital accumulation within their own region, most of the resultant capital was accumulated in the North.

Anyone who visited purely agricultural sections of Appalachia during the twentieth century's first three decades would have found the region's preindustrial way of life apparently in full swing. Many men in their prime years, however, would have been absent, for they were "working out," generally at mining or logging. Women in their prime years were often running the home and looking after elders as well as raising children.[15]

The full implications of such "working out" lifeways have only gradually been explored by economists. After World War II, the

Dutch economist J. H. Boeke put forward the idea that many colonial countries contained two separate socioeconomic systems. On one hand was a capitalist, modernizing sector whose participants embraced Western values; on the other hand a precapitalist sector continued to pursue traditional goals and maintain traditional values.[16] A well-known application of this model to Appalachia is Jack Weller's book *Yesterday's People.*

A number of Third World economists based case studies on Boeke's concept of a "dual economy," but for others it did not sit right. Critics of the theory could easily demonstrate that economic behavior within the traditional sectors was often profoundly changed if a capitalist sector existed in the same country, or even in a neighboring country. Thus, where Boeke had seen only "pockets" of market-oriented activity, his critics could often document that remote, tradition-oriented villagers were producing commodities for those markets or were traveling to the markets to sell their labor. Those people were practicing dual employment, just as many Appalachian people were doing.

Writing in 1960, Jonathan Levin modified Boeke's thesis, rediagraming the dual economy as not modern versus traditional but as export versus domestic. Levin argued that domestic (traditional) sectors are not "backward" per se, but that they *become* backward if the new capitalist sectors are based mainly on exports and if export earnings are not brought back and reinvested in the domestic economic sectors.[17]

This line of reasoning prompted a Latin American specialist named Andre Gunder Frank to talk of "the development of underdevelopment." Frank thesis was that the capitalist development of a center (or core) will automatically foster the underdevelopment of its economic hinterland or periphery. He suggested that the process of "primary capitalist accumulation" has historically been dependent on the " 'noncapitalist' work of family members or others [that helps to] support the wage earner" by providing one or more of the "vital processes that are necessary for the continued supply of labor power to capital."[18]

As in many Third World colonies, subsistence-style child rearing and aging continued in Appalachian long after many of Appalachia's rural breadwinners were employed, at least occasionally if not permanently, away from their home farms. In other words, many people found that during their prime work years they had to deny some or all of their labor to the agriculture that had not only succored they themselves but that still was largely supporting their spouses, children, and elders. The writings of Jonathan Levin and Andre Gunder Frank explain how this "subsistence reproduction of labor power" underwrites low-wage, labor-intensive production methods, and how it prompts employers to sweat workers destructively in their prime years, leaving them physical wrecks to be later sustained by subsistence agriculture back at their home locations.[19]

Some 1910 and 1920 figures will help to suggest the extent of Appalachia's reproduction of labor power at that time relative to its extent in the United States as a whole. According to the 1910 census, only 43.9 percent of the total U.S. population, urban as well as rural, was then aged twenty or under. But in 1910 in Older Appalachia (the Valley subregion), 48.3 percent of the total population was aged twenty or less. And in Newer Appalachia (the Plateau subregion), 53.2 percent of the total population was aged twenty or under.

Ten years later, in 1920, only 42.4 percent of the total U.S. population was aged twenty or under. In Older Appalachia, meanwhile, the proportion had risen slightly: 49.9 percent were now aged twenty or under. And the 1920 figure for Newer Appalachia was still a very high 53.1 percent of the population aged twenty or younger.[20]

In other words, Appalachia's adults were parenting far more children than were most American adults. For every 1,000 U.S. adults in 1910 there were 783 children aged twenty or under—but for every 1,000 adults on the Appalachian Plateau there were 1,137 children. By 1920 the U.S. proportion had fallen to 736 children per 1,000 adults, but the Appalachian Plateau proportion had hardly fallen, standing at 1,132 children per 1,000 adults.

These figures reflect, of course, the reproduction of labor power regardless of how that was accomplished—whether by subsistence farming or otherwise. Indeed, most of the rural United States in the 1880–1900 period was still reproducing labor power largely through home production rather than through money purchases. Part of the higher percentage of children in Appalachia was a result of the larger proportion there of rural population. But another factor was that in Appalachia, farming was less capital intensive than it was elsewhere in the United States. Subsistence farming, lacking access to investment capital, was inherently labor intensive and, by that token, tended to foster a demographic tableau skewed toward youth. A major exception to such demographic skewing as a result of subsistence farming was Japan from the 1720s to the 1860s, but we have already noted the grueling labor that small family sizes required from Japan's subsistence farmers.

The special characteristics of the Plateau economy tipped the age "imbalance" furthest there. Outside Appalachia, and particularly outside Plateau Appalachia, the rural United States tended to *export* a large percentage of its matured youth. As migrants with no further economic ties to their subsistence background, these workers then generally had to be paid a fully family-supporting wage. Rural Appalachia, by contrast, kept (until about 1942) a far higher percentage of its matured youth than the rural areas of other regions. It kept them not so much as full-time farmers than as wage workers who, together with their families, supplemented their meager paychecks with subsistence agriculture. Although the farm population of Appalachia grew only 5 percent between 1900 and 1930, the region's rural but *non*farm population rose more than 75 percent, and most of these rural nonfarm people kept one foot in subsistence agriculture despite not qualifying as farm households by the census definition.[21]

Because labor-intensive farming prompted the raising of large families, Appalachia provided America's industrial sector with more than its share of workers. And by subsidizing these workers with home production, it subsidized the U.S. economy's industrial sector. But Appalachia's function as a labor "staging area" for industry did not automatically relegate it to an inferior status politically. Had Appalachia been a colony politically, regional regulations could have been established to institutionalize and perpetuate its subsistence reproduction of labor for the benefit of other regions in the United States. Elsewhere in the world, travel passes and work certificates have successfully been used to such effect. Someone "working out" who lacked a valid pass could have been ordered back to his Appalachian "homeland" or summarily jailed.[22]

South African-type "pass laws" were politically untenable to regulate U.S. citizens, but the pill that Appalachia's people had to swallow was also bitter medicine. For the more that Appalachia's people once contributed to the United States in subsistence labor reproduction, the more they have had to pay since 1940 in migration away from home. From 1940 to 1960, net migration from the region totalled 1,700,000.[23]

Was any alternative possible? Had something been done differently, might some of those 1,700,000 people have been able to maintain their mountain lives? To help answer this, we can look at a very different pattern of interaction between subsistence farming and industrialization that occurred in Taiwan. In the process, some comparisons will be possible. Taiwan's industrialization has occurred largely since 1949, and like the industrialization that occurred earlier in both Appalachia and Japan, it has been heavily subsidized by subsistence labor reproduction. And Taiwan's case has resembled Japan's in the resultant benefits staying at home. This is the opposite of Appalachia's case, however, for the benefits from Appalachia's subsidized labor have been dispersed throughout the United States.

During the fifty years before 1945, Taiwan was a colony of Japan, and its economy was shaped by Japanese investments. What the Japanese wanted from Taiwan, however, was not at all what northern U.S. investors have wanted from Appalachia. The Japanese wanted a food product, rice, which also constituted much of the Taiwanese diet. Agriculture's crucial role in Taiwan's twentieth-century development began with rice-growing innovations that Japanese economists established in Taiwan before 1945, and it continued as the Taiwanese, building on that strong rice-growing base, industrialized their country after 1949. Besides rice-growing innovations, the Japanese also established a power industry in Taiwan and built up other infrastructure such as roads and railroads, but most of that was destroyed during World War II.

Taiwan had come under Japanese rule in 1895, a spoil of the Sino-Japanese War. Some limited Japanese initiatives began soon, and then after Japan's 1918 rice riots, the Japanese instituted a crash program to heighten Taiwan's rice productivity and to export the surplus rice to Japan. Biological and chemical innovations were established that increased the labor demands on Taiwan's farmers per unit of land. This contrasts with the tractor-and-mechanization innovations that at that very time were starting to *de*populate most U.S. farms, but it parallels Appalachia's rural population rise. Taiwan's rural areas, like Appalachia's, were gaining population. Taiwan's rural families continued to need their sons and daughters just as did Appalachia's. And in both cases subsistence farming was subsidizing the production of an export product. But Taiwan's export product (rice) was produced by self-employed farmers and it was their own primary food staple, whereas Appalachia's export (coal) was produced for wages and was locally little used.

Taiwan's farm families faced rising outlays for fertilizer and irrigation, but their rice productivity grew faster than their costs, providing families with a heightened living standard.[24] Taiwanese farm families' average propensity to consume dropped from 96 percent of their current income during the 1911–1915 era to only 88 percent by 1936–1940. Thus, by the time of World War II, about 12 percent of Taiwan's farm-family income was being saved.

In 1911 the Taiwanese—rural and urban together—had consumed 84 percent of their total food production. By 1940 they were consuming only 58 percent of it, and yet they were consuming more calories per person than they had in 1911. They were also consuming more of the basic nonfood goods and acquiring more education.

Meanwhile, in sharp contrast with Appalachia's experience during those years (1911–1940), Taiwan's industrial labor force was growing far slower than its total population—for Taiwan's export production was keeping its people busy producing a basic food crop, whereas Appalachia's was mainly extracting and exporting coal and thus transferring labor pell-mell into the industrial sector.

Between 1911 and 1960, Taiwan's agriculture provided a net real capital outflow to the rest of its economy, and did so at an increasing rate. By 1960, Taiwanese farm families' average propensity to consume was down to 71 percent and their savings rate was up to 29 percent.[25]

The Japanese had not set out to enhance Taiwan's well-being but, rather, Japan's own well-being. Until 1945, the surplus from Taiwan's rapidly increasing rice productivity was exported to Japan. Indeed, between the early 1910s and the early 1940s, the amount of rice available for consumption in Taiwan fell by 24 percent per person. Caloric intake rose because sweet potato consumption quadrupled per person and the availability of pork (Taiwan's principal meat) rose per person by half. Even per capita sugar consumption doubled, and vegetable and fruit consumption also evidently increased. When Japanese rule ended in 1945, the Taiwanese tossed sweet potatoes out of their pantries and into their livestock fodder. And the island's food exports dropped from the 1936–1940 level of 42 percent of food production down to a postwar level of only 6 percent.[26]

Since 1945, Taiwan has been able to keep almost all of its rice for domestic consumption. What is striking, however, is that after 1945 the proportion of the rice crop that farm families put on the market fell below the level they had marketed way back in 1911, before Japan's significant interference had even begun. Not only was Taiwan now keeping more of its rice for domestic in-country consumption, but its farm families were keeping more of their home-grown rice for actual home consumption. As compared with the years 1911–1915, the years 1956–1960 saw 28 percent more consumption on the home farm of food that was produced on the home farm.[27]

What was happening? For one thing, a major land reform in the early 1950s freed many Taiwanese farm families from the need to sell most of their rice crop in order to pay rent. Further, a very pro-farmer ceiling was set on land rents, and often they were made payable in kind (e.g., in rice). Also, after 1948 the government was both boosting rice output and husbanding financial resources by trading fertilizer to farmers in exchange for rice at a pro-farmer ratio. Sometimes the government also provided farm families with cotton cloth and other necessities in exchange for rice.[28] Such bartering reduced Taiwan's need to create money.

Two scholars speak of the years "between the early 1950s and the late 1960s to early 1970s" as displaying a "remarkable success achieved by Taiwan in eliminating poverty and malnutrition."[29] And yet Taiwan's farm population was increasing between 1946 and 1969 from 3.5 million to more than 6 million, and the island's average farm size was falling from about 5 acres down to less than 2.5 acres. Already by 1960, 37 percent of Taiwan's farms held less than one and one-quarter acres— and yet less than 35 percent of the income of those small-farm families came from off-the-farm sources.[30] Can we imagine an agriculture that productive in Appalachia? This favorable food trend accompanying Taiwan's post-World War II industrialization contrasts dramatically with the threatening subsistence crisis that earlier had hastened Appalachia's industrialization. When Taiwan's industrialization took off in the 1950s, its subsistence farming was vibrantly healthy, unlike the worrisome subsistence situation that had existed when Appalachia's industrialization took off.[31] The two scholars who wrote of Taiwan "eliminating poverty and malnutrition" between "the early 1950s and the late 1960s to early 1970s" provide a simple explanation for why that happened. They call it "an especially clear example of the effectiveness of the labor supply/demand situation in leading to widespread increase in returns to labor."[32]

In other words, it was only after Taiwan's domestic food supply was guaranteed that the country industrialized. As early as 1952, Taiwan was exporting more than five times more processed food, beverage, and tobacco goods than it was importing. And as late as 1986, it was still exporting almost twice the value of those consumption goods that it was importing.[33] Clearly, Taiwan's domestic food supply continued secure. Here was a country whose population far more than doubled from 1952 to 1986,[34] and yet its food production rose more than one-quarter more than did its population.[35] Furthermore, throughout the 1950s Taiwan supplied its own domestic demand for basic consumer goods (for nonfood consumer goods) by using tariff barriers to encourage import substitution. Only after domestic manufacturing was supplying its domestic market did Taiwan begin—about 1960—to export a significant proportion of its industrial output.

A result of this sequence was that when the growth in Taiwan's agricultural productivity finally slowed about 1970, that happened not only because Taiwan's arable land was reaching the limit of its productive capacity but also because a shortage of industrial workers was driving up industrial wages and thereby enticing farmers out of their fields.[36]

Rampant urbanization was nonetheless avoided. As late as 1986, 21.8 percent of the Taiwanese still lived on farms, and many Taiwanese industries had located in rural areas to gain access to rural residents as employees.[37] As of 1986, Taiwan's average manufacturing employee was earning the equivalent of $1.78 an hour.[38] Direct testimony and statistics of consumption attest that those employees were well off.

An official 1974 Taiwanese publication summed up what had occurred there: "For two decades the growth of [Taiwan's] economy has been fueled by the rural sector. Industry took root rapidly because of the foreign exchange, domestic food supplies, and manpower resources that could be drawn from what was fundamentally a farming economy. These contributions of the rural sector were absolutely indispensable to economic modernization in the cities and in industry."[39]

Rural Appalachia made similar contributions toward the industrialization of the United States. Appalachia's coal contributed both directly and indirectly to American foreign-exchange earnings. Appalachia's

local provision of food and other subsistence supplies allowed low wages
in mining, timbering, textiles, and other industries. Its labor was made
available to industries without requiring that the industries pay enough
to support the workers' families. But Appalachia is not a country. The
benefits of Appalachia's contribution were dispersed throughout the
United States and have gone unnoticed.

In natural resource endowments, Appalachia was better off than
both Japan and Taiwan.[40] But in the crucial categories of self-
sufficiency and self-financing, Appalachia was worse off. Contrasts between Taiwan and Appalachia are dramatic on both of these scores.
With respect to financing, the onset of Appalachia's industrialization
saw many members of the mountain elite selling or leasing much of
their land to outside investors—whose agents, land-buyers, and law-
yers they often then became.[41]

Mountain land had not bred much money until major railroad, timber, and coal investments began arriving from outside sources in the
1870s and 1880s. The more outside capital flowed into Appalachia, the
more dependent the mountain economy became on the region that controlled most of that capital, the North. Appalachia became an increasingly "peripheral" region within an emerging "core" country, the
United States.

It is important to understand why Appalachia became financially
dependent. The fact that a major portion of the region's land and resources had long been controlled by absentee owners was part of the
reason,[42] but the main reason was that many of Appalachia's people
found themselves able to maintain their living standards only by acquiring increasing amounts of income that were apportioned to them
from outside the region. The crucial transactions were not those occurring between naïve farmers and savvy "mineral hunters" or land
buyers. Some farmers admittedly alienated their mineral rights for only
25 cents an acre, but had they charged the mineral hunters $25 or $250
an acre, that would not have insured greater local control over Appalachia's industrialization.

Nor can Appalachia's growing dependency be explained by the behavior of those who supervised the region's mining or those who controlled the capital invested. Richard Simon has suggested that if West
Virginia's mine operators had automated sooner, dependency might have
been avoided. The coal operators automated too late, he says, and what

prevented earlier automation (thereby also preventing higher wages) was "destructive competition" among the region's coal operators.[43] This is apparently a circular issue, however, for Appalachia's coal fields would not have been developed to the extent that they were if mountain people had not been willing to dig coal for wages lower than northern workers. In the economic picture, lower pay compensated for Appalachia's greater distance from coal's main markets—from the coal-burning factories, locomotives, and power plants of the North. Despite the high cost of transporting so heavy a commodity,[44] the mountains' bountiful cheap labor enabled Appalachian coal to sell at a competitive price— until hindered from doing so by the price-and-wage supports established under the National Recovery Administration in 1933. And when wages then shot upward, the mechanical coal loaders that had long waited in the wings were soon being used—greater mechanization suddenly becoming the easiest way to maximize profits in most Appalachian coal operations.

The New Deal thus changed the coal industry's ground rules, but prior to 1933, Appalachia's coal operators generally perceived their maximum profitability to lie in policies of postponing automation, continuing to use relatively labor-intensive mining methods, and refusing to bargain with labor unions. The anti-union policy was made workable by the existence of company towns.[45] As long as they could successfully squelch unionism, almost all Appalachian coal operators continued to pay miners to shovel coal rather than buying underground coal-loading machinery.

The fact that Appalachian coal operators were slow to automate does not necessarily verify Richard Simon's claim that they possessed less "development-minded leadership" than did northern coal operators. Indeed, many or most of Appalachia's operators were of northern origin, and many of them also, southern as well as northern, enjoyed considerable access to capital.[46] Appalachia's operators, like their counterparts elsewhere, tried to produce coal in the amounts and by the methods that would yield maximum profits. Appalachia's operators automated slowly because that was the pace that their cost-benefit analysis suggested would prove most profitable.

As midwestern mines began adopting mechanization in the form of automatic coal cutters in the 1880s, thereby reducing the manpower required per ton of coal production, the proportion of coal income paid out as wages in the Midwest temporarily dropped to a level of parity with the proportion being paid as wages in Appalachia.[47] Back in 1870 and 1880 (as noted in chapter 2), the share of Appalachian coal income that went to miners had been much smaller than the share of midwestern coal income that went to miners. (See table 4 for those percentages.) But by 1890 this was no longer the case. Although midwestern miners then received wages almost 6 percent higher per ton than Appalachian miners, this was only a hair below the amount by which the value of midwestern coal exceeded that of Appalachian coal at the mine head. By 1890 in both regions, workers were receiving about 74 to 75 percent of total coal income.[48]

Besides coal-cutting mechanization in the Midwest, other factors may have worked to hold labor's share of midwestern coal income down that low. By the 1880s—for one reason—the supply of good land near the Midwest that was available cheap, or was available free under the Homestead Act, had been exhausted. For another reason, the late 1880s saw several large and highly capitalized coal ventures begin in Appalachia in the Flat Top-Pocahontas area that straddles southwestern Virginia's U-shaped border with southern West Virginia. Rapid expansion there required operators to draw on the pool of experienced miners in Pennsylvania and the Midwest[49]—and that required paying wages comparable to, or perhaps a whit higher than, those paid in Pennsylvania and the Midwest.

Soon, however, midwestern miners devised a way to regain their previous economic leverage. By the 1890s good homestead land was no longer an alternative against which midwestern coal operators had to bid for labor, but midwestern miners now turned to "combination," forming a consolidated labor union they called the United Mine Workers of America (UMW). By 1902, when the largely non-unionized miners of Appalachia were reduced to receiving only 63 percent of the value of the coal they mined, midwestern miners were largely unionized and were still receiving the 74 percent that they had received in 1890.[50] An econometric study estimates that as early as 1909–1913 the UMW was responsible for increasing its members' wages 38 to 43 percent over what their wages would have been without the union.[51]

While midwestern miners were thus constructing a new foundation under their self-interest, Appalachia was instead seeing *operators* seize the initiative—by shepherding miners into company towns where union organizing could be outlawed under property-owners' prerogatives. The first company town for Appalachian miners went up in 1885, and by 1910 about 70 percent of the region's miners lived in such towns. At that time, meanwhile, only 8.5 percent of Indiana and Illinois miners lived in company towns.[52]

It is also important, however, to realize that unionization could benefit only a limited number of Appalachian miners. "Better late than never" applies here, but the effects of late unionization included traumatic mass unemployment that, for many miners, became permanent unemployment. We should not let marginal acts of roguery like operators' coal-weighing tricks, or their company-store price gouging, obscure more fundamental realities that have kept Appalachia's coal industry profitable. When decisive unionization finally did occur in Appalachia in the 1930s, it inspired operators to abandon their relatively labor-intensive mining methods and, in the process, to permanently abandon a large portion of their pre-Depression work force. When union membership became the rule and pushed up wages, mechanization in Appalachian mines began to catch up with midwestern mines (which before 1933 had not only undercut almost all of their coal by machine but had also begun *loading* much of it by machine at the coal face).[53] As of 1933, only 1.2 percent of West Virginia's underground coal loading was yet mechanized, whereas 58.9 percent of Illinois's loading was mechanized.[54] Then, with their wage costs increased after 1933, many Appalachian operators likewise embraced maximum mechanization. Loading machines, which many Appalachian operators now hastily acquired, reduced the total labor needs of a mine by at least 10 percent and by up to 40 percent.[55] Among those miners who found themselves permanently excluded from the industry were a disproportionate number of black miners, many of whom then left the region.[56]

Prior to 1933's successful United Mine Workers organizing drive, however, union organizers had faced an uphill struggle—a struggle not only against the Appalachian "bosses" and their company-town system but also against the average miner's slowness to adopt class antagonism. For example, by the time the famous "Coal Creek rebellion" erupted in east-central Tennessee in 1891, coal had already been exported from Coal Creek by rail for twenty years (since 1871). The grievance that provoked Coal Creek miners to armed rebellion was the use by operators there of unpaid convicts as workers in the mines. That grievance had been rankling since 1877.[57] By contrast, at newly opened mines located near Middlesboro, Kentucky—where conditions were no less oppressive than the conditions inspiring class warfare just fifty miles away at Coal Creek—no major strike broke out until 1931. Unlike at Coal Creek, no cadres of convict labor competed with wage labor at Middlesboro, but other serious grievances had existed from the first opening of the Middlesboro mines around 1890.[58] Middlesboro conditions were poor in the 1890s, but, unlike Coal Creek, class antagonism had not yet had time to develop at the Middlesboro mines. Over time, class antagonism slowly grew in Appalachia's coal districts.

This growth of class antagonism should be seen in the context of narrowing chances for upward mobility.[59] In many Appalachian areas, outsiders had not been the first to *attempt* a capitalistic approach to development—not been the first to seek control of sufficient productive resources to compete, for instance, in the northern coal markets of places like New York and Chicago. Of the Flat Top-Pocahontas coal field (straddling the Virginia-West Virginia border) one scholar says that "locals tried like hell to exploit the coal, but lacked the necessary means to mount a large-scale operation. The locals [then] acted as middlemen, arranging sales of land and right-of-way to Philadelphia entrepreneurs who financed the thing."[60]

And how did they finance it? Figures helping to answer that question were recorded after West Virginia appointed a state bank examiner in 1891. Most of the Flat Top-Pocahontas coal field lay in West Virginia, and four state-chartered banks already existed in that coal field's West Virginia portion by that time. When visited by West Virginia's new bank examiner in 1891, however, their combined cash holdings totalled only slightly more than fifty thousand dollars.[61]

That same year miners' wages in the West Virginia portion of the Flat Top-Pocahontas coal field ran about $112,000 a month and $1.18 million for the year.[62] Thus, not enough cash was available in the area to meet even a single fortnightly coal payroll. The four area banks together held $291,235 in checking deposits,[63] but capital invested in the area's coal mining already exceeded that. Indeed, by 1890, $10.5 million was already invested overall in West Virginia coal mining, although the state's banks held only $8.1 million in all forms of deposits.[64] And coal mining was not the only development that was being financed from outside the region. The year 1892 would see West

Virginia lead the nation in miles of railroad track completed within that year.[65] Both coal mining and railroads were major Appalachian industries using large amounts of money, but often that money merely shuffled between northern bank accounts. Of the investment money that *did* enter Appalachia, most probably never became cash.

The region's cash drought was not rapidly ameliorated. Eleven years later, in 1902, West Virginia's part of the Flat Top-Pocahontas coal field could count six local banks—one of them a national bank that had been founded in 1891. The local banks' checking deposits had multiplied eight and a half times since 1891, to $2.46 million. But their cash on hand had failed even to triple, growing only from $50,000 to $138,000.[66] Meanwhile, coal output in the area *had* tripled from 1891 to 1902,[67] and because the Plateau miners' average wage per ton was down only from 68 cents a ton to 67 cents,[68] the area's available cash had fallen in relation to its aggregate coal wages.

Furthermore, it was not likely that very much cash could have been sent to the Flat Top-Pocahontas coal field for payroll purposes from elsewhere in West Virginia. By 1902 that state's monthly coal wages were totalling at least $1.4 million, and meanwhile all the banks in the state at any given time, including the national banks, held only about $3.8 million in cash. The banks' combined holdings of deposits, however, stood by 1902 at $54.7 million.[69]

In view of these financial realities it is clear that had early attempts to unionize the coal fields been successful, they might have slowed Appalachia's journey into economic dependency but would not have reversed it. Successful early unionization would have driven much of the highly capitalized mining out of the region. This would have left mostly the option of subsistence farming, but the population was already too large for the land available.

On the other hand, had there been large cash-on-hand holdings in the Flat Top-Pocahontas coal-field banks—indicating significant cash holdings among the general population—a local market for a variety of local products could have been created. The fact that by 1902 the local banks held almost eighteen times more in checking deposits than in cash reflects the fact that most of the money in the area was not at the disposal of either local purchasing decisions or local production decisions. The company stores where miners made their purchases, using company scrip instead of money, offered many standardized outside products—the kind of products that the local coal companies could import in bulk from elsewhere by writing checks.[70]

Much of the money invested in Appalachia's coal production and railroads stayed in the North. Money controlled from the financial "core," indeed, soon became instrumental in a transfer of Appalachian political leadership out of the hands of traditional political-party bosses whose wealth was in land rather than in money. Studying the politics of this period, Gordon McKinney finds that a "new professional middle class created by the industrial revolution . . . came to dominate mountain society." The Republican party had controlled most of the Plateau's politics since the Civil War, and now within that party, says McKinney, "businessmen and the professional middle class sought to bring order to mountain society by challenging the old mountain Republican machines." But the old "bosses did not give up power easily. They controlled the party structure, and they still spoke for many of the mountain people who resented the changes coming to mountain society." The new middle class could afford to reward its campaign workers with money, however, and a drastic pruning of federal patronage jobs in favor of civil service appointments also worked in its favor. McKinney concludes that "by 1896 the issue had been settled . . . and the Republican Party's commitment to local interests had disappeared." Indeed, during the 1893–1896 depression, even "the Democratic party split into business and agrarian factions" in Appalachia as throughout the country.[71]

But where did northern interests acquire so much money to invest, including to invest in politics? A great deal of it, ironically, came from peripheral regions of the country—from the very regions that then had to look north and east to find investment capital. As of 1900, about one-third of the money on deposit in the national banks of Boston, Detroit, Cleveland, and Minneapolis consisted of "bankers' balances" (that is, of money from other banks). In Chicago, Kansas City, and St. Louis, bankers' balances constituted about *half* of the deposits of national banks, and in New York City the proportion was much higher. Such balances in New York City as of 1900 amounted to $339.3 million, on which the New York City banks paid about 2 percent interest in good times and bad. This vast financial resource derived from the Gilded Age's shift away from cash and toward deposit money. Back in

1870, New York City's central banks had held only $65.9 million in bankers' balances.[72]

Viewing this from a regional perspective, we find that only 10 percent of the outside deposits placed by state or national southern banks in other (national) banks were placed in the national banks of the South's three major financial centers (Richmond, Dallas, and Atlanta). Some of the South's bankers' deposits doubtlessly did go elsewhere in the South—but 35 percent of them went to New York banks, and another 20 percent to banks in Chicago, St. Louis, and Philadelphia.[73]

Money thus gravitated to the North. One of the major reasons it did so was because that was where large borrowers went to draw their loans. Large borrowers—large developers and industrialists, including Appalachia's—could not be adequately financed by small banks with limited funds and high overhead. Furthermore, interest rates were lower in the North than they were in the South, including in Appalachia. A situation evolved whereby from 1888 to 1911, interest rates on loans rested 1 to 5 percent lower in the northeastern United States than in the rest of the country—averaging between 3 and 4 percent lower in the Northeast than in the South.[74]

Throughout this whole period, interstate branch banking was prohibited, yet a complex network existed for the transfer of funds nationwide. The transfer of funds out of banks in peripheral regions such as Appalachia went far beyond the bankers' balances that were held in large cities. And not only did funds arrive from the periphery to be apportioned at the will of central bankers, but much of the risk for those large loans was in turn apportioned back out to the periphery in the form of "commercial paper."[75] ("Commercial paper" referred to a range of negotiable instruments backed by promissory notes rather than by actual collateral. Businesses issued the initial promissory notes to acquire ready cash or credit, and brokerage firms distributed the promissory-note-backed "commercial paper" in instruments of all denominations throughout the country, spreading out the investment risk to those holding the paper.)

After the financial crisis of 1897, and particularly after that of 1907, many outlying banks began to invest heavily in commercial paper—thereby diversifying their portfolios in order to guard against bankruptcy and to fulfill new banking laws. Partly a bank's scale of operations, but also the diversity of its portfolio, determined whether it could fulfill the increasingly stringent banking laws, both federal and state, that were legislated during the late nineteenth and early twentieth centuries. As for the danger of bankruptcy, even a local panic or local depression could sink a local bank if it used all its savings-deposit money to issue local loans.

By the early twentieth century, a situation had evolved whereby large industrialists generally had little difficulty gaining credit from financiers for their unbacked promissory notes. These notes in turn constituted the backing for the "commercial paper" issued by the financiers. Northern financiers such as J. P. Morgan had perfected methods for what an economic historian calls "easy access to the pooled resources of the country's savers, directly and via the intermediation of collection." The historian adds that now "the country had a machine for the mobilization of capital."[76]

Finance capital thus fled the periphery and accumulated ever more at centers that were already bursting with it. A situation evolved in which, as the same historian puts it, "the American industrialist had access to big money but not to small."[77] The optimal course for a peripheral region such as Appalachia would have been to accumulate, within the region, sufficiently large and concentrated savings to finance its own industries. But this was not feasible as long as the region was importing a major share of its necessities and was paying for those imports with its "foreign exchange" assets (that is, with its U.S. dollar income).

The case of Alabama illustrates this. Why were insufficient local savings accumulated in Alabama for that state to build up large banks and thus to begin financing its own mining and manufacturing? Alabama's case calls into doubt any theory that Appalachia could have avoided economic dependency by manufacturing more products within the region—such as by manufacturing more steel. The economic historian Richard Simon has suggested that perhaps West Virginia's dependency derived partly from having coal but not having much iron ore. Simon writes that "perhaps the presence of iron ore in addition to coal, as in Alabama, would have induced expansion of steel manufacturing in West Virginia. But West Virginia had no great deposits of iron ore." Simon hypothesizes that "underdevelopment was the result of the incomplete industrialization."[78]

But the different natural-resource endowments of West Virginia and Alabama cannot explain West Virginia's economic dependency, because Alabama too, despite its development of steel manufacturing, fell into dependency. This occurred because despite its steel making, Alabama like Appalachia became a major field for investments from the northern United States.

Indeed, Alabama's steel industry, despite financial control from the North, possessed insufficient capital until Birmingham's main steel mills were sold in 1907 to their primary competitor, U.S. Steel Company. U.S. Steel then imposed what were called "Pittsburgh Plus" prices on the output of Birmingham mills, meaning that U.S. Steel's Birmingham products could not be sold anywhere for a price lower than it would have cost to supply the same steel from Pittsburgh.[79] The profit margin that this created between high Pittsburgh Plus prices and Birmingham's low production costs (including its low wages) was then withdrawn to Pittsburgh.

Why did Birmingham's steelworkers, under those circumstances, not claim a share of the immense profits? Because the labor force had still poorer prospects outside the steel mills than it had in them. That is, Alabama's steelworkers were replaceable by still poorer workers. Under such circumstances—and even if sweated workers do manage to unionize and to force up wages—W. Arthur Lewis reminds us of "the propensity of manufacturers to move from low-wage centres to lower-wage centres." Lewis goes on to ask, "Is there no way to break out of unfavourable factoral terms of trade? Simply to raise productivity in the exporting sectors (whether manufacturing or agriculture) does not do the trick, if exporters' wages remain tied to low productivity in food; since export prices then fall *pari passu* with rising productivity."[80]

The point here is that despite Alabama's participation through manufacturing in the "value added" column of economic statistics, Alabama's dependency on the North grew from the same root as did the dependency of Plateau Appalachia with its almost solely extractive industry. W. Arthur Lewis's insight points us back to the importance of the subsistence potential of a region's agriculture. People able to maintain a satisfying living standard through subsistence farming, or through locally marketed agricultural production, are not likely to undertake wage work for a pittance. For many Appalachians, agriculture alone could no longer maintain their previous living standard, but neither could industrial work alone accomplish that. So agriculture continued in Appalachia, much of it now carried on by the region's industrial workers, including those who lived in company towns. This constituted a subsidy from agriculture to industry, a "subsistence reproduction of labor power." In Appalachia, as elsewhere in the world, such a subsidy has allowed low wages. But unlike Japan and Taiwan, Appalachia did not capture the benefit of its low wages—the U.S. North did.

5

The New Deal
and Appalachia's Industry

We relied on PWA [the Public Works Administration] to activate the heavy industry at once and thus increase the *total number of purchasers*. We relied on AAA [the Agricultural Adjustment Administration] to increase farm purchasing power immediately and thus still further add to the *number of purchasers*. These added to NRA additions would so far increase *volume* that I thought (and I still think) the increased labor cost could be absorbed without much increase in price. The President specifically asked industry to take this gamble.

—Hugh Johnson, *The Blue Eagle from Egg to Earth*

From the 1880s on, and particularly after 1920, Appalachia's highly competitive mines enforced a curb on the profits attainable by northern coal operators. In 1920 the mines of West Virginia and Kentucky supplied only 23 percent of the country's bituminous coal, but by 1927 they were supplying 41 percent. [1] Already by 1924, production in Ohio, Indiana, and Illinois had fallen 27 percent from its 1920 level, whereas production in West Virginia and Kentucky had risen 23 percent from its 1920 level. As for the size of the work force, that fell more than two-fifths from 1923 to 1929 at the bituminous mines of Pennsylvania, Ohio, Indiana, and Illinois. [2]

Low-priced coal from Appalachia's largely non-unionized mines defeated efforts by the United Mine Workers (UMW) to enforce compliance by northern coal operators with the February 1924 Jacksonville Agreement. Under that agreement, most northern miners received $7.50 a day at a time when most Appalachian miners were non-unionized and receiving about $3.00 a day. In 1927 northern operators shook off the last vestiges of the Jacksonville Agreement. A 1927 strike by two hundred thousand UMW miners failed to resurrect the agreement and, in that one year, fifty-five thousand northern bituminous mining jobs were permanently abolished. Throughout the 1920s, indeed, midwestern operators slashed their high-cost labor force by installing new underground machines to load coal. By 1929, more than one-third of Illinois's deep-mined coal, and more than one-fourth of Indiana's, was machine loaded. By contrast, in Appalachia as of then only 2 percent was yet machine loaded.[3]

Ideally, Appalachia's mines should have been unionized from their first days. Had that happened—had coal miners achieved collective bargaining as early in Appalachia as in the North—coal mining might have developed as a stable industry, and an optimal allocation of the industry's resources might have been possible. In that case, much less mining would have occurred in Appalachia. Fewer Appalachian miners, in turn, would have meant fewer part-time farmers adding to agricultural demands on the region's eroding hillsides. From many angles, an earlier unionization of Appalachia's mines would have been beneficial. The only sour note might have been a longer history of class antagonism in the region. Perhaps, however, an earlier origin of class antagonism might have moderated its intensity. As it was, the dichotomy between the unionized North on one hand and non-union Appalachia on the other engendered unstable conditions for the entire coal industry east of the Great Plains.

The willingness of Appalachian miners to dig coal for low wages did not mean that their wages were always pegged low, just usually. It allowed Appalachian coal operators to respond faster than northern operators to any change in market conditions. When demand for coal was strong, its market price shot upward. At the end of World War I, some Appalachian operators paid wages as high as $25 a day, taking advantage of high coal prices. Such temporarily high wages drew miners into Appalachia from Pennsylvania and the Midwest. But when demand for coal plummeted again to much lower levels, Appalachian miners' wages fell as low as $1.50 a day in the late 1920s and early 1930s. Wage variability gave Appalachian operators great flexibility in their operating costs, for about 65 percent of total operating costs consisted of wages. Thereby, Appalachian operators generally managed to increase their share of the coal market through both good times and bad.[4] Even the seasonal alteration between high wintertime demand for coal and low summertime demand helped Appalachia's flexible non-union operations at the expense of the less-flexible union operations in the North.[5] Furthermore, when major strikes hit the unionized North, Appalachia's mines achieved marketing gains that the unionized areas could not easily reverse after their strikes ended. The dependability of coal deliveries from Appalachia's usually strike-proof mines earned them a lower hauling rate per mile than the railroads were willing to grant mines in the North and the Midwest.[6]

Because Appalachia's wages were generally low, mechanization in its mines commonly lagged behind mechanization in midwestern mines. When demand for coal shot upward, this translated into not only higher Appalachian wages but also faster Appalachian mechanization. Back in 1909, for example, only 41 percent of Appalachia's coal production was yet being undercut by machines. (The rest was either undercut by hand-pick or was "shot from the solid.") Meanwhile, 51.4 percent of the coal produced by midwestern mines (those of Ohio, Indiana, and Illinois) was already being undercut by machine.[7] By ten years later in 1919, however, World War I's tremendous coal demands had inspired Appalachian operators to have 70.7 percent of their coal output machine cut—surpassing the Midwest's proportion at that time of 66.3 percent machine cut.[8]

About 1923—a time of weak market demand but strong union demands—midwestern mines began using underground machinery to *load* a significant portion of their coal production. In Appalachia, by contrast, machine loading remained insignificant until the New Deal era of the 1930s. (By 1940 the mountain region would mechanize to the extent of machine loading approximately 27.1 percent of its underground coal production, but by then the Midwest would be machine loading 70.6 percent.)[9]

The coal industry, all this while, could mine far more coal than the United States could consume. Even at the height of market demand in 1918, when the price of coal soared to astounding heights, less than two-thirds of the coal industry's effective capacity came into use.[10] During the 1920s, the obstacles to any agreement among coal operators for equalized production cutbacks proved insurmountable. This was the decade that saw the UMW cripple northern mines through strikes while a large percentage of the Midwest's coal production migrated to Appalachia.[11] Then too, the 1920s also saw oil and gas make enormous strides in replacing coal as an energy source—and also saw major technical improvements that increased coal-burning efficiency in various industries, thereby further restricting demand for coal.

Problems in the 1920s' coal industry inspired many of the ideas that would later be imposed throughout American industry under the New

Deal's National Industrial Recovery Act (NIRA). In 1928 a congressional committee considered the Watson Bill, which was supported by the UMW and by some coal operators whose mines had long been unionized. A similar Davis-Kelly Bill followed in 1932 and gained considerable support—but again not enough to pass. Both of these bills foreshadowed the fundamental business-labor trade-off that finally became law in 1933 under the NIRA. Both the Watson and the Davis-Kelly bills called for price supports, as desired by northern operators with their high-cost mining operations. Both bills would also have guaranteed workers' rights to organize and to bargain collectively. [12]

When Franklin Roosevelt took office in 1933, however, he did not give immediate attention to industrial and commercial recovery. Roosevelt hesitated in those areas to seize the mandate that his landslide electoral victory offered. After the new administration's first month slipped past without any major "recovery" initiative, the Senate passed a recovery bill introduced by Senator Hugo Black of Alabama. The Black Bill called for reducing the industrial work week to thirty hours per worker. Because Black's bill contained no minimum wage requirement, Roosevelt feared it would lower workers' purchasing power, and a small army of presidential advisors began creating an alternative bill before Black's bill, already through the Senate, could move on through the House of Representatives and confront Roosevelt as a fait accompli.

Roosevelt's recovery bill initially emphasized direct employment increase ("direct economic start-up," this was called) including massive public works. But by the time the bill went to Congress on 17 May 1933, its provisions for public works were smaller than they originally had been. Instead the final bill emphasized a plan for *indirectly* increasing employment and restarting the economy by devising "codes of fair competition" for each of the country's major industries. These codes would fix prices within agreed parameters (thereby increasing profits) and would limit production (thus limiting competition). Beyond that, the administration's recovery bill repeated some popular themes of the Black Bill, including minimum standards for working conditions and also labor's right to organize and bargain collectively—two provisions appearing in the new bill's famous Section 7(a). [13] On 13 June 1933, this bill passed Congress as the National Industrial Recovery Act. On 16 June, Roosevelt signed it and named Hugh Johnson, a veteran of World War I's War Industries Board, to head a National Recovery Administration (NRA). A Chicago lawyer named Donald Richberg was appointed as Johnson's assistant.

The NIRA provided benefits primarily for large and influential participants in the American economy, including big labor as well as big business. It added governmental power to the powers already inherent in bigness, proving detrimental to three other major (but less organized) interest groups: farmers, small business people, and consumers.[14]

Much of Appalachia's coal mining was admittedly carried on by large companies, but not generally by the large northern coal companies that stood to benefit from the NIRA.[15] Nor, in the spring of 1933, were very many Appalachian coal miners represented by the coal industry's only major union, the United Mine Workers (UMW).

Northern coal-operator associations joined John L. Lewis of the UMW in helping to draft Section 7(a) of the NIRA—the section protecting collective bargaining. Because most northern mines had been unionized long before 1933 and could not be *de*unionized, their owners had long sought the unionization of Appalachia's mines as the ultimate solution to Appalachia's low coal prices (which were now castigated as "unfair competition" to fit the NIRA's *Weltanschauung*).

John L. Lewis of the UMW went into the new NIRA era open eyed. Like his archrival William Green of the American Federation of Labor, Lewis accepted what amounted to price fixing under the NIRA. De facto price fixing was the price that business leaders demanded, and that labor leaders accepted, in exchange for labor leaders' treasured Section 7(a) of the legislation.[16] Lewis reportedly said at this time that he was only looking out for current miners. Miners' sons, he reportedly said, would have to look for work in the cities.[17] Lewis was manifestly not, however, looking out for *all* current miners. His initial proposal for a nationwide daily minimum wage of five dollars for all coal miners[18] would have ruined many Appalachian operations, throwing their miners out of work.

Meanwhile, before the NIRA passed Congress and went to Roosevelt for his signature, John L. Lewis set in motion a successful UMW whirlwind campaign that largely unionized Appalachia's coal fields. Before the National Recovery Administration (NRA) ended its hearings about wages and hours for a bituminous coal "code of fair competition," the UMW had already lassoed Appalachian operators into a September 1933 "Appalachian Agreement" that raised wage levels in the mountain region enormously. Representatives of the major Appalachian operators testified at the NRA's code-formulation hearings that those high wages could only be maintained if the NRA stimulated "increased demand and increased prices" for coal.[19]

Before the UMW's well-timed organizing drive, wages as low as $1.50 a day had been common in Appalachia's mines. Now, as the bituminous coal code negotiations ended, Appalachia's major coal mines were already unionized and their operators had already agreed to pay almost three times that much. In their NRA-sponsored code they reaffirmed their agreement to pay about $4.20 a day—only forty cents below Pennsylvania and Ohio's standard minimum and only sixty cents below that of Illinois.[20]

During the hearings, industry spokesmen pointed out that labor costs constituted 65 percent, on average, of the total operating costs of producing coal. The logic of the situation called for *lower* coal prices, said one industry spokesman, because oil and natural gas were rapidly displacing coal as an energy source. In 1923 bituminous coal had provided 63.5 percent of U.S. energy, but by 1930 it was providing only 55.7 percent, and the Depression was seeing coal use fall faster than the use of its major competitors (oil being its prime competitor, with natural gas next). Under such circumstances, asked the coal industry spokesman, was it logical to raise the price of coal? No, he said, but because miners' wages had already been raised, the price of coal would have to go up too.[21]

Replying on behalf of the NRA, Donald Richberg made no objection to coal prices going up, but Richberg did object to any continuation of the "open shop" in Appalachian coal mines. Like John L. Lewis, Richberg favored the "closed shop." To bring about "fairly uniform standards of hours and wages" among U.S. coal miners, Richberg desired what he called "an equal organization of the employees uniform to compare with the organization of the employers." A coal industry spokesman counterargued that the employers had only become so organized because the NRA had demanded it.[22]

Prior to the New Deal, as we have seen, most Appalachian coal operators had perceived their maximum profits to lie in relatively labor-intensive mining methods combined with anti-unionism. As for the miners, they and their families had in general subsisted partly off the land. The miners had tended to raise large families who helped them

maintain their agricultural pursuits but who at the same time constituted a pool of surplus labor, undermining the miners' bargaining position vis-à-vis the mine operators.

The transition that now occurred in 1933 insured only that *some* of
Appalachia's miners would share in the extra profits that accrued to operators through price supports—for the new wage gains of 1933 con-
vinced many Appalachian operators to minimize their labor needs by
mechanizing more thoroughly. Many more operators waited for the
NIRA's constitutionality to be challenged, thinking that wage levels
might then be reducible in a post-NIRA situation, but their hope
proved futile. The NIRA's demise in 1935 inspired a new National Labor Relations Act (the Wagner Act), which reinstated labor's right to
organize and to bargain collectively. Indeed, 1935 also saw Congress
pass a Bituminous Coal Conservation Act (the so-called First Guffey
Act), which provided for a new coal code to set minimum wages and
hours and to decree minimum and maximum coal prices. This First
Guffey Act imposed a 13.5 percent tax on the coal produced by any
bituminous operator who did not abide by the new code.

The Supreme Court voided this First Guffey Act in 1936 for the
same reasons it had struck down the NIRA in 1935; but, despite losing
those two battles, ultimate victory went to high-price and high-wage
adherents when the Supreme Court in 1937 upheld the National Labor
Relations Act, and when Congress that year passed a Second Guffey Act
similar to the first.[23] These 1935 and 1937 New Deal victories became
the signal for a heightened pace of mechanization in Appalachia's
mines.[24] Appalachian coal operators' savings through lower wages now
no longer exceeded the midwestern operators' savings through higher
productivity per worker, so Appalachian operators now also sought to
maximize productivity per worker.

If low-wage labor was ever at a premium in the mountains, it was
during the Depression. And yet, in reaction to the new high wage levels, Appalachian operators reduced their labor needs through a renewal
of the mechanization drive they had begun during World War I but had
then abandoned. World War I and its immediate aftermath had created
an unprecedented demand for coal that had resulted, temporarily, in
high coal prices, high union membership (two-thirds of all U.S. miners
were then unionized, including, temporarily, many Appalachian miners), and high wages. Now in 1933, these same three results were

achieved despite *low* demand for coal. In 1933, high coal prices, high union membership, and high wages were achieved in effect by government fiat. A renewed surge of automation was provoked by the high wage demands and was made financially feasible by price supports. After 1933—and especially after 1938—Appalachian coal production rose far faster than employment rose in the mines.[25]

Meanwhile, because the NRA and the AAA (Agricultural Adjustment Administration) had caused a sharp rise in consumer-goods prices, real wages for the miners were not rising quite as much as their nominal wages. Already by 15 August 1933 a national survey found food prices 16 percent higher than they had been five months earlier.[26] Indeed, by mid-July, after four New Deal months, overall U.S. wholesale prices had already risen an average of 27.5 percent—although overall retail prices were still reflecting backlogged inventories of durables and semidurables and had risen only 6 percent during those first four Roosevelt months.[27]

Also meanwhile, automation proved a mixed blessing even for some of the miners who were not replaced by machines, for automation increased the coal dust that causes black lung disease. The principal culprits in creating dust were the cutting machines—and already by 1919, as noted, 70.7 percent of Appalachia's coal production was machine cut. When the U.S. Public Health Service finally studied black lung disease among Appalachian miners in the 1960s, it found fully one-third of former cutting-machine operators suffering from black lung—a far higher percentage than the 19.3 percent average incidence among former miners who had been employed in any capacity whatsoever at the coal face.[28]

Use of cutting machines went back as far as the late 1880s in a few mines, and by the end of World War I, most U.S. coal production was undercut by machine, but not until 1963 was any systematic study begun of the health damage caused by different types of mining in the United States. In 1931 Great Britain had begun to require that limited compensation be paid to miners for any "respiratory disability which could not be attributed to silicosis."[29] (Compensation in Britain for silicosis had begun even earlier.) But in the United States the New Deal ignored this whole subject, including the medical toll exacted by the mechanization the New Deal itself inspired, and not until 1947 did the federal government undertake a general survey of "all forms of tuberculosis" among coal miners. This survey catalogued miners' lung problems, and their resultant mortality, state by state and even county by county, but it did not distinguish between the different jobs performed underground.[30] A more analytic study was carried out on more than four hundred patients at a West Virginia hospital in the early 1950s and revealed not only the existence but also the probable extent of black lung disease in the United States.[31] No significant prevention was yet attempted, however. Finally, between 1959 and 1961, the state of Pennsylvania X-rayed the lungs of sixteen thousand working miners and compared those findings to X-ray data about the general population.

Pennsylvania's study set the stage for a study begun in 1963 by the U.S. Public Health Service, which surveyed 3,740 Appalachian miners and former miners, all of them chosen at random to prevent self-selection because of lung problems. About one-third of those examined were retired miners—who, as retirees, tended to have longer exposure to coal dust than did still-working miners.[32]

We have already seen what this survey found among former cutting-machine operators—that fully one-third of them suffered from black lung. As for loading-machine operators, the study found that 22.5 percent of former loading-machine operators had black lung, whereas only 14.9 percent of former hand loaders (shovel workers) did so.[33] The transition from hand loading to a significant degree of machine loading in Appalachia was initiated by the high-wage policies of the New Deal.[34]

Black lung is a disease that denies its victims sufficient oxygen to sustain normal levels of exertion. Many black lung victims desire death long before it arrives. Black lung existed as a human cost for more than half a century before it was acknowledged as an economic cost to its victims and to society. The human cost of black lung, as well as its personal economic cost, was already stupendous when federal black lung pensions were finally legislated by the Coal Mine Health and Safety Act of 1969.[35]

Admittedly the mechanization of Appalachian coal loading drastically reduced the number of miners—perhaps to such an extent that the absolute number of Appalachia's black lung victims was falling rather than rising by about 1960.[36] But this does not exculpate the New Deal, for in the 1930s the British government was already initiating underground dust control and other preventive measures. The British thereby cut the average death toll among their miners significantly between

1932 and 1950.[37] Similar preventive measures should also have begun in the United States in the 1930s rather than waiting until 1969. And, over and above the black-lung question, the instigation of a trend toward capital-intensive mining in the midst of a depression was not only economically unsound but inhumane.

Rexford Tugwell exonerated the NRA of human costs because a welfare net was unfurled beneath its victims. Looking back from the vantage of 1977, Tugwell managed to see the NRA philosophically. In retrospect he saw a silver lining in the fact that already by 1934 the New Deal had begun inspiring a *political* realignment that might prove auspicious. "As this alignment went on," Tugwell mused, "it did not matter much, politically, . . . that the NRA was likely to fail. What was important was that people's immediate needs were being satisfied." After all, Tugwell continued, the NRA's fundamental "mistakes meant nothing immediately to the sufferers from the depression. If they were still unemployed, they had relief or there was public work."[38]

This ignores, unfortunately, the fact that the NRA's two-year sabotage of recovery left deleterious results for decades. The NRA coal code, for instance, hastened conversion to coal's primary competitor, oil, and thereby contributed to today's potentially disastrous U.S. oil dependency.

Tugwell, in his 1933 reenactment, called the NRA "likely to fail." Ironically, however, the NRA only failed to the extent it succeeded. Its failure was in conception rather than in execution. The NRA did in fact largely establish the wage and price "standards of fair competition" that it advocated. How, then, had such a poor idea managed to gain sufficient support to become law? The short answer is that Franklin Roosevelt's pursuit of political expediency had overly influenced his perception of what was economically desirable.[39] Roosevelt found it politically expedient to pursue two contradictory recovery policies simultaneously.[40] On taking office, what Roosevelt mainly sought was to avoid serious, possibly revolutionary, political challenges for which the Depression was creating a constituency. German political developments in that spring of 1933 were not reassuring. Roosevelt considered the specifics of recovery efforts less important than that something or other be tried. "This nation asks for action, and action now," he declaimed at his inaugural. "We must act and act quickly."[41]

In human terms there was undeniably much to admire about the New Deal. Unfortunately, admiration for Franklin Roosevelt and many of his associates has contributed to postponing analytic research about the New Deal. Analytic research about the New Deal's effect on Appalachia is only just beginning. At the national level, however, an econometrician has demonstrated what others have long guessed: the NRA was not economically neutral but was actively counterproductive. As that econometrician summarizes his findings:

> Monetary expansion after June 1933 was mainly due to gold inflows [and thus the] 14 percent average annual rate of increase in the money supply during the two-year NIRA period can be considered an exogenous shock—independent of the NIRA legislation itself. . . . [Meanwhile] the industrial codes contributed to prices approximately 14 percent per year during the NIRA period. The codes exactly nullified the monetary expansion! Despite nominal expansion of the money supply, there was literally no expansion of the *real* money supply. Thus there was no stimulus to any real variables in the economic system. In the absence of the codes, the monetary stimulus would have been expansionary; in the presence of the codes, the monetary stimulus was impotent. . . . The combination of the monetary stimulus and the NIRA-induced inflation left real output virtually unchanged. Thus the contradictory impact of the codes can be measured, at least in part, by what contributions to real output and [to] employment the monetary stimulus would have made in the absence of the codes.[42]

Nor were NRA-type price supports permanently terminated when the Supreme Court voided the NIRA in 1935. Like NRA-type wage supports, price supports soon reappeared. Congress reenacted significant price supports through the Robinson-Patman Act of 1936 and, more strongly, through the Miller-Tydings Enabling Act of 1937.[43]

The NRA was a fundamental flaw in the early New Deal and a major cause of prolonging the American Depression far beyond Europe's recovery. Let us now look at the New Deal's agricultural policies and their more mixed effects.

6

The New Deal and
Appalachia's Agriculture

The National Recovery Administration . . . [has] so encouraged the
business people of this country that they are setting about their affairs
with renewed energy. . . . The manufacturer, with his people working
full-time, is engaged in producing commodities and articles for the use
of the people of this country. . . . There must be placed within the reach
of the people in the rural sections of our country purchasing power before
this problem will be solved, and that is the situation with which the Federal Government is wrestling.
—H. G. Kump, governor of West Virginia, 21 July 1933

In May 1927 a torrential, once-in-a-century rainstorm struck much
of the Appalachian Plateau, tearing topsoil and clay off its plowed
hillsides in sheets. Three years later, from Arkansas to West Virginia
in a west-to-east belt, the 1930 growing season saw the onset of a
major drought. In northern West Virginia, the Monongahela River
and the Tygart Valley River shrank to isolated pools that were transferred downstream through water hoses so that the cities of Morgantown and Elkins could receive drinking water.[1] As far east as
Roanoke, the year 1930 saw only 16.27 inches of precipitation, well
below half of that Virginia city's annual average.[2] In Kentucky, the
Red Cross sent county-by-county surveyors through the state, and
from eastern Kentucky they predicted that tremendous suffering lay
ahead during the coming winter, making a relief program inevitable
there. In October 1930, Kentucky's Red Cross director visited four
counties in eastern Kentucky and found "people getting along as
best they could on a very narrow margin, but each day consuming
their winter supply which in a normal year would not be touched
by this season."[3] Many of the residents had sold their livestock,
which doomed them to malnutrition over the winter unless they were
given relief.

In reporting these conditions, Kentucky's Red Cross director predicted that relief would have to start in November. But on 20 October

1930, the national Red Cross closed its Kentucky relief offices.[4] By November in eastern Kentucky's Rowan County, the county judge was committing children to institutions because their parents could not feed them and a Red Cross field representative was warning that "people will starve to death unless something is done soon."[5] In adjacent Morgan County, the same field representative found three deaths from pneumonia and found people begging from door to door. Here too she predicted starvation unless relief began soon.

Nothing was done soon. On 27 November 1930 eight inches of snow fell on eastern Kentucky and the temperature dropped to 16 degrees fahrenheit. By mid-December the Kentucky Red Cross director was reporting that "the picture of distress . . . in the eastern part of our state is almost unbelievable. . . . There is a growing army of itinerants travelling on foot."[6] Other people were selling their household furnishings to traveling peddlers to obtain money for food. Still others were robbing tobacco wagons. Kentucky's infant mortality rate had climbed 10 percent in the previous four months, and some schoolchildren were found bringing nothing in their school lunch buckets except green nuts.[7] Similar reports came from West Virginia.[8]

Finally in January 1931 the national Red Cross reopened its Kentucky and West Virginia relief offices. Many of the people who were then helped had never before received any form of charity. Their average ration, however, was only two dollars a month per person, with a maximum for the largest families of twenty dollars a month. According to Kentucky's Frontier Nursing Service, this sufficed only to buy a low grade of grain and provided "no margin to give a man working-calories, to give children growth, to enable an expectant or a nursing mother to carry her baby, or to stave off the ravaging effects of pellagra or tuberculosis. No provision whatever is made for milk for the young children."[9] And yet, as of 11 February 1931, the national Red Cross had barely distributed half of the money it had collected for its Drought Relief Fund.[10]

For many full-time Appalachian farmers, the 1930–1931 drought proved more traumatic than the Depression that was then beginning. In Appalachia's mining areas, on the other hand, it was not so much the drought as the Depression that brought impoverishment. In the coal fields, not only spring 1931 but many springs saw small children dying of bacillary dysentery (the "bloody flux"), deaths often precipitated when hungry children rapidly ingested too many raw weeds. In spring 1931 in Kentucky's highly industrialized Bell County, at least thirty-five children died of the bloody flux. [11]

Such conditions did not suddenly cease when Franklin Roosevelt took office. As of September 1933 desperation still characterized the coal fields. From southern West Virginia's coal fields that month, county relief supervisors reported that relief was providing only enough money for food. Despite approaching winter, home evictions for unpaid rent were beginning to snowball. Medical care was desperately inadequate. In the coal fields of West Virginia's McDowell County, epidemics of typhoid, diphtheria, and dysentery were threatening. Equally severe conditions were still being reported in November 1933 among at least some of East Tennessee's miners and their families. [12]

By 1933, federal relief for many of Appalachia's unemployed and underemployed wage workers was not only necessary but had been overdue for years. Entailing as it did widespread destitution among wage workers, the Depression temporarily reversed America's long-term trend toward increased urbanization. Even among intellectuals a back-to-the-land mood manifested—marked by nostalgia for simple rural lifeways but also by a lot of economic rethinking. Certainly in Appalachia's preindustrial era, by all accounts, starvation had been virtually impossible. And during the region's industrialization period, roughly 1880 to 1930, all indications point to a fall, rather than any rise, in average living standards. [13] In fact, by the time of the 1927 flood and the 1930 drought, many Appalachian farm families had been sliding toward poverty for decades.

Concerted and consistent federal programs tailored to meet the actual needs of such families were able to yield long-term benefits, but only a few New Deal programs fell into that category. Most New Deal programs that affected Appalachia did so merely accidentally, and their long-term results have proven mixed. Initially the New Deal emphasized restoring the nation's commodity markets. Only gradually did the Roosevelt administration tackle the issue of rural poverty. Indeed, no unified conception controlled the New Deal or completely dominated any separate New Deal agency. Many officials desired a unified approach, but Roosevelt preferred operating with only vague aims, leaving the means for accomplishing those aims ad hoc and sometimes contradictory. [14]

One contradiction has been identified by Rexford Tugwell. Tugwell influenced the contents of the Agricultural Adjustment Act (AA Act) and was appointed assistant secretary of agriculture under Henry A. Wallace, but he never actually worked within the Agricultural Adjustment Administration (AAA). Later Tugwell set forth the view that the operation of the AAA brought about "what was plainly to be a disaster" for many southern farmhands, sharecroppers, and tenant farmers:

> In spite of what [Henry A. Wallace] said, the small farmers who were so much praised had miserably few government benefits from the operation of AAA. These would go to the larger operators, not the smaller ones. They would either sink into poverty where they were or move to city slums in search of other employment. The problems of another generation were created by the policies of 1933, and absolutely nothing was done to avert what was plainly to be a disaster. [15]

Tugwell's point here is mainly about the Deep South, where because of the AAA, as he goes on to say, "wages were supplanting the sharecrop arrangements in force since the abolition of slavery and where laborers were being replaced by machines." These two interrelated effects of the AAA, says Tugwell, created a new and desperate clientele for Harry "Hopkins' social workers who previously had had no rural responsibilities." [16] And the subsequent northward migration of displaced tenants, sharecroppers, and farm laborers to city slums has indeed created Tugwell's "problems of another generation." [17] The NRA-hastened elimination of many Appalachian mining jobs (described in the previous chapter) was thus paralleled by an AAA-hastened elimination of many sharecropping jobs in the Deep South.

As for Appalachia's agriculture—although the AAA attempted to reduce the output of Appalachia's two basic subsistence products, corn and hogs, participation in that "corn-hog" limitation program was voluntary, and most mountain farm families did not participate. The AAA also, however, limited production of one of the mountains' main farm products of a purely commercial nature, tobacco. In this case participation was made effectively mandatory. Most of Appalachia's counties grew little or no tobacco, but in several dozen of them it was a vitally important cash crop. [18]

The New Deal's method of limiting agricultural production was called *allotment*. It originated in the ruminations of a former Montana wheat farmer named M. L. Wilson. Wilson had given up farming to become a Montana State College agronomist. In the mid-1920s he had become an official of the U.S. Agriculture Department. Wilson devised the allotment plan as a means of reducing U.S. wheat production, which had overexpanded during and immediately after World War I, and which since the early 1920s had glutted its market. Faced with wheat's overproduction crisis, many individual wheat farmers produced still more wheat in a desperate bid to maintain their family incomes and meet their debt payments—ironically increasing their production to survive the overproduction. The allotment idea called for annual quotas of wheat production. Farm-by-farm quotas would be allotted by the government to farmers who were willing to cooperate with the program—their cooperation being purchased through "rental fees" that the government would pay for the acreage they removed from wheat production.

By February 1933, however, Wilson had developed second thoughts about any *general* applicability of his allotment idea, suspecting himself of being, as he put it, "more or less gripped in the provincialism of the Northwest."[19]

Meanwhile, nonetheless, Rexford Tugwell had already by July 1932 secured Roosevelt's rejection of "a Cornell [University] opinion looking toward the saving of the family farm, [in favor of] a western one wanting to bolster the big wheat producers."[20] "It was necessary, however," Tugwell himself tells us, "to be aware of the South; and there was some question whether [the allotment approach] would do for cotton what [M. L. Wilson] promised it would do for wheat."[21]

There is no sign that any attention was given—either before the passage of the AA Act, or before its powers were invoked—to asking how it would affect Appalachia or any other region as a region. The AA Act was not formulated region by region but commodity by commodity. With respect to allotments, the AA Act authorized the government to limit the production of certain farm products—wheat, cotton, corn, hogs, rice, tobacco, milk, and milk products.[22] By imposing production limits, the market value of each of these commodities was to be raised. The field crops on the list were to be limited mainly by allotting only a certain number of acres for planting to each of them, and livestock was to be limited by allotting only so many head to be raised.

Appalachia produced significant amounts of four of these farm products—corn, hogs, tobacco, and milk. As for secondary "milk products," these in the mountains consisted mainly of butter, which was churned not so much for sale as for home use and barter. Cheese making was important in several parts of Older Appalachia (the Valley subregion), but it was uncommon in most of the region, especially in Newer Appalachia (the Plateau subregion).[23]

The two basic subsistence products of the region overall were corn and hogs. These also happened to be the only two AAA reductions administered in tandem. That is, a farmer could only receive money for reducing his corn acreage if he also reduced his hog numbers, and vice versa. The other reductions were all administered separately.

The compensatory payments mailed to farmers who participated in the corn-hog program reimbursed them at approximately the pre-AAA market value of the corn production and of the hogs that they forewent. And in situations in which the corn and hogs involved were destined for market, this level of compensation seems justified. Most Appalachian farmers, however, raised corn and hogs less for sale than for subsistence, and the true cash equivalent of their lost production was therefore not how much they could have previously sold their corn and hogs for but how much it would cost them to replace them—that is, the current store price. A considerable difference existed between these two amounts.

The corn-hog program operated for two years, 1934 and 1935, and the "base period" that it adopted was 1932–1933. In other words—to consider only corn for a moment—1932–1933 was the base period whose farm-by-farm statistics of corn acreage planted and corn bushels harvested were used to calculate the farm-by-farm corn acreage that the AAA allotted to the farmers participating in its corn-hog program. In 1932 and 1933, however, bumper crops had made it cheaper for many farmers to buy corn than to grow it. The 1932 corn crop had sold at an average on-site farm price of $0.29 a bushel, and during the winter of 1932–1933, the price had fallen as low as $0.188 a bushel. Then in 1933–1934 a major drought afflicted the Plains states, raising the nation's average on-site corn price by December 1934 to $0.79 a bushel. In eastern Kentucky, and perhaps elsewhere in Appalachia, corn prices went as high in 1934 as $1.00 a bushel.[24]

The fact that the 1934 corn harvest totalled less than half as many bushels as the 1932 harvest was a consequence mainly of the Great

Plains' 1934 drought and only secondarily of the AAA's reduction efforts. But in Appalachia, unaffected by that drought, the cause of corn's dearness was immaterial. What mattered in Appalachia was that corn now cost $0.79 to $1.00 a bushel and that farmers who had signed up for the AAA's corn-hog program were being reimbursed for their sacrificed production (of 20 to 30 percent of their 1932–1933 corn production) at only $0.30 a bushel.[25] One Tennessee livestock marketing specialist complained to Washington that "because it was cheaper in the base years for a man to buy corn at $.25 cents a bushel than to grow it, I see no reason why our Program should compel him to continue buying it at an increased price." To compel a farmer to buy expensive corn rather than to grow his own cheap corn, this expert said, might well "interfere with, or prevent, a balanced set-up" on Tennessee farms.[26] It could also prevent earning a livelihood from farming.

This specialist was asking, in effect, that Tennessee farmers who had registered for the 1935 corn-hog program be allowed nonetheless to practice "import substitution." But to substitute home corn production for corn purchases would have undermined the entire allotment approach to solving the glut of corn and hogs on the market. Further, if we glance at the political situation, we find midwestern interests more or less controlling U.S. agricultural policies. In November of 1933, for instance, five midwestern governors felt so pressured by the direct action tactics of Milo Reno and the Farm Holiday Association that they went to Washington and almost managed to stampede the Roosevelt administration into pegging farm prices and allocating to all individual farmers the amounts that they would be allowed to sell, irrespective of market demand.[27] In such a political atmosphere, it simply was not feasible to antagonize midwestern farmers by allowing AAA-contracted farmers elsewhere in the country to grow their own livestock feed—by allowing farmers elsewhere to quit buying seventy-nine-cent midwestern corn, in this case, even though they had formerly bought twenty-five-cent midwestern corn. I could find no answer from Washington to the Tennessee specialist's fear that the AAA threatened balanced farming.

Indeed, not only the AAA's production restrictions per se threatened balanced farming but also rules prohibiting alternative profitable uses for the land removed from corn production. Rules governing alternative crops and land uses were much more stringent in the corn-hog program than they were in other AAA programs. The AAA even had rules governing alternative uses of the farm labor and equipment removed from corn production.[28]

With respect to hogs, the 1934 corn-hog contract mandated a 25 percent reduction (below the 1932–1933 average number) of 1934-born hogs raised for sale. Participating farmers who possessed extra hogs could either trade them or give them away. Compensation from the AAA to the farmers came in the form of a five dollar bounty for each market-intended hog that *was* permitted.

For Appalachian people enrolled in this program, the most onerous aspect of its hog provisions was that hogs raised for home consumption were restricted to the average annual number per farm raised for home consumption during the two base years (1932–1933).[29] This was burdensome because the AAA's intervention came at a time of growth in the subsistence demands on Appalachian agriculture. Already in 1929, before the Depression, Appalachia had contained 166,000 "self-sufficing" farms—one-third of the U.S. total concentrated in about 3 percent of the country's land area.[30] With the Depression's onset, industrial cutbacks within the region itself and in its diaspora meant that subsistence agriculture not only had to support people who were returning to Appalachia's farms from residence elsewhere but also had to provide a larger portion of income for many people who had maintained continuous rural Appalachian residence but who now needed to increase their subsistence farm activities as their off-the-farm wage work declined or disappeared.

In eastern Kentucky, part-time farming was denser than anywhere else in the United States. There the federal Bureau of Agricultural Economics reported that an almost 30 percent "increase in the number of farms from 1929 to 1934 was brought about largely by change of occupation from mining to farming. That is to say, the same families were involved, but because of less employment in the mines or forests, they did relatively more farming and became classed as farmers in 1934. There was, however, a limited amount of immigration and emigration."[31]

The number of farmed landholdings increased during the years 1929 to 1934 throughout Appalachia—although nowhere else so dramatically as in eastern Kentucky—and even the number of residents per farm inched slightly upward. In Older and Newer Appalachia combined (but with eastern Kentucky excluded), 1930 had found 5.45 residents per farm on average, whereas 1935 found 5.6 per farm—an increase of slightly over one person per seven farms. In eastern Kentucky, meanwhile, the number of mouths to feed per farm *decreased* by about that amount. But this occurred concurrent with the amazing 30 percent increase in the number of eastern Kentucky holdings being seriously farmed, as mentioned above.[32] Throughout Appalachia, farms were being called on to provide a greatly increased proportion of their residents' income.

By basing its overall corn allotments and its subsistence hog allotments on earlier production per farm—rather than taking into account the number of people, and the proportion of their income, that each separate farm actually had to provide—the AAA effectively hindered some of its Appalachian participants from supporting themselves with the skills tradition had given them. Beyond doubt this contributed to driving some people onto relief.

Such regional dynamics set in motion by the AAA's allotment program were easily overlooked. The AAA had no institutional mechanism for monitoring how its allotment program affected farmers' overall economic life. Rural Rehabilitation committees were created under the Federal Emergency Relief Administration partly to monitor the overall welfare of relief recipients, but those committees had very little power, and certainly had no influence at all on the AAA.

The AAA's acting administrator, H.R. Tolley, stated in April 1935 that "commercial slaughter is the important item for a corn-hog program" and that therefore it did not make much difference that up to 150,000 fewer "small producers" had chosen to sign 1935 corn-hog contracts than had signed 1934 corn-hog contracts.[33] As for why so many small farmers chose to eschew the 1935 corn-hog program after participating in 1934, presumably they decided that the costs of participation outweighed the benefits. In West Virginia, 1934 had seen 2,169 farmers sign the AAA's corn-hogs contracts, but in 1935 only 1,425 farmers signed up. The number of participating farms thus fell by 34.3 percent, but in the process the base corn acreage on participating farms dropped off only 28 percent,[34] indicating that farmers who had found the 1934 corn-hog program disadvantageous tended to have smaller operations than those who had found it advantageous.

A specialist on the AAA has written that in 1933 many farmers "saw at once that this program had little to offer small producers, that marginal [rather than fertile] land would be taken out of production thus minimizing reduction of surpluses, and that the program might interfere with sound rotation practices."[35]

One might reply to such objections, of course, that the AAA at least offered *something* to small producers, making it partly justified on that ground alone. But in the market, small farmers had to compete with large farmers. The substantial money payments received by large farmers from the AAA helped them mechanize and fertilize, thereby increasing their productivity relative to small farmers' productivity. And more directly as competitors, large farmers could use their AAA payments to buy out small farmers.[36] What helped large farmers tended automatically to hurt small farmers within the overall context of market competition.

In Plateau Appalachia the main crop grown strictly for marketing was tobacco. Tobacco was a cash crop important to the livelihood of many small farmers in eastern Kentucky, western West Virginia, southwestern Virginia, eastern Tennessee, and western North Carolina.[37] How did small tobacco growers fare under the AAA's tobacco program relative to large tobacco growers? John B. Hutson, who was chief of the AAA's tobacco section, recalled later that "there were some pressures for minimum acreages for producers"—by which he meant that some people wanted a minimum size to be established for the AAA's tobacco allotments. Then, no matter how small a farmer's tobacco plot may have been in previous years, if the farmer had previously grown any tobacco at all (say, a mere one-sixteenth of an acre), that would have entitled him under the AAA program to grow a plot of an official minimum size (one-half acre, say, or perhaps one acre). Hutson recalled that "that kind of problem did at one stage receive considerable backing by Congressmen and Senators. In those early years we took the position that it was not possible to establish minimums. . . . We pointed out that it would be extremely difficult to really favor small producers by establishing these minimums, because we would cut, obviously, the large operator."[38]

The formula for apportioning tobacco production cuts could easily have included a provision establishing a minimum acreage size. Technically no difficulty existed. The obstacle would have been opposition from large operators. The choice to lump small with large farmers was a political choice reflecting the distribution of power in farm organizations and in American politics generally. Because Appalachia's tobacco growers were almost all small growers, the AAA's decision against setting a minimum size for allotments hurt Appalachia as a region. I make this explicit because although an initial AAA bias against small farmers has generally been acknowledged, the regional implications of this bias are still ignored.

In the case of eastern Kentucky, we saw in chapter 5 that the National Recovery Administration prevented mine operators there from applying their earlier hard-times response of selling coal cheaper and prevented the miners themselves from applying *their* customary response to hard times, working cheaper. That decreased eastern Kentucky's previous share of the national coal market.

And now, in the workings of the government's tobacco program, eastern Kentucky was hurt once more. Because small holdings were the rule in eastern Kentucky, full-time subsistence farming was generally not feasible,[39] but this area's traditional cash crop, tobacco, was a highly intensive crop, and if the government had not interfered with tobacco plots of less than one or two acres per farm, fewer eastern Kentuckians would have needed welfare.

Technically, the participation of farmers in the tobacco program, as in all other AAA programs, was voluntary. But the distinction between "voluntary" and "mandatory" retained little meaning after the Kerr-Smith Act of June 1934 levied a 24 percent marketing tax on every pound of tobacco grown outside the program. The tax was explicitly meant to prevent anyone from doing better by ignoring the AAA tobacco program than by cooperating with it.

Nor did the tobacco program fall by the wayside as did the hog part of the corn-hog program when the AA Act was ruled unconstitutional in January 1936. By the time that Supreme Court ruling occurred, the U.S. Agriculture Department had already prepared legislation to imbed the AAA allotment program within a new program for soil conservation.[40] Crops that had formerly been called "surplus" were now relabeled "soil depleting," and the program continued. Indeed, the government's tobacco contracts now became more restrictive, specifying that acreage removed from tobacco production could not be used for any other similarly soil-depleting crop. In 1938 a West Virginia county agent tried to convince the second AAA (newly created that year) that contracted acres removed from tobacco production should be permitted for use in subsistence production. He argued that "if all tobacco growers in West Virginia quit growing tobacco and grew additional acreage of corn, oats, wheat and such like it still would all be consumed on the farm and the amount produced for sale would not be increased."[41] Unfortunately, that argument only fit the 1933–1935 reason for crop reductions. The county agent's argument was now three years out of date. Corn, oats, and wheat were no longer officially "surplus" but "soil-depleting," and as such they could not be grown on government-contracted land, even for home consumption.

Meanwhile, farmers in a position to farm more capital intensively found little difficulty in circumventing the output limitations at which the AAA aimed. In the case of cotton, for instance, the acreage planted by 1939 had fallen 47.2 percent from the acreage that had been planted to cotton back in 1929—and yet cotton production had only fallen 21.2 percent over those years.[42] Between 1935 and 1940 alone, cotton's average productivity per acre was increased 33.4 percent.[43] Overall, for all crops by 1939, thirty-eight million fewer acres were harvested than in 1929 and yet total farm production was up 10 percent.[44]

The acreage cutbacks of both the first and second AAAs inspired an immense acceleration of American agriculture's chemical revolution—involving vastly increased use of fertilizers, herbicides, and insecticides. In the case of corn (which was still slated for reduction after 1935 although hogs were not) not only the chemical revolution but also new hybrid corn seeds helped to maximize per-acreage production. Requiring far more chemical fertilizer than ordinary cross-pollinating corn, hybrid corn leapt from obscurity in 1933 to cover 75 percent of midwestern cornland by 1940. Hybrids averaged 15 to 20 percent greater output per acre than the cross-pollinating corn that remained Appalachia's staple.[45] The result was more intense corn cultivation in the Midwest. In the United States overall, 1939's corn acreage was down 11 percent from 1929's corn acreage, but harvested production was up 7.8 percent.[46] Large-scale producers of corn—as of cotton and wheat—defeated the intent of the allotment program by raising their productivity per acre.

But was this option theirs exclusively? Could not Appalachian farmers keep pace by increasing their own productivity? Did not every farmer in the United States have an equal right to use inputs that would raise production per acre? The answer to this, unfortunately, is that external constraints on production per acre were more pronounced in Appalachia than in, say, the Midwest. Capital not being available to subsistence farmers, they could not make their methods capital intensive. In 1929, for instance, wholesale fertilizer sales as a proportion of all wholesale business was already four times lower in West Virginia than in the United States as a whole.[47]

Appalachia's relative lack of chemical applications doubtlessly had its good side in terms of health, but not all progress was similarly double-edged. One input of unqualified benignity was lime. By lowering the acidity of soil, lime enables farmers to establish the pH level most likely to aid their crops. Between 1932 and 1940 the total use of lime in American agriculture increased seven fold.[48] Appalachia's Valley subregion is rich in limestone, and numerous lime sources had been developed there prior to the New Deal. In Pendleton County—part of West Virginia's Blue Ridge area—a progressive farm movement during the World War I era had established six lime grinders where previously none had existed.[49] But in Appalachia's Plateau subregion, lime was often difficult for farmers to acquire. As late as 1938 an "acute lime problem" afflicted most of West Virginia, with no solution in sight.[50] A similar shortage of agricultural lime existed in much of eastern Kentucky.[51]

For some purposes, such as to neutralize soil acidity in pastures, lime could be replaced by agricultural phosphate (also known as superphosphate). And toward the end of the 1930s the government did achieve considerable success in distributing phosphate at a subsidized cost.[52]

Following the transition period in 1935–1936, indeed, the government's agriculture program began to benefit Appalachia in various ways. Regional considerations began to enter the New Deal's agriculture program after 1935, along with a farm-by-farm approach. As the emphasis shifted away from rescuing commodity markets, increased attention was paid to saving the land. In Appalachia, the farm programs of this "second New Deal" helped to inhibit, and occasionally to reverse, the region's twin curses of soil depletion and soil erosion. Much of the attack on these two problems was driven by the same sort of financial incentives (money payments to farmers) as drove the AAA allotment program. Improved methods of land use were in-

creasingly rewarded under the Soil Conservation Service inaugurated
in 1937.

The federal government's ecological initiatives after 1935 were im-
pressive. This environmental vision of the second New Deal was often
unaccompanied, however, by any comparable social vision. Lewis C.
Gray, who coordinated the U.S. Agriculture Department's elaborate
1929–1935 study of Appalachia, described himself as "a hard-boiled
economist" who was not sociological in his outlook.[53] Gray's foremost
recommendation for solving Appalachia's economic and social problems
was the "conversion of the land to public ownership and its utilization
for public forests, parks, or game preserves."[54]

Much land *was* converted to public ownership in the 1930s. Through
such land buying as well as through the Agriculture Department's late
1930s emphasis on better land use, environmental destruction was
slowed in Appalachia—but in the process the region's economic dependency was increased, helping to set the stage for the 1940–1960
mass population exodus from the region. This exodus in turn exacer-
bated urban problems in the cities where migration deposited Appalachia's emigrants.

Some of this bleak social result was avoidable. As early as 1916 the
principles of a prosperous and sustainable Appalachian agriculture had
been enunciated by the well-known economic geographer J. Russell
Smith. Smith had challenged American agronomists to "develop and
teach a mountain agriculture that will make the mountaineer prosperous and leave him his mountain."[55] Smith's main point was that Appalachia needed tree plantings that would increase the region's
production of fruits, nuts, and seeds—especially for animal fodder.
Without neglecting orchard fruit trees, Smith emphasized certain forest
trees with great potential as food sources. For tree-grown fodder, Smith
suggested "the mulberry, the persimmon, the honey locust, the acorn,
and the chestnut, [which] are primarily forage crops, chiefly pig feed,
but also good for poultry, sheep, goats, and cows." (The American
chestnut, of course, subsequently succumbed to a blight that has yet to
be defeated, but the Chinese and Japanese chestnut remain available.)
For supplemental human consumption Smith recommended walnuts
and pecans, adding that "the pig also dearly loves both of these, but
they are too good for him." Because Appalachia's people were accustomed to eating pork, and because excess hogs could be marketed,

Smith emphasized forest trees that produced good hog fodder—including, besides the trees mentioned, pawpaws.[56]

Smith's ideas for forest-grown animal fodder were important because they offered the best basis—perhaps the only basis—not merely for reversing Appalachia's soil erosion and depletion but also for sustaining the region's subsistence reproduction of labor power and, with it, the region's competitive standing in U.S. commodity markets. Smith pointed out that mulberry trees drop their ripe fruit continuously for ten summer weeks and are "considered by many Carolina farmers to be as valuable as corn, acre for acre. The persimmon," he added, "is equally valuable in the autumn."[57] Farm Extension agents ignored, however, Smith's case for providing animal fodder through such "tree crops" planted on hillsides that corn and other row crops were eroding.

Then in 1933–1934 the first chairman of the Tennessee Valley Authority (TVA), Arthur E. Morgan, began promoting tree crops within the context of a reforestation-and-wood-industry program in the Tennessee Valley. By October 1934 Morgan was able to report that "studies are being made for small cooperative industries based on special uses for particular woods. A forest policy is evolving. Abandoned lands are being acquired, several million trees are being raised for reforesting, and a training program for practical foresters is being prepared." Regarding forest tree crops, Morgan announced that "the raising of tree crops to supply food for hogs, and tree products for sale, is being promoted, and large research and breeding nurseries are already planted. Hickories, pecans, walnuts, Japanese and Chinese chestnuts, Japanese and Chinese persimmons, mulberries, paw-paws and other tree crops are being developed for land too hilly for plow crops."[58] Thus J. Russell Smith's tree crops were temporarily promoted—and planted in nurseries—by one New Deal agency, the TVA.

Of the TVA's three directors, Arthur Morgan served not only as chairman but as the director in charge of the TVA's forestry programs. What he was advocating in this case, however, was the use of forests to produce animal fodder—and soon his encroachment on "agriculture" was rejected. Later, Arthur Morgan wrote that what he sought through tree crops was one means of reversing the Tennessee Valley's history of being "confined to subordinate functions in great industries." He added that the tree-crop "program was stopped by the other two members of the [TVA] board voting as a majority, and the men who were working in the program were summarily discharged. Much of the land was then made available, at fifty cents to two dollars an acre, to lumber companies and others, who then stripped it of its forests."[59]

So the TVA's experiment with tree-produced animal fodder was aborted. A less-ambitious reform sponsored by the TVA director in charge of agriculture, Harcourt A. Morgan, proved more acceptable, at least temporarily. Utilizing the TVA's immense capacity to produce fertilizer, Harcourt Morgan determined that the TVA's fertilizer should be plentiful, cheap, and should not consist of the *nitrate* needed by row crops but rather of the *phosphate* that grasses and legumes needed.[60] This new "phosphate gospel" was both preached and administered by Harcourt Morgan, and it pushed Tennessee Valley farming away, temporarily, from soil-abusing row crops such as corn and cotton and pushed it toward livestock raising. Then during the later New Deal this phosphate gospel was expounded throughout the Appalachians by the Agriculture Department and by state extension services. The TVA itself, however, began abandoning Harcourt Morgan's phosphate gospel ten years later, in the late 1940s, returning a great deal of Tennessee Valley acreage to row crops (and especially to corn) by ceasing to provide farmers with cheap phosphates and instead giving them cheap nitrates.[61] Appalachia, by contrast, has not abandoned the phosphate gospel with its concommitants of hay, pasture, and livestock.

Thus the later New Deal years set Appalachia on a long-term course that has taken a great deal of land out of corn and other high-erosion crops, putting it into hay and pasture. Hay has displaced corn as the region's dominant harvested crop. Corn is a far more intensive crop, of course, but even when compared acre by acre, corn had dominated Appalachia's harvested acreage on the eve of the 1930s. Aside from feeding farm families and their livestock, much of this corn had been raised by wage workers to increase their family living standards, and during the Prohibition years of 1920–1933 a good many mountaineers had increased their corn acreage to participate in the moonshining boom.[62] As of 1929 in the region's 190 counties, 125 counties were harvesting more farm acreage of corn than of any other crop. Hay had followed corn in 1929 by leading harvested farm acreage in forty-six counties—but only in West Virginia had hay-led Appalachian counties outnumbered corn-led Appalachian counties. The farther south one went in Appalachia, the more hay was dominated by corn, until in Georgia and Alabama it became cotton, not hay, that contended with corn for acreage dominance. In four of Alabama's five Appalachian counties, as of 1929, cotton acres outnumbered corn acres, and the same was true in five of Georgia's twenty Appalachian counties. The only other exception to Appalachia's corn-hay syndrome occurred in the eight Virginia counties that made up the Shenandoah Valley and its environs. In seven of those counties, wheat acreage led the acreage of all other crops, and in the eighth county, fruit acreage led.[63]

By the second half of the century, that 1929 picture had changed a great deal. In 1959, only fifty Appalachian counties still harvested more acres of corn than of hay,[64] and by 1982 only eight still did so.[65]

In a topography as hilly as Appalachia's, the decline of corn acreage and rise of hay adds up to considerable environmental progress. It cannot be labeled a complete solution as hillsides growing grasses and legumes do not completely cease to erode. They merely erode less than they would if planted in row crops. Probably only the production of animal fodder through forest tree crops can place Appalachia's agriculture, and with it the region's traditional lifeways, on a permanently sustainable basis.

7

The Welfare of Rural Appalachia

> We must raise our guard against placing a penalty upon industry or a
> premium upon indolence. . . . We must not permit our people to be-
> lieve that the government will do for them what they should do for
> themselves.
>
> —H. G. Kump, governor of West Virginia, 14 January 1937

New Deal policy makers betrayed no misgivings about the usefulness of
pumping money into "backward" areas such as Appalachia. Harry
Hopkins and his assistants often bucked local political opposition to at-
tain their relief quotas. And Franklin Roosevelt, from 1934 on, frequently blamed the South's low living standards on its dearth of
money—money with which southerners could buy goods and also could
pay taxes for better roads, schools, and social services. When New Deal
money injections into the rural South did *not* revive its economy, the
government's prescription nonetheless stayed the same. At a March
1939 press conference, Roosevelt reiterated that anything done "to im-
prove this economic problem No. 1 [the South] ultimately comes back
to a question of greater purchasing power on the part of the average
Southern family."[1]

There is nothing inherently wrong with government intervention.
In fact, since at least the 1920s, Appalachia has suffered from region-
wide economic liabilities that cry out for planned solutions. Early in
1929, before the stock market crash, Appalachia was singled out for
study by the U.S. Agriculture Department's Bureau of Agricultural
Economics. Cooperation in that first major social and economic survey
of the region came from the extension services of Virginia, West Virginia, Kentucky, and Tennessee—four of the five main Appalachian
states.[2] As the Depression worsened, the study continued, and by early
1933 a draft of its recommendations was circulating among policy
makers. Most of those recommendations were eventually tried before
the New Deal was over. But at first, in the formative flurry of 1933,
regional distinctions were buried beneath the national drive to somehow revive markets for America's major commodities, agricultural and

industrial alike. The first New Deal approached the economy commodity by commodity, not region by region.

Thus, despite the federal government's longstanding regional approach to some fields (such as electric power), and even despite its new multipurpose Tennessee Valley Authority overlapping the southwestern flank of Appalachia, it proved slow to adopt the Bureau of Agricultural Economics' regional approach to Appalachia. That bureau itself did inaugurate an Appalachian Regional Office in 1934, but its headquarters were in Washington, D.C., and it attempted little before 1939. Meanwhile the New Deal's agricultural adjustment program began to veer toward regional thinking in its second incarnation (beginning early in 1935),[3] but in this new scheme the bulk of Appalachia was divided between two of the country's twelve AAA farming classifications: "general farming" and "self-sufficing."[4] (Not until 1965, when the Appalachian Regional Commission was established, did the federal government design explicitly Appalachian policies. That commission's diagnosis and policies lie beyond the scope of this book.)[5]

As applied to Appalachia, the New Deal fell into three broad categories: industrial, agricultural, and relief (now called welfare).

In the industrial category, the National Recovery Administration of the 1933–1935 "first New Deal" sponsored wage and price minimums that damaged the ability of Appalachian coal to compete with northern and midwestern coal[6]—and this at a time when the Depression was curtailing opportunities for people to migrate out of Appalachia. Although the Supreme Court invalidated the NRA in May 1935, that merely abolished coal's price supports until the First Guffey Act was passed three months later, in August 1935. And *wage* minimums were effectively reenacted even sooner, in July 1935, by the Wagner Act— inspiring Appalachian coal operators to hasten their replacement of miners with machines. This mainly involved installing automatic coal-loading machines, which, as has subsequently been revealed, increased the incidence of black lung disease among Appalachian miners.[7]

Turning then to the New Deal's agricultural program and its effect on Appalachia, we found the AAA working to the disadvantage of many Appalachian farmers by inspiring unprecedented advances elsewhere in crop productivity per acre. Tobacco and corn-hogs were the two AAA programs most directly relevant to Appalachian farmers, and both of those programs worked against many of the region's small farmers. In the later 1930s, on the other hand, the New Deal's growing emphasis on financial incentives for land-use improvements helped to slow the rate of Appalachia's soil depletion and erosion.

Like the New Deal's industrial and agricultural programs, its relief programs did not completely achieve what any of their varied constituencies hoped for. Social visions abounded in the 1930s. One visionary who made the most of her position was Eleanor Roosevelt. Eleanor Roosevelt's visit to depressed West Virginia mining communities in August 1933 triggered a chain of projects that continued as long as the New Deal itself. Traveling incognito for several days in West Virginia, Eleanor Roosevelt came to believe that the government should expand various community development projects that had been started in the mountains by the American Friends [Quaker] Service Committee working in league with state extension services. This led directly to the founding of five government-sponsored communities for "stranded" unemployed coal miners: Westmoreland in Pennsylvania; Arthurdale, Red House, and Tygart Valley in West Virginia; and Cumberland in Tennessee. These five communities soon weighed like five albatrosses around the federal neck—becoming among the most controversial of the ninety-nine new communities eventually sponsored by the government's subsistence homestead program.[8] The head of West Virginia's extension service later wrote that "instead of [Eleanor Roosevelt's] visit leading to needed additional Federal aid to carry out the program already underway with the guidance of Extension and Friends, the Federal Government took all responsibility away from the local agencies and people"—substituting "government help from the top down [which] eventually ended as a dismal failure."[9]

Arthur E. Morgan, who chaired the Tennessee Valley Authority (TVA) from 1933 to 1938, saw the difficulties faced by intentional communities. When Morgan returned to private life he lauded the strengths of organic, non-intentional communities that were based on family ties and lifelong connections.[10] As for economic issues, Morgan deemphasized national objectives in favor of instead achieving "a large degree of local and regional self-sufficiency." Morgan believed that "with highly developed regional self-sufficiency, a great part of our economic maladjustment could be solved. For planning the most satisfactory degree of self-sufficiency, a minimum region may be no larger than a local neighborhood or a township. A village and a surrounding area of ten or twenty square miles may be regionally self-sufficient in many respects. This area in turn might be part of a larger region of perhaps four or five hundred square miles, with many more elements of self-sufficiency."[11] Arthur Morgan was not a localist or regionalist in any cultural sense. He evinced no affection for local color or provincial traits. Perhaps because of his background as an educator, however, he saw pitfalls in the path of people who were shifting from a low-money life-style to the broader horizons and greater individualism that are possible in money-supported lives.[12] This was not a concern shared by the TVA's two other directors. One of them, David Lilienthal, a brusque young lawyer, opposed any goal for the TVA less definable than the production and distribution of kilowatt-hours. ("I don't have much faith in 'uplift,' " was one of Lilienthal's sayings.)[13] But the educator Arthur Morgan saw self-discipline as part of any worthwhile grassroots monetization. "In rural America," Morgan said, "there are millions of people living in families where even in prosperous times the total cash income is less than one hundred dollars a year. . . . For children in such families economic opportunity is primary and vocational training is the first essential, but unless it is accompanied by the cultural growth of discrimination and self-discipline, the waste of personality which will accompany the increase of income, may be very great."[14]

Arthur Morgan not only pondered human development in tandem with economic development but he thought about the future of Appalachia. To minimize the mountain region's dependence on the larger U.S. economy, Morgan suggested the creation of local self-help cooperatives that could produce for local consumption and could distribute what they produced. With respect to agriculture, Morgan considered it counterproductive for Appalachia to attempt much exporting of staple products to regions that were turning out the same things with higher productivity. Agriculture, said Morgan, was not the ideal way for Appalachia's people to fulfill their cash needs. Rather, he said, "agricultural products ought to be something to live on at home, so that we will not have to buy things from the outside. Agriculture ought to be like the home garden that sustains people, but is not primarily the source of income. . . . Agriculture in the southern mountains . . . ought to support this region in food but not to supply its money except from special crops. . . . If we use our agriculture to feed our own region and then begin to manufacture the things we need at home, we shall have [an] answer to the problem of balancing agriculture and industry."[15] This approach parallels the path that Taiwan has followed to economic success since World War II.

The speech containing Arthur Morgan's regional prescription became the most controversial of his career, for it also contained a suggestion that "local money" could usefully be issued to supplement U.S. money. Morgan suggested that "to a certain limited degree this region might well set up its own local economy. It can produce its own goods and deal with itself. But if a region is going to build up a new economy by making things it needs at home, it will in a limited sense have to build up a whole economy and not a fragment of an economy. . . . I would have a central purchasing organization, a central sales organization, a distributing organization, and I think I'd have that cooperative organization have its own tokens of credit,—a sort of local money."[16]

This idea was controversial at the time and it will be controversial again if it receives another hearing. Arthur Morgan was in effect prescribing the sort of financial prerogatives that Appalachia had enjoyed before the Civil War. Arthur Morgan delivered his speech in Knoxville in November 1933, at a time when Knoxville's city government was issuing one of America's most successful local currencies. In mid-June 1932, Knoxville had begun paying its city employees with "tax warrants," which were claims on the city's future tax income. The tax warrants paid 6 percent interest. Almost all Knoxville merchants accepted them. They could not be deposited in banks, and thus they circulated faster than U.S. dollars, stimulating Knoxville's economy. The tax warrants helped rescue the city government finances, for after six months of paying city employees with them the city began receiving them into its coffers as tax revenues faster than it was paying them out as salaries.[17]

Once the New Deal got under way, most industrial wages in Appalachia began rising rapidly, which was a boon for the workers involved. Unfortunately, however, these wage increases were subsidized not so much by industrial recovery as by price increases. Appalachia's main employer was the coal industry—an industry whose previous response to hard times had been to pay lower wages and to sell coal cheaper. In 1933 this kind of response was suddenly penalized by the NRA-sponsored "codes of fair competition," which set minimum prices and minimum wages. The NRA damaged Appalachia's competitive position in coal markets, and that damage in turn helped to inspire the New Deal's homestead projects. A picture emerges of government intervention trying to offset the effects of previous government intervention. An in-house study reported that "when some of the codes of the National Industrial Recovery Act began to have the effect of closing down, or threatening to close down, still more mines, in the late summer of 1933, thus to leave still more stranded miner communities, the suggestion was made in some quarters that one section of N.I.R.A. should be used to undo the incidental damage wrought by another. Whether or not this was the deciding force, it was decided to establish four subsistence-homestead projects for stranded miners."[18] Actually, counting the Red House project in West Virginia, which was run by Harry Hopkins's relief agency rather than by the Division of Subsistence Homesteads, five projects were started for stranded miners.[19]

One means for extending aid in a *non*community setting was the New Deal program of rural rehabilitation loans. This program made federal advice available without subordinating farmers to federal supervision. Research conducted by Benita J. Howell shows in detail why rural rehabilitation loans proved more successful among a number of mountaineers than planned communities proved.[20]

As the New Deal continued, on-site federal officials divided among themselves as to what policy could best deal with isolated mountain people and with the headwater land those people often abused. In West Virginia, some federal personnel felt that fully one-fifth of the state was so rugged and inaccessible that the government should buy it up and prohibit farming there. These officials cited not only excessive erosion in such areas but also the high cost of providing social services there. Other officials counterargued that people who lived in remote locations "seem reasonably well content at present," and that therefore "the best solution lies in rehabilitation of these families in their present locations."[21]

A survey made of the southern nubbin of West Virginia's Lewis County in February 1941 offers a closer look at one of those remote locations. The survey found 326 people living there in 63 households. Demographically, however, these were not normal American households, or even normal West Virginia households. Their age distribution was extremely skewed toward youth. In the United States as a whole at that time only 34 percent of the population was aged 19 or under—and in West Virginia as a whole only 42 percent of the population. But in that remote southern tip of Lewis County a full 52 percent of the population was aged 19 or under. Indeed, 44 percent was aged 14 or younger. The area was making an unrecognized contribution to Appalachia's economy by performing subsistence reproduction of labor power. In the words of the survey, "The principal export product of this area appears to be children." Almost two-thirds of the households had received relief in 1940. One-third of them had no other cash income, and this one-third averaged half again more cash income than the other households. [22]

In chapter 4 we saw that an age spectrum skewed toward youth was chronic in Appalachia. And in fact, during the industrialization period of 1880 to 1930, West Virginia's population pattern grew increasingly skewed toward youth. [23] But the point to note here is that *before* any significant relief money appeared, West Virginia's southern Lewis County farm households, and tens of thousands like them throughout Appalachia, must somehow have managed to subsist *despite* their handicap of an age spectrum weighed heavily toward children. Before the New Deal, the southern Lewis County households had received little if any relief money. Now one-third of them depended on relief for their entire money income. How then had those families managed to support themselves prior to the New Deal? How many of their breadwinners had "worked out"—living and working away from home—and how much had other members of the families damaged their home farms in the process of farming them?

Only partially does the southern Lewis County survey help us puzzle out such questions. The district contained, it says, "relatively few young adults and older adolescents, aged 15 to 30 years." This age group had evidently "tended to migrate from the area when the opportunity came." [24] As of February 1941 not many of these absent youth were "working out" at wage jobs. Apparently their opportunity to leave the area had instead come when the federal government took over responsibility for supporting their elders and their younger siblings, freeing these young adults and older adolescents to try bettering their own condition elsewhere. Before the Depression, working out had been common among mountaineers. But as of early 1941, the Depression was not yet quite over and the survey found that only half as many sons as daughters were then making their homes outside the district. Four-fifths of the absent daughters were absent because they had married elsewhere. By and large, they had thereby acquired greater affluence.[25] Left behind were disproportionate numbers of children and older adults. The survey concluded on a note of concern about the children: "Inasmuch as the principal export product of this area appears to be children, it is of utmost importance that their health and education should be one of the principal aims of any adjustment program."[26] The surveyors betrayed no hint, however, that people were already adjusting their lives to the government's relief payments.

In 1932, relief payments in West Virginia had barely exceeded $2 million. Then, from the beginning of 1933 through the middle of 1940, relief payments in West Virginia (including paychecks issued by the Civilian Works Administration in 1933–1934 and WPA paychecks issued from 1935 on), combined with paychecks dispersed to West Virginians by the Public Works Administration, the Civilian Conservation Corps, and the National Youth Administration, totalled about $320 million.[27] If evenly dispersed, that would have given $23 every year to every West Virginian regardless of age, more than $100 a year to every West Virginia household. In 1993 dollars it would have been more than $800 a year for every household.

As of 1939, the WPA called 23 percent of its West Virginia employees "displaced from agriculture" (as compared with 47 percent "displaced from industry").[28] This tells us that West Virginia farm households received WPA jobs roughly in proportion to their percentage of the population.[29] Rural workers were limited to fifteen hours of WPA work weekly, however, whereas urbanites could work for the WPA up to twenty-four hours a week. That delivered greater than half again more WPA income to urbanites than to rural workers, but nonetheless many farmers on the WPA rolls were making more money income than they ever had.

An increased dependence on money income was not a consequence *intended* by this federal outlay. Nor, for that matter, were WPA or other relief payments ever explicitly designated for the purpose of decreasing agricultural pressure on mountain land. And although farmers' high relief payments helped to set the stage for later mass emigration from Appalachia—yet out-migration too was never explicitly intended to result from high relief payments.

In retrospect, despite our present-day realization that some of Appalachia's present problems derive from welfare, we must ask whether in fact there was any alternative to providing high relief payments to farm families—or any alternative to their later mass emigration from Appalachia's farms—if wholesale erosion and soil depletion were to be reversed. Neither at the micro level in such places as West Virginia's southern Lewis County, nor in a West Virginia land-use planning effort that began about 1940, do we find any suggested means to stop erosion except by terminating agriculture. West Virginia's land-use planning committee had no major alternative income to offer hill farmers unless they quit cultivating their fields and planted trees in them, thereby qualifying for a one-time payment of five to thirty-five dollars an acre from the Agricultural Adjustment Administration.[30]

And only certain trees qualified for this one-time payment. The plantings had to be of AAA-approved "forest trees," which in West Virginia consisted of four species of pine and two of spruce, plus yellow poplar, black locust, and black walnut.[31] None of these trees provided good animal fodder, with the single exception that hogs were willing to eat black walnuts, and thus the AAA's financial incentive to plant fields and pastures with AAA-approved trees offered no real hope for maintaining rural Appalachia's way of life. The mountains' native oaks, with their acorns, provided better hog fodder than walnuts—and oaks are easier to grow than walnut trees on cleared land—but the AAA did not subsidize oak plantings, perhaps because oak logs fetched less money at sawmills.

As a state almost entirely hilly, West Virginia did devise guidelines for the degrees of slope that were considered usable for cultivation and for pasture. Those guidelines, however, were prescriptions for disaster. As of 1939, the West Virginia extension service was advising farmers that slopes of up to twenty-five degrees were suitable for cultivation under certain conditions, and that slopes of up to thirty-five degrees were "suited generally for pastures."[32] This did perhaps prompt some progress during a decade when Civilian Conservation Corps workers were finding corn cultivated on slopes of up to eighty degrees.[33] But in the absence of terraces to inhibit water runoff, twenty-five degrees was far too steep for row crops, and thirty-five degrees far too steep for pasture. As recently as 1977, 1982, and 1987, West Virginia has led the nation in pasture erosion—its 1987 soil loss estimated at an average annual rate of 6.7 tons per acre of pasture.[34]

In a 1926 meeting, a Tennessee extension agronomist had announced that "mountain lands can never compete with good lands; but since the people will not move out of the mountains to better farming sections, the only thing to do is to help them use what they have to the best advantage."[35] Yet little help was forthcoming. Indeed, after the Cumberland Homesteads project was established in east-central Tennessee's Cumberland Plateau area, the Tennessee extension service had "to make an investigation to ascertain crop possibilities in the area" before it could advise the homesteaders about even their cash-crop options.[36]

Later in the 1930s, however, there was more mountain-farm research. In 1937–1938, for instance, a TVA supervisor in southwestern Virginia made important long-term calculations of the amount of erosion prevented on average open hillside pastures through the application of ninety-six pounds of agricultural phosphate per acre. Fifteen months after applying the phosphate, the TVA supervisor found legumes covering 40 percent more surface of the phosphated pastures than of similar pastures left unphosphated. During those first fifteen months, the phosphated pastures lost four-sevenths less soil through erosion than the unphosphated pastures, and one-third less water ran off the phosphated pastures.[37]

From the perspective of any farm family that intended to continue farming, here surely was an improvement that was preferable to planting hillside pastures with AAA-approved forest trees. Improved pasture, besides lessening erosion, would enable a farm to raise more livestock. And already by 1936 (when the government was paying only $5 an acre to farmers for planting forest trees) the government financial incentive for phosphating pastures was at least $2.50 an acre.[38] But remember that even after phosphating, those open pastures would still lose about three-sevenths of the soil they had been losing without phosphate. Thus phosphating would slow the destruction of hillside pastures but would not prevent it. Was a choice thus required between phosphating pastures (thereby maintaining an area's population density, at least for awhile) or reforesting hillside pastures with the expectation that most people would soon have to leave such a reforested area? Those seemed the only choices offered by government policy.

And yet, as mentioned in chapter 6, the principles of a prosperous and sustainable Appalachian agriculture had long been publicized by J. Russell Smith, who in 1916, we noted, had challenged America's vast agricultural research establishment to "develop and teach a mountain agriculture that will make the mountaineer prosperous and leave him his mountain."[39] For hillside fields, Smith emphasized terracing— something that New Deal officials were unaccountably slow to recommend to mountain farmers and were loathe to support with financial incentives.[40] After terracing hillside fields, Smith recommended the evenly spaced planting of mulberry, persimmon, honey locust, oak, chestnut, and pawpaw trees—all of which provide excellent animal fodder, especially for hogs.[41] Smith's ideas may well have represented— and may still today represent—the only sustainable way to practice agriculture on the hillsides of the Appalachian Plateau.

Conclusion

If the roots of the changed economy of the 1980s lie before 1960, we must find those roots and explore them. . . . The perspective of our history from the inflationary stagnation of the late 1970s and early 1980s is different than it was when an earlier generation of economic historians chronicled our victorious march through the troubles of the 1930s to the apex of American world prestige at the end of Eisenhower's presidency.

—Jonathan Hughes, *American Economic History*

The stagnation of which Jonathan Hughes speaks is still with us in the 1990s, and I venture to say it has grown systemic to American capitalism. This rethinking of Appalachia's odyssey began with Frederick Jackson Turner's comment that early American settlers poured "their plastic pioneer life into geographic moulds."[1] As we have seen, they were also pouring their lives into the molds that we call economic systems. Even in a single region, no one mold—no one economic system—molded the behavior of everyone. Many of Appalachia's people poured their efforts into subsistence-barter-and-borrow systems, many others into the capitalist system, and many into both.

Concurrently—and within either system—auspicious material conditions called forth enterprise but inauspicious conditions evoked an obsession with obtaining subsistence. In the pioneering, frontier period of Appalachia's history, self-sufficiency came easily to most people. Under those easy conditions the average farm family could be entrepreneurial without jeopardizing its subsistence. Indications abound that Appalachia as a region was self-sufficient in food prior to 1860. Many pioneers invested in guns or animal traps not merely to provide for their families but also to trade animal pelts for nonnecessities. All the evidence indicates that prior to 1860, Appalachia exported large amounts of commodities proportional to its population—its food exports generally occurring as livestock "on the hoof." But Appalachia's exports used exchanges that were at least partly financed by credit provided from outside the region—and this proved, under later conditions, to be a seed of economic dependency. Within the region as well, money was being created by state-chartered banks—and this suggests that a less-dependent odyssey of capitalist development might have been possible than what eventually occurred. Meanwhile, most of the region's economic exchanges involved no transfer of money at all. The region prior to 1860 was clearly not economically dependent.

As we turned to the agricultural production levels achieved in Appalachia during the forty years preceding the beginnings of its major industrialization (that is, between 1840 and 1880), we found, in absolute figures, that most forms of agriculture registered increased production during those years. But when the amount of agricultural production *per capita* was calculated, a rapid decline could be seen. This decline of food production per person was particularly precipitous in the region's Plateau area west of the mountains proper. The Plateau subregion experienced a population boom during those years—from 130,018 people in 1840 to 501,655 people in 1880, a growth of 286 percent.[2]

During those forty years before the Plateau's major industrialization began, the number of hogs per person fell by more than half. The number of cattle and work animals per person fell by almost half. Grain production per person fell by one-third. At the same time, potato production per person increased slightly and so apparently did dairy production—both indicating a shift toward less desired foods that required more work to produce.[3] This is understandable, because the Plateau's average farm size decreased by more than half in just thirty years (1850 to 1880).[4]

The farmers who raised surplus livestock, and the intrepid drovers who canvassed the various districts to gather herds and drive them to market, were almost all independent operators, almost all self-employed.[5] After the depredations of the Civil War, however, and after the subsistence demands of a postbellum population boom, there no longer existed so much surplus livestock to export on the hoof from Appalachia. Other forms of enterprise then began expanding. It is in this period that Altina Waller's book *Feud* shows us Devil Anse Hatfield as an extremely entrepreneurial timber operator along the Tug Fork River. Devil Anse lacked any significant money to invest. He operated on credit, promising future payments or future timber deliveries, in exchange for immediate merchandise for his family and work crew.

Devil Anse Hatfield's low-money timber business dissolved when he lost his timber lands in 1888. This was symptomatic of a Gilded Age trend throughout Appalachia, particularly in Plateau Appalachia. The finding of an expert on the Flat Top-Pocahontas coal field (which straddles the West Virginia-Virginia boundary) bears repeating: outsiders were not the first people to try to exploit that coal field. "Locals tried like hell to exploit the coal," he says, "but lacked the necessary means to mount a large-scale operation. The locals [then] acted as middlemen, arranging sales of land and right-of-way to Philadelphia entrepreneurs who financed the thing."[6]

The type of small, low-money, high labor-investment enterprise that had often succeeded before the Civil War was much less likely to succeed after the Civil War. Why?

The primary reasons were probably technological. Decentralized, low-capital forms of enterprise faced increased competition throughout the United States after the Civil War from newly available technologies. Concentrated, capital-intensive means of production offered economies of scale that investors of capital found attractive. But the increasing deployment of such means of production is not all that is important. We have also asked *who* controlled their deployment and why they controlled it. We have asked why Appalachia's own entrepreneurs often found themselves confined to relatively low-capital, old-fashioned production methods while outside investors often were financing the deployment of up-to-date technologies under their very noses.

Prior to the Civil War, "easy money" periods had predominated in the United States, whereas "tight money" periods had usually lasted only a few years in the wake of each financial panic. The panics occurred about every twenty years, generally precipitated by eastern bankers' demands that western and southern bankers redeem their banknotes in specie (metallic money). The western and southern practice of requiring only low specie reserves behind local banknotes made possible rapid economic development in "new" areas, where the bulk of assets consisted not of financial holdings but of potential, of natural resources (e.g., land, timber, and mineral holdings).

Then in 1863, as a war-finance measure, Congress passed a national banking act that offered bankers the option of replacing their state charters with federally issued charters. Under a federal charter they could still issue banknotes (as they had done as state banks), but now they would have to back their banknotes 111 percent with U.S. bonds. The intent of Congress was to sell more U.S. bonds to raise money for the war, but the actual effect was to make federal charters unattractive to bankers. Congress heightened bankers' aversion by failing to sanction the use of land, timber, minerals, or other real estate as collateral that national banks could accept to guarantee loans. In March 1865, however, Congress (by a single vote) passed an act imposing a 10 percent fee on any bank of any sort that passed a banknote of any nonnational bank—in effect thereby outlawing state-bank banknotes—and suddenly bankers stampeded to acquire federal charters. Prior to 1862, which was when government "greenbacks" had begun appearing, all banknotes had been issued by state-chartered banks. Now suddenly none were.

This is not to say that easy money disappeared. Only cash became relatively scarce after 1865 (that is, only specie and banknotes). Easy-money practices continued in the realm of checking-deposit money. In 1865 deposit holdings exceeded cash in the United States by a ratio of only one and a half to one. By 1914 deposits would exceed cash by almost nine to one.[7]

Thus the money growth that accompanied America's rapid postbellum industrialization was a ballooning growth of deposit money accompanied by stagnation in the amount of cash that was circulating. This was something new. Prior to the Civil War, cash had expanded faster than deposit money. From 1834 to 1860, cash in circulation (specie and banknotes together) had grown 251 percent, whereas bank deposits had grown only 204 percent.[8]

The most important long-term effect of the 1865 law terminating state-bank banknotes was the financial advantage that it conferred on the region that held the most financial reserves as of then. This was not a "natural" advantage. Indeed, the Northeast had itself acquired its substantial financial assets largely by issuing banknotes against other forms of assets—slaves, land, timber, fish, rum, etc.[9] In effect, the 1865 law denied to other regions the right to follow the Northeast's path to acquiring large financial reserves.

Meanwhile, by the 1880s, out-migration was ceasing to offer Appalachian farm families hope of retaining their life-style if they relocated elsewhere. The Ozarks had absorbed a stream of Appalachia's young people from the 1830s onward,[10] but by 1880 the average farm size in the Ozarks was down to 121 acres, almost 50 acres below Appalachia's average farm size.[11]

Agricultural production per capita continued its decline in Appalachia, and one consequence of this decline was that employers could obtain low-wage labor from at least some of the Plateau's farm families. Even a low wage enabled hard-pressed farm families to live better, initially, than they would have lived without any wage income at all. The evidence suggests that most of the Appalachian farm families who turned to wage labor did so because, solely as farmers, they were becoming poorer. Most of those who did begin wage labor also continued to farm part time, or to alternate between farming and wage work. Their turn toward wage work does not mean that they were completely impoverished, but it suggests that they saw their living standard declining. The wages offered by coal operators generally stayed relatively low in Appalachia, but those wages could be attractive because when combined with continued farming they tended at the time to increase living standards at least slightly.

As major industrialization thus got under way, many of the region's farmer-miners continued calculating within a different economic system than did their employers. In Antonio Gramsci's terms, the farmer-miners and their employers participated in different *historical blocs*.[12] Appalachia's farmer-miners did not necessarily seek a different *goal* than the coal operators who employed them. Although most of the region's farmer-miners entered the mines primarily for subsistence goals, some of them surely did so to acquire more than their subsistence needs. The crucial difference was that most farmer-miners held values rooted in their subsistence-barter-and-borrow systems, whereas most coal operators held values rooted in the cash-credit-and-wage system (capitalism). These two different economic systems fostered different evaluations of any given behavior. Within Appalachia's subsistence-barter-and-borrow systems, the most advantageous investments were generally investments of labor and land—whereas in the capitalist system labor was subordinate to capital investment, which held the initiative and generally proved more advantageous.

Appalachia's industrialization initially served the short-term interests of both financial investors and miners, but eventually the economic interests of the financial investors were served far better than those of miners. To see why this occurred, I analyzed Appalachia's low-money economic systems. Some might call them systems of "household economy." Here I have put less emphasis on production than on exchange (on distribution) and have therefore called them subsistence-barter-and-borrow systems. Their means of production were mainly labor-intensive subsistence farming and their means of exchange were mainly barter and borrowing. These systems were driven primarily by voluntary reciprocity. Simultaneous two-way exchanges held lower priority than exchanges in a time-lapse pattern to suit mutual convenience.

These "traditional" economic systems did not cease to function when, more than one hundred years ago, Appalachia's major industrialization began. What occurred then was a meshing: capitalist relations meshed with Appalachia's "traditional" economic relations. The burgeoning capitalist relations were characterized by contracts (such as labor in exchange for cash wages, or for "in kind" wages, or for company-scrip wages) and by cash or scrip purchases of store goods. Meanwhile, the continuing, and indeed thriving, "traditional" relations remained based on networks of voluntary reciprocity, including labor exchange.

But why, if the subsistence-barter-and-borrow economy *thrived* during Appalachia's industrialization era, did so many of Appalachia's people eventually find themselves in need of federal relief when the industrial economy faltered?

The answer is that, by continuing alongside outside-controlled industrialization, the continuing networks of mutual aid served to reduce wage demands and thus to transfer Appalachia's wealth (in the form of labor's products) outside the region. The long-term effect of continued low-money networking among industrial workers was that the workers subsidized U.S. industry at their own eventual expense.

Looking back over the full train of thought that leads to this conclusion, each step in the logic of this present book has been prefigured by earlier economic paradigms. In the process of criticizing earlier ideas I am also making use of them. Walt Rostow's too-optimistic five-step paradigm of economic development, for instance, prefigures my own formulation of five steps that have led Appalachia into economic dependency. Rostow's five steps were (1) the traditional society, (2) the preconditions for take-off, (3) the take-off, (4) the drive to maturity, and (5) the age of mass consumption. Similarly I have found five steps in Appalachia's economic past, but they have led to dependent development.

First, there indeed used to be a "traditional society" functioning in Appalachia, but that society was not preoccupied with attaining merely its subsistence. Most of the region's earliest white settlers were intent on attaining both subsistence and profits.

Second, from 1840 to 1880 there then occurred "preconditions for take-off," but what Appalachia's preconditions actually prefigured was dependent, not independent, growth. For internal as well as exogenous reasons, Appalachia by 1880 was starting to grow dependent on outside sources for some of the food it consumed and for a great deal of money that helped to mediate its own internal economic exchanges.

Third, what followed between 1880 and 1930 (the region's industrialization era) can then accurately be called a "take-off," but what took off, again, was dependency. Appalachia's industrialization constituted a dependent economic development. Independent economic development in this low-capital region would have required greater agricultural or financial autonomy than Appalachia enjoyed. Sufficient autonomy in those two areas eluded the region for reasons both economic and political.

And then, following Rostow on to a fourth step, the New Deal helped drive Appalachia's dependency on to "maturity" by encouraging even many of the region's full-time farmers to increase their dependence on a money system based outside the region. The fact that completely sustainable mountain agriculture was not promoted by the New Deal, and that local autonomy was not encouraged, constituted two major missed opportunities.

With the New Deal's liquidation in 1942, the region moved on to a fifth stage, but rather than a stage of "mass consumption" this was a stage of mass emigration. Even this did not solve the region's problems, however—perhaps because people tended to emigrate during their most productive phase of life. During the 1960s, major federal transfer payments were reinitiated in the region and continue today.

The causes of the century-plus path toward dependency have included acts of commission as well as acts of omission. Not merely things that were not done, resources that were not available, helped to cause dependency, but also things that *were* done. To a considerable extent, therefore, my findings have paralleled Andre Gunder Frank's idea of "the development of underdevelopment" and have paralleled Richard Simon's earlier application of that paradigm to Appalachia (in a study as yet unpublished). [13] But I have modified Simon's analysis after finding that not merely industrial conditions fostered dependency but also agricultural and financial conditions. The present study nonetheless builds on the groundwork already laid by Simon and others.

Lest I leave the impression that I think everything was shifting sand in Appalachia's past—totally opposite the region's popular image— let me point out that three invariables have pushed Appalachia toward ever greater dependency and have demanded emphasis in this book. Appalachia's dependency (1) invariably increased with its growing per capita imports of manufactured products, (2) invariably increased with its growing per capita imports of agricultural products, and (3) invariably increased with the increased role of outside money in its economic relations.

Of these three causes of dependency, the first resulted more or less automatically from general U.S. industrialization, because Appalachia was not as well suited to urbanize (and thus to achieve high productivity in manufacturing) as was most of the United States. But to a significant degree the second cause, Appalachia's agricultural imports, occurred because the region failed to maintain its most favorable agricultural option, namely, multiple-use trees that could supply not only wood products but also tree-produced fodder for livestock. The destruction of forests, and the type of agriculture then practiced on the deforested land, helped cause the need for high agricultural imports, and by lowering the region's wage demands it also maximized coal-mining. In both of these ways deforestation and subsequent agricultural practices increased the region's dependency.

As for the third cause, the increased role of money that entered Appalachia from outside the region, here the crucial factor was the March 1865 congressional act that imposed the 10 percent tax on the passing by any bank of currency issued by a nonnational bank. Appalachia's liability of importing money rather than locally creating it heightened the region's first two liabilities. Under these circumstances, it was in the long-term interest of Appalachia's people to avoid dependence on outside money—on money wages and even on money passed out free by a well-intentioned government. To avoid such dependence was often not possible. But the presence of *money in a form capable of buying outside products* (I emphasize this because purely local forms of money are also possible) automatically drew the relatively cheaper outside products into Appalachia and lowered the value of all competing local products and thus of all competing local labor, paid or unpaid. In other words, as the relative cost of imports into Appalachia fell, and as their amount grew, the value of the local labor that competed with those mass-produced imports fell. Not only the value of Appalachia's competing wage labor fell but also the value of unpaid home labor that competed with imports.[14] What is unequal in "unequal exchange" is the amount of time and effort required to produce the same amount of economic value.

Despite this long-term disadvantage inherent in Appalachia's growing dependence on outside money, individuals often possessed little choice about contributing to it. During the region's industrialization, for instance, most wage earners enjoyed less choice about their degree of money dependency than most full-time farmers enjoyed. And when the Depression struck, unemployed wage earners enjoyed less choice than full-time farmers about whether or not to accept welfare payments.

Going back, then, to the question of why capitalism won its contest with Appalachia's traditional economic system, we now can see that the region's true traditional system, its true pre-1865 economic system, was hobbled by its own productivity lag and also by certain federal policies. The region's true traditional economy has more and more had to hobble along on only one of its two initial legs—namely, on its subsistence-barter-and-borrow leg. Appalachia's economy, virtually shorn of its internal market for its own products, became excessively dependent on its subsistence-barter-and-borrow systems. And the built-in labor intensivity of those systems hastened the day when too many rural mountaineers would compete for the use of too little land. Until that demographic squeeze came about, however, the benefits derived from children in rural Appalachia remained comparable to the benefits that children conferred during other historic population explosions, such as Java's and Northern Ireland's. Some of Appalachia's children made their economic contribution to the region's industries, but most children made their contribution in the subsistence agriculture that formed a necessary complement for Appalachia's low wages and thus for the competitive market position of its exports.

While conducting interviews with people born in the early twentieth century, I was told by a woman born in 1905 in West Virginia's Lincoln County that as an adolescent she used to ask her mother why their family was so large. (Eight of her parents' children lived to adulthood.) Her mother would answer, "So we'd have someone to help with the farmwork." The daughter continued, "I always said, 'Why? . . . Why so many children?' Cause, see, it put a burden on me. I was the second child in the family. And I helped raise all those children from about the fourth or fifth one down, down below me. . . . Not only babysitting. I was washing diapers, and feeding children, and cleaning up after them, and a little bit of everything. Took them with me when I went places." When I asked this woman whether she thought that people in the early twentieth century generally *could* do better on a farm by having more children, her answer was, "*I* never could see it."[15]

This woman's recollections reflect the constricted economic opportunities that had resulted from several generations of land subdivision, soil depletion, and soil erosion. But even by the 1920s Appalachia's large families had not necessarily outlived their usefulness. This woman's family farmed full time, but both full- and part-time farming helped to subsidize Appalachia's coal industry. As a result, when the U.S. demand for coal quit growing in the 1920s, thereby intensifying competition within the coal industry, Appalachia managed to compete very successfully and to acquire a much larger share of total U.S. coal production. Concomitantly and inseparably, however, the 1920s saw the worst ecological abuse yet inflicted on Appalachian farmland. By that time, fifty industrializing years had seen more and more mountain farm families becoming involved in wage labor. By the time the Depression began, many mountain farm families, perhaps most, were drawing on supplemental sources of income outside agriculture. The full-time farmer of one year might be only a part-time farmer the next year. A farmer could dig coal or cut timber during the winters—or when farming was not going well or cash was particularly needed—but his family could retain its land and thereby retain the option of farming when it chose, or when mines and lumber camps were shut down. In many cases workers in their prime years worked away from their home farms while spouses or grandparents stayed on the farms overseeing the farm work of children. A 1937 statistical study of West Virginia found that "between the ages of 25 and 55 the farm loses its relative strength in the total population, but beyond fifty-five, it exceeds in ratio either the urban or rural non-farm groups. This condition has existed in West Virginia for at least forty years due to a very large number of our young people leaving the farm, and perhaps also leaving the state, when they have reached maturity. Our farm families today are composed in a major part of young people and old people."[16]

During the Depression, when the industrial sector faltered in supplying the money component (or the company scrip component) in the income of part-time farmers, Appalachia's coal operators were able to cut wages to almost nothing because most mining families still raised much of their own food.[17] Thus Appalachia's coal operators could maintain a strong competitive position in what coal market still existed—until in 1933 the National Recovery Administration enforced nationwide wage-and-price supports. Both the wage and the price supports penalized labor-intensive operations in favor of those more capital intensive. The NRA's intervention thus increased the number of mountain miners and farmer-miners constrained to accept relief.

Admittedly, major relief payments were desperately needed before 1933 in Appalachia's more money-dependent areas, including its coal fields. Not merely the relief payments made to unemployed or underemployed full-time wage workers were needed but also the relief payments made to part-time wage workers. Economic intervention by the NRA increased the amount of relief needed by both of these groups, but the NRA did not cause the original problem.

When I looked at Appalachia's full-time subsistence farm families, however, I began to suspect that, on average, they did *not* need all the relief money they received. That relief, including work relief under the WPA, increased the money dependency of many full-time farm families, weaning them away from their intense networks of borrowing and barter. Thus it increased their dependency on the larger economy, over which they exercised no control.

That still was not the full story, however, for a look at Appalachia's pre-New Deal conditions of soil erosion and soil depletion made me ask if perhaps it was *necessary* to de-agronomize much of the region's farming population in order to save the land. This was concluded by the U.S. Agriculture Department after its elaborate 1929–1935 study of the *Economic and Social Problems and Conditions of the Southern Appalachians*. That study found the region's population had grown 55.8 percent from 1900 to 1930 and recommended that it be shrunk again, gradually, by much of that amount. The study found that Appalachia's actual farm population grew only 5 percent during those thirty years, but it pointed out that the region's "more isolated areas" produced "a more or less continual outward movement of people (mostly young folks) to cities" and to industrialized parts of the countryside (such as to coal fields).[18] The report failed to recognize, however, that such subsistence reproduction of labor power contributed to the region's and the nation's economic competitiveness.

The Agriculture Department's study made five major recommendations, and each of the five was to some extent attempted by the New Deal. As summarized by Appalachian scholar Ronald Eller, those recommendations were: "(1) conversion of land to public ownership; (2) establishment of small, rural, farm-forest communities; (3) development of local manufacturing; (4) combining employment in the mines with part-time work in small factories or on the farm; and (5) emigration."[19]

Any one of those recommendations could potentially involve the relocation of mountain farm families, and relocation was often a more compelling policy the more aims a given project tried to fulfill. Only subsequently did many federal officials begin to realize how traumatic relocation usually became for subsistence farm families—how little their way of life lent itself to mobility, either economic or psychological. Of course, only a small percentage of Appalachia's farm families were relocated directly by the New Deal. But relief payments often raised farm families' money income above what it had been prior to the Depression, and this tended to encourage their migration out of Appalachia a few years later, when relief payments ended at the same time World War II was creating jobs outside the region.

I have not tried to estimate how much relief Appalachia's full-time farmers actually needed during the Depression. Primarily it was the *form* in which relief came—money—that weakened the region's low-money economic systems of subsistence production and reciprocity. The results left many full-time farm families genuinely dependent on regular money income by the time nine years of government aid had ended. Many of these farm families then followed the trail of government money in the 1940s and took defense-related jobs outside Appalachia.

Admittedly, the American economy had exploited these people more on their mountain farms than it exploited them later when it had to pay them fully family-supporting wages. One of my points, indeed, is that both Appalachia's regional economy and America's national economy benefited more from these people when they were self-sufficient and supplied subsidized workers to industry than it has benefited from them since they have joined more fully in the money economy. So I grant that

previously they were more exploited and that now they are less exploited. But to be less exploited is not necessarily to be better off.[20]
How willingly did these people undergo the changes in their way of
life? How willingly did they abandon an economic system suffused with
voluntary reciprocity and enter a system virtually void of it, based instead on binding contracts? How glad were these people to leave their
farm homes and how glad later were they to have left? Simply because
they made the transition does not mean they made it willingly.[21] A
family's choices can be narrowed by choices that other families have
made. Once telephones enter most homes, for instance, the nontele-
phone grapevine tends to atrophy, and it becomes a hardship to live
without a phone. It is not merely a question of "keeping up with the
Joneses" by installing a phone. If the cost-free communication network
ceases to function, a phone can become a necessity.

Or consider horses. In West Virginia's Lincoln County the number of
farm horses and mules was finally outstripped in the late 1950s by the
number of farm motor vehicles.[22] Once that occurred, a spectrum of
horse-related supplies and jobs rapidly grew scarce. Horses and mules
were of course produced locally, but not motor vehicles. As local production for local use declined, it became an increasing hardship to lack
sufficient money to buy imported items. A reduced provision of regional
products to the region's own markets, in other words, and a higher proportion of necessities coming in from outside, increasingly hindered the
Appalachian people's acquisition of necessities through barter and borrowing. To hanker after store-bought goods is one thing, but to leave
home to get them is another matter. What drove most out-migrants to
leave home was not so much a hankering for store-bought goods as a
need for them. The disappearance of alternatives to store-bought goods
coerced many families to emigrate from rural Appalachia.

Later, in the 1960s and 1970s, many of Appalachia's émigrés began returning to the region as retirees, and some of them were then
able to "cash-in" on favors they had rendered in northern cities to
other émigrés from their home neighborhoods in the mountains. In
the 1960s, for instance, some returnees to West Virginia's Wayne
County could retire comfortably in their old neighborhoods by bringing home what John Lozier and Ronald Althouse call "a combination
of cash and a specialized coin whose exchange value is limited to the
local system."[23]

Nonmonetized economic relations have been crucial in many mountain people's lives but have often failed to interest economic analysts. Robert Heilbroner incorrectly supposed that subsistence farming had helped to cause the Depression. Subsistence farmers in the 1920s had numbered half the nation's farm population. Ignoring their immense economic contribution in the form of subsistence labor reproduction, Heilbroner complained that their low level of money expenditures constituted a drag on the economy.[24]

From our perspective in the 1990s, several problems are evident in thus equating a high GNP with economic health. People who raised their children largely outside the money economy—children who then went to work in wage jobs while raising their own children partly off the land—subsidized American industry by helping to keep its products competitive. When New Deal relief, including work relief, put money into the hands of such people, what resulted was not (as one might have wished) the mechanization of their farms and thus the attainment of higher productivity. Not enough money was provided to make that possible—except to the tiny minority of farm families allowed into the Rural Rehabilitation program. Furthermore, relatively few Appalachian farms were suited for mechanization. Relief money went to buy consumer goods rather than producer goods, and one economic result was to reduce Appalachia's subsistence reproduction of low-wage labor.

The New Deal's massive relief program was only one of the two main means by which an enlargement of purchasing power was attempted in the 1930s. The other major means was the New Deal's high-wage policy. The NIRA of 1933, the Wagner Act of 1935, the two Guffey acts of 1935 and 1937, and the Fair Labor Standards Act of 1938 contributed to raising wage levels in Appalachia and raising, with them, the prices of Appalachian-produced goods. In the nation as a whole, the New Deal's insistence on wage enhancement outdid its relief programs in distributing money. Even in Appalachia, despite its long relief rolls, wage hikes dispensed more money than relief payments dispensed.

Franklin Roosevelt's strategy of priming the economic pump by subsidizing consumers proved only temporarily more successful than Hoover's supply-side strategy of underwriting investment—for the New Deal's internal contradictions prevented a genuine recovery. Rexford Tuxwell writes that when Roosevelt took office "the enormous sum

(for those days) of $3.3 billion was presently requested for unemploy-
ment assistance when obviously the government had no such funds to
appropriate. . . . [Roosevelt] meant to raise the price level so that
[this] vast burden of debt could be liquidated."[25] The government
would borrow money for relief purposes, in other words, and then
would inflate prices so it could pay the money back in dollars worth less
than those it had borrowed.

There is thus no point in asking how
Roosevelt hoped to avoid the bleak result that Michael Weinstein's
econometric study of the NRA found, for Roosevelt did not *wish* to prevent price rises that would nullify the benefit of an increased money
supply. Tugwell reports that Roosevelt's intention in reflating the currency was precisely to raise prices. "The idea," Tugwell says, was "to
'reflate' by manipulating the price of gold in a [gold] market monop-
olized by the government. . . . Perhaps when prices had been restored
to their former levels the process [of reflation] could be stopped." The
only danger, according to Tugwell, was that inflation might *not* occur:
"The catch in the plan had seemed plain enough. It was that currency,
in fact, was no longer so closely related to gold that the value of dollars
would be greatly affected [i.e., lowered] by what happened to [the
gold] price." And as Tugwell feared (but should have hoped), buying
gold to increase the money supply did not in fact raise prices significantly. It took the NRA's industrial codes to do that. In any case, Tugwell tells us, "Roosevelt concluded that he could not ignore the demand
for raised prices."[26]

Not until the 1970s did the wage-and-price hikes of the New Deal
years begin coming home to roost. Indicators of the American people's
well-being continued rising until the early 1970s, but since then many
of those indicators have been pointing downward. This is basically because U.S. goods tend to cost more to make than goods produced elsewhere. More, for instance, than comparable goods made in East Asian
countries such as Japan and Taiwan. In 1986, when Taiwan's average
manufacturing employee was being paid the equivalent of $1.78 in
U.S. dollars, the wages of manufacturing employees in West Virginia
were averaging $10.38 an hour.[27]

In the 1930s, competitiveness abroad remained a moot issue because
the Depression had inspired most foreign countries to establish high
tariffs and strict import quotas, thereby reserving their home markets
for their own products.

As early as 1935, however, the director of the Brookings Institution saw trouble ahead. In weighing what he called "different methods of disseminating the benefits of progress," he pointed out that

attention must be called to their bearing upon international competition. Insofar as an increase in money wages is accompanied by increasing prices, the ability of American manufactures to meet competition in foreign markets is obviously impaired. . . . Consideration must also be given to the import side of the problem of international competition. High money wages in the United States are made the basis for demands for protection of American wage levels against cheap foreign-made goods. The American-made goods may be quite as *cheap* as the foreign in terms of the amount of human energy required to manufacture them; they are dear only in the price sense—the result of the higher level of money wages. . . . Distributing benefits of progress by means of progressively lower prices rather than by means of advancing wages [is] the broad highway along which continued economic progress must be sought. . . . When this road is followed the benefits of technical improvements are conferred automatically upon all divisions of the population.[28]

Another prescient forecaster predicted that unless New Deal policies were reversed, the continued viability of the U.S. economy would depend on making fundamental changes in the nature of both U.S. and international banking.[29] Such changes did occur through the Bretton Woods conference of 1944, which created the International Monetary Fund. The Bretton Woods system helped to postpone the need to lower U.S. prices until after Richard Nixon broke the dollar's final link to gold in August 1971. As one scholar says, "The Bretton Woods monetary system lent the United States an ability to finance its payments with its own liabilities."[30]

Meanwhile, from $7.2 billion in 1946 the investment of U.S. corporations in their foreign subsidiaries rose by 1975 to $133 billion.[31] U.S. corporations acquired large percentages of the productive assets of many IMF countries. (Not of Japan, however, for Japanese law prohibited virtually all foreign direct investment.)[32]

The new U.S. corporate owners of productive foreign assets often turned those resources toward producing goods for the U.S. market. American consumers then acquired the cheap "foreign" products flooding the market by running up huge balance-of-trade deficits. Meanwhile, revolutions broke out in many of the countries whose productive resources were being turned so heavily toward exports.

With the early 1970s, however, a turning point was reached within the United States. Foreign direct investment inside the United States from abroad rose from a mere $13.3 billion in 1970 to $183 billion by 1985.[33] Today's U.S. deficits, both public and private, are fed by (among other things) Americans' efforts to outbid foreign purchasers of productive assets in the United States. This has proven self-defeating.

The primary available alternative is to foster nonmonetized (or, more specifically, nondollarized) sectors in the U.S. economy, so that fewer dollars will suffice to carry on economic exchanges within the United States, leaving a higher proportion of dollars to be used for paying foreign debts. Every dollar issued by the Federal Reserve System creates a potential foreign claim against U.S. assets, and thus we now need ways to conduct more internal business without using so many dollars.

In the 1930s the New Deal helped to liquidate, in Appalachia, the very sort of money-of-account barter systems that we now stand in need of. The unpleasant alternative to such decentralized barter systems might be a centralized and regimented national barter system.

Only now, as we traverse the 1990s with our manufactures uncompetitive in many foreign markets and less and less retaining a remnant of our own domestic market—only now are the dragon's teeth sown by the New Deal ripe for harvest. They are not a harvest that we can plow under.

Notes

Introduction

1. U.S. Department of Commerce, Bureau of Economic Analysis, Regional Economic Information System data series. Released April 1992.

2. Besides Theotonio Dos Santos's definition of dependency quoted in the Preface, other concise summaries of the concept appear in Richard White, *The Roots of Dependency*, xv–xix; Bauzon and Abel, "Dependency," 43–69; and Matthews, *The Creation of Regional Dependency*, 38–76.

3. But for a rigorous definition of "internal colonialism," and for an argument that the term does *not* describe the condition of Appalachian whites, see Walls, "Central Appalachia in Advanced Capitalism," 69–83.

4. On the early compatibility of subsistence farming and commercial farming, see Noe, "Southwest Virginia," 25.

5. Robert D. Mitchell, *Commercialism and Frontier*, 37–39, 96–100.

6. Regarding such intra-Appalachian migration, Ronald Eller notes that after 1900 people "poured by the thousands out of the mountains of Tennessee and North Carolina into the nearby coal fields of Kentucky, Virginia, and West Virginia." Eller, *Miners, Millhands, and Mountaineers*, 126. In the subregions of the present study, this constituted a population shift from Older and Intermediate Appalachia to Newer Appalachia.

7. Within the overall boundary of Appalachia as defined by Ford, ed., *The Southern Appalachia Region*, my three subregions of Older, Intermediate, and Newer Appalachia will follow, as closely as possible at each census, the boundary lines of the state economic areas and the standard metropolitan areas as first used by the 1950 census. Older Appalachia contains ten state economic areas and two and a half standard metropolitan areas. Intermediate Appalachia contains four state economic areas and one and a half standard metropolitan areas. Newer Appalachia contains five state economic areas and two standard metropolitan areas. (The boundaries of all these areas are drawn in Ford, ed., *The Southern Appalachian Region*, p. 4 map.) For an outline of the system at the national scale, see Bogue, "Economic Areas as a Tool for Research and Planning." In that 1950 article, Donald Bogue proposed the delineation of a "Southern Appalachian Economic Sub-Region" (414). Also see Bogue and Beale, *Economic Areas of the United States*, a large volume replete with maps, photos, and statistics.

8. Wilkinson, *Poverty and Progress*, 5.

9. The usual one-way model of a linear development from tribal relations through slaveholding and feudalism to capitalism and then socialism has been convincingly challenged by a model that derives from prerevolutionary Chinese historiography. This Chinese-based model sees feudalism and capitalism as alternating in long cycles, with socialism as a blend of the best features from each. See Schrecker, *The Chinese Revolution in Historical Perspective*, preface.

10. Robert D. Mitchell, *Commercialism and Frontier*, 37–39, 17 map, 48–52 maps.

11. The new rural history case study concerned with the Shenandoah Valley is Robert D. Mitchell, *Commercialism and Frontier*. Mitchell's study will contribute to the argument here in chapter 1.

12. The study that nibbles Appalachia's southern edge in Georgia is Hahn, *The Roots of Southern Populism*. Hahn's study will contribute to the argument in chapter 2.

13. The study set in the heart of the Appalachian Plateau is Waller, *Feud*. Waller's study will also contribute to the argument in chapter 2.

14. Rohrbough, *The Land Office Business*, 234.

15. Rockoff, *The Free Banking Era*, 50—63, esp. 59 table.

16. With many variations, economic systems based on subsistence production combined with barter and borrowing can still be found throughout the Third World. Such a system in the Philippines that is now facing market and government penetration is described by Thomas Gibson, *Sacrifice and Sharing in the Philippine Highlands*, 39—48.

17. Vickers, "Competency and Competition," 4.

18. Ibid.

19. Weiman, "Families, Farms and Rural Society," 255.

20. How profit can be achieved in a low-money economy based on voluntary reciprocity is spelled out by Weiman, "Families, Farms, and Rural Society," 255—60. Weiman finds, however, that rural America's "communal arrangements effectively transferred wealth to those at the lower end of the distribution." 259.

21. Merrill, "A Survey of the Debate," 9—10.

22. In this regard, see Heinemann, *Depression and New Deal in Virginia*, 121—22.

23. For some examples, see enclosures accompanying H. D. Hatfield (senator from West Virginia) to Walter H. Newton (secretary to Herbert Hoover), 21 February 1931; Herbert Hoover Presidential Library, West Branch, Iowa; Presidential Papers, Subject Files, Box 118, Folder "Drought Correspondence 1931, Jan.—March." Also see Woodruff, *As Rare as Rain*, 142—55.

24. Cohen, *Women's Work, Markets, and Economic Development*, 36.

25. On supplementary subsistence farming by southern textile workers, see Tippett, *When Southern Labor Stirs*, 31—32; and on barter and borrowing in addition to subsistence production among southern textile workers, see Jacqueline Dowd Hall et al., *Like a Family*, 146—72. Subsistence farming was combined also with lumbering in the Smoky Mountains. See Bush, *Dorie: Woman of the Mountains*, chaps. 6 through 13.

26. On the danger of hillside erosion leaving insufficient humus to grow "either corn or good timber," see the "Statement of the Kentucky Agricultural Experiment Station for Appalachian Travelling Conference, October 30—November 4, 1939," 2; National Archives (hereafter cited as NA), Bureau of Agricultural Economics (hereafter cited as BAE), Appalachian Regional Office, 1934—45; Box 2, Folder "KY-030 Conferences, Southern Appalachian Traveling, Oct. 30—Nov. 4, 1939."

27. Schwarzweller, Brown, and Mangalam, *Mountain Families in Transition*, 40.

28. For example, Taylor, "Depression and New Deal in Pendleton," 124—27, 133.

29. Stephenson, *Shiloh: A Mountain Community*, 128—29.

30. Ardrey, ed., *Welcome the Traveler Home*, 18—19.

31. A 1950 exposition by Prebisch in English is Prebisch, *Economic Development of Latin America.* For a virtually complete bibliography of works by Prebisch, see DiMarco, ed., *International Economics and Development,* 487–99.

32. Love, "Raúl Prebisch," 62–63.

33. Prebisch, *Economic Development of Latin America,* 12.

34. Hayami and Ruttan, *Agricultural Development,* 34.

35. Prebisch, *Economic Development of Latin America,* 8. See also 9 table.

36. Love, "Raúl Prebisch," 47–60. The variables explained thus by Prebisch are viewed from somewhat different assumptions by W. Arthur Lewis, "Economic Development," 158. Also see Klarén, "Lost Promise," 14–20.

37. W. Arthur Lewis, "Economic Development," 182–91.

38. W. Arthur Lewis, *The Evolution of the International Economic Order,* 16.

39. Rostow, *The Stages of Economic Growth,* 4–7.

40. Ibid., 7.

41. Jack Fugett (president, Capels Resources, Inc.), "Commentary Response to Andrew Maier," 5 June 1990, West Virginia Public Radio, transcript.

42. Rostow, *The Stages of Economic Growth,* 7. See also 8, 17–18. For an earlier discussion of investment rates in connection with economic development, see W. Arthur Lewis, "Economic Development," 155–60.

43. Rostow said little about what he called "lagging" regions within mature national economies. He asserted that they "resist—for whatever reason—the full application of the range of modern technology." Rostow judged the United States to have become a mature economy by 1900 despite "the South, whose take-off can be dated only from the 1930s. The technological definition of maturity must, then," Rostow concluded, "be an approximation when applied to a national society." Rostow, *The Stages of Economic Growth,* 67.

44. Ibid., 18.

45. Ibid., 8.

46. Ibid.

47. See Hayami and Ruttan, *Agricultural Development,* 167 table. For the 1880–1980 century as a whole, the average compound growth rate for both Japanese and American agricultural productivity was about 0.9 percent a year. For related information, see 165 table. In this regard, the Japanese people's traditionally high rate of savings and investment at all levels of income has historically acted to spread Japan's productivity gains across the full spectrum of investment from small scale to large scale.

48. Rostow, *The Stages of Economic Growth,* 68.

49. How the Japanese did this is summarized by W. Arthur Lewis, "Economic Development," 174.

50. Kemp, *Industrialization in the Non-Western World,* 22. Douglass North criticizes Rostow's paradigm for overemphasizing capital investment and ignoring "human investment." North writes that "it is probably capital broadly conceived to include human investment as well as physical investment that is the proper criterion, and this does not figure at all in Rostow's scheme." North, *Growth and Welfare in the American Past,* 88.

51. See, for example, Heilbroner, *The Making of Economic Society,* 147 including note.

142 Notes to Pages xxxiv–4

52. Thomas C. Smith, *Nakahara*, 4–5, 8–14, 109.

53. Forest conservation, for example, has been practiced assiduously in Japan since the 1600s. See Osako, "Forest Preservation in Tokugawa Japan," 136–45.

54. Takafusa Nakamura, *Economic Growth in Prewar Japan*, 45–51. Also see Wilkinson, *Poverty and Progress*, 82–83.

55. B. R. Mitchell, *International Historical Statistics: Africa and Asia*, 89.

56. Takafusa Nakamura, *Economic Growth in Prewar Japan*, 113 table. See also 112–25.

57. Kada, *Part-Time Family Farming*, 45 table, and 46 table 3.7b. In that year (1975) Japan's farm families derived 67.8 percent of their income from nonfarm sources (46 table 3.7a). For theory, see Jussaume, *Japanese Part-Time Farming*, 9–11, 19–35, 155–66.

58. B. R. Mitchell, *International Historical Statistics: Africa and Asia*, 89; and U.S. Census Bureau, *Historical Statistics of the United States: Colonial Times to 1970*, pt. 1, 127.

59. Issawi, "Middle East Economic Development," 396.

60. Note, for instance, Kagawa's influential work in Japan with forest-type tree crops, as summarized by Douglas and Hart, *Forest Farming*, 36–38.

1. Early Settlement and Self-Sufficiency

1. Turner, *The Significance of Sections in American History*, 38.

2. Robert D. Mitchell, *Commercialism and Frontier*, 37–39, 96–100; and Noe, "Southwest Virginia," 7–11.

3. U.S. Census Bureau, *Historical Statistics of the United States: Colonial Times to 1970*, pt. 2, 1168.

4. Summaries of Appalachia's settlement include Rice, *The Allegheny Frontier*, 3–9, and maps on 60, 68; and Abernethy, *Three Virginia Frontiers*, 37–82. On early settlement in northeastern Tennessee, see Hsiung, "How Isolated Was Appalachia?" 339–47.

5. Hofstra, "Land Policy and Settlement," 105–12, 115–16. During East Tennessee's early settlement, conflicting land claims created a chaos described by Abernethy, *From Frontier to Plantation in Tennessee*, chap. 11. The use of forged land warrants in early East Tennessee is described by Rankin, *Abolitionist*, 4.

6. On Cherokee "oldfields," see Blethen and Wood, "The Pioneer Experience to 1851," 71; Pillsbury, "The Europeanization of the Cherokee Settlement Landscape," 67; and H. David Williams, "Gold Fever." The settlement of northwestern North Carolina is summarized by Beaver, *Rural Community in the Appalachian South*, 8–19.

7. Pillsbury, "The Europeanization of the Cherokee Settlement Landscape," 60; and H. David Williams, "Gold Fever."

8. U.S. Census of 1830, *Compendium*. For statistical purposes, Appalachia will be defined (unless otherwise specified) as closely as possible to the 190 counties labeled "Appalachian" by Ford, ed., *The Southern Appalachian Region*, 4 map. Total continuity for the region's boundary cannot be achieved for the early period, because county subdivisions and boundary adjustments were frequent before the Civil War and occurred occasionally afterward. Some of these changes affected the outline of Appalachia as a whole, but only slightly. For county lines, census by census, see Thorndale and Dol-

larhide, *Map Guide to the U.S. Federal Censuses, 1790–1920,* 11–23, 79–90, 122–32, 245–58, 314–25, 349–58, 367–76.

9. Robert D. Mitchell, *Commercialism and Frontier,* 4–6.

10. Cuppett, "Harrison Hagans and His Times," chaps. 2 and 4. Hagan's network of stores that paid those 1822 prices for peltry was located in what is today Preston County in north-central West Virginia.

11. Rice, *The Allegheny Frontier,* 165–66. The merchant family was named Mathews.

12. In North Carolina's mountains, in fact, Cherokees had already by the end of the eighteenth century seriously depleted ginseng to use it in trade. Silver, "Vanishing Indians, Vanishing Animals," 13.

13. Wilhelm, "Animal Drives," 328.

14. McMaster, "The Cattle Trade in Western Virginia," 143. See also 142–45.

15. Ibid.; and Stealey, "Notes on the Ante-Bellum Cattle Industry," 39–42.

16. Berry, *Western Prices Before 1861,* 215. This 1805 cattle drive from Chillicothe to Baltimore was achieved by George Renick.

17. Quoted in Rice, *The Allegheny Frontier,* 158; see also 163.

18. Ambler, *West Virginia: Stories and Biographies,* 342, 166–67.

19. Thorp, "Doing Business in the Backcountry," 387–408.

20. Gump, "Half Pints to Horse Shoes," 3, as revised May 1993. Other early East Tennessee merchandising details appear in Hsiung, "Isolation and Integration in Upper East Tennessee," 90–104.

21. Atherton, *The Southern Country Store,* 91. Of course, not *all* frontier settlers exhibited enterprise. See Rice, *The Allegheny Frontier,* 167–68.

22. Thorp, "Doing Business in the Backcountry," 391–92, 399, 402; Atherton, *The Southern Country Store,* 90–95. Also see Inscoe, *Mountain Masters,* 13–20, 37–44, 154; Noe, "Southwest Virginia," 27–28; Robert D. Mitchell, *Commercialism and Frontier,* 152–60; Eller, *Miners, Millhands, and Mountaineers,* 14; Hahn, *The Roots of Southern Populism,* 32; and Rice, *The Allegheny Frontier,* 165.

23. Merrens, *Colonial North Carolina in the Eighteenth Century,* 134–37. On the cattle drives that funneled north through the Shenandoah Valley, see Robert D. Mitchell, *Commercialism and Frontier,* 147–49.

24. Blethen and Wood, "A Trader on the Western Carolina Frontier," 160. On livestock drives from southwestern Virginia—some traveling north but others south—see Noe, "Southwest Virginia," 25–26.

25. Otto, "The Migration of Southern Plain Folk," 191.

26. Blethen and Wood, "Scotch-Irish Society in Southwestern Carolina," 16–17.

27. Blethen and Wood, "A Trader on the Western Carolina Frontier," 162–64; and Inscoe, *Mountain Masters,* 45–52. East Tennessee's earliest roads are mapped in Hsiung, "How Isolated Was Appalachia?" 342, 345. All of the South's main droving routes are mapped in Hilliard, *Hog Meat and Hoecake,* 194. For estimates of the number of animals driven over the major routes, see McDonald and McWhiney, "The Antebellum Southern Herdsman," 160–62.

28. Atherton, *The Southern Country Store,* 129–34. Also see Hsiung, "How Isolated Was Appalachia?" 345–46. Initially, northern wholesalers provisioned southern stores largely with products imported from Europe. Sydnor, *The Development of Southern Section-*

alism, 253–54. Gradually the North substituted its own manufactures for European imports, and these northern "import substitutes" then came to dominate northern wholesalers' shipments to southern stores.

29. Blanche Henry Clark, *The Tennessee Yoemen*, 157.

30. For North Carolina, Inscoe, *Mountain Masters*, 59–86. For the Shenandoah Valley, Robert D. Mitchell, *Commercialism and Frontier*, 238.

31. U.S. Census population figures, 1790–1860.

32. Regarding antebellum public attitudes toward abolitionism in eastern Kentucky and southeastern Ohio, see Rankin, *Abolitionist*, 49–61. By 1837 one observer could no longer discover a single antislavery society anywhere in the South, including Kentucky and western Virginia. Sydnor, *The Development of Southern Sectionalism*, 242. See also 241–44.

33. Blanche Henry Clark, *The Tennessee Yoemen*, 126–27. Large livestock exports also took place from early eastern Kentucky. Moore, "An Historical Geography of Economic Development," 20, 27, 29, 172. On livestock exports from the upper South in general, see Gray, *History of Agriculture*, vol. 2, pp. 876–78.

34. U.S. Censuses of Population and Agriculture, 1840–1870.

35. John C. Inscoe sees western North Carolina's settlement sequence as progressing roughly through bottoms, creek mouths, and hollows to the higher coves. In Appalachian Virginia the same sequence, he says, had been enacted about fifty years earlier. Inscoe, *Mountain Masters*, 12–13.

36. Otto and Anderson, "Slash and Burn Agriculture," 136–38.

37. Gallman, "Self-Sufficiency in the Cotton Economy," 6–8, 22–23; Hutchinson and Williamson, "The Self-Sufficiency of the Antebellum South," 606–9; and Hilliard, *Hog Meat and Hoecake*, 234–35.

38. Earle, *Geographical Inquiry and American Historical Problems*, 290–91; and Earle, "Regional Economic Development," 191–93.

39. Ransom and Sutch, *One Kind of Freedom*, 151–53.

40. U.S. Census of 1860, *Population*.

41. Wilkinson, *Poverty and Progress*, 175.

42. Eller, *Miners, Millhands, and Mountaineers*, xx, 6. A corrective to Eller and others on this point is Shifflett, *Coal Towns*, chap. 1. The ideological spin associated with various versions of Appalachia's early history is explained by Beaver, *Rural Community in the Appalachian South*, 142–45.

43. Ronald L. Lewis, conversation, 11 June 1990.

44. In parts of West Virginia, oil and natural gas extraction also reached major proportions. By the turn of the twentieth century, says a West Virginia agricultural historian, "employment on drilling rigs, hauling pipe, or feeding and lodging the itinerant oil field workers provided cash earnings which made part-time farmers out of many of the land owners." Frame, *West Virginia Agricultural and Rural Life*, pt. 1, 17. Also see Mylott, *A Measure of Prosperity*, 199–202.

45. Takafusa Nakamura, *Economic Growth in Prewar Japan*, 45.

46. For the Japanese half of the natural resource comparison, see Ackerman, *Japan's Natural Resources*. For the Appalachian half of that comparison, Caudill, *Night Comes to the Cumberlands*, chaps. 6 and 7; and Bowman and Haynes, *Resources and People*, chap. 1.

47. James I. Nakamura, *Agricultural Production*, 20–21, 155.

48. Thomas C. Smith, *The Agrarian Origins of Modern Japan*, 211.

49. Ibid., 209, 210.

50. Ibid., 211.

51. U.S. Censuses of Population and Agriculture, 1840, 1850, 1860. The census livestock figures omit all hogs, cattle, sheep, and horses born in the year the census was taken. The figures also do not include livestock which was not on farms. As of 1870, by census calculations, 90 percent of horses *were* on farms, and 90.5 percent of cattle, in the combined states of Alabama, Tennessee, Virginia, Kentucky, and West Virginia. 1870 Census, *Compendium*, 697.

Not until 1880 did the census begin to apply an explicit definition to determine what was and was not a "farm." The census then defined a farm as a holding of three or more acres, and added smaller holdings from which money income exceeded $500. Later the money income required from holdings smaller than three acres was lowered to $250. Even so, few if any Appalachian holdings qualified as farms under this supplementary provision.

Pitfalls to avoid in using the three antebellum agricultural census counts are detailed in Gallman, "Changes in Total U.S. Agricultural Productivity." Significantly, Gallman finds there that overall U.S. agricultural output per farm worker grew faster between 1800 and 1840 than between 1840 and 1900. (See his 206–10.) This is one more indication that most pioneers were relatively secure economically. By the decade of the 1910s, in fact, the *absolute* agricultural output per U.S. farm worker was actually in decline. (Heilbroner, *The Making of Economic Society*, 145.) Since that time, however, farm mechanization has vastly *increased* output per U.S. farm worker. See U.S. Bureau of the Census, *Historical Statistics of the United States: Colonial Times to 1970*, pt. 2, 953.

52. Lewis Cecil Gray, quoted in Pudup, "The Limits of Subsistence," 67. The quotation is from Gray, *History of Agriculture*, vol. 2, p. 884. See also the table in Gray's vol. 2, p. 876.

53. Butler, "Reminiscences," 66–67; and Hilliard, *Hog Meat and Hoecake*, 92–104.

54. U.S. Censuses of Population and Agriculture, 1840, 1850, and 1860. County boundary changes during the intervals between the census counts do not significantly affect these figures because I am comparing the *proportion* of farm livestock and crops to the total human population of each subregion as that subregion was constituted at the time of each given census.

55. Blanche Henry Clark, *The Tennessee Yoemen*, 126.

56. U.S. Censuses of Population and Agriculture, 1840, 1850, and 1860. The census figures suggest that noncorn grain production fell faster per capita in the 1840s than in the 1850s. (See table 2.) This may be deceptive, however, because census officials considered their 1850 wheat count too low, and, beyond that, the 1850 wheat crop was short compared to the years immediately before and after. See 1850 Census, *Statistics*, 170. For maps that show the antebellum census grain counts per capita, see Hilliard, *Atlas of Antebellum Southern Agriculture*, 59–66.

57. U.S. Censuses of Population and Agriculture, 1850 and 1860. These work-animal figures include work oxen.

58. U.S. Censuses of Population and Agriculture, 1840, 1850, and 1860.

59. Nationwide, milk yield per dairy cow grew about 8 percent in the 1850s. All states with Appalachian sections stood far below the national average of milk yield per cow in absolute census figures, but county level counts were not published. See Bateman, "Improvement in American Dairy Farming," 257–58 tables.

2. Accelerated Agricultural Decline and Adverse Federal Policy

1. U.S. Censuses of Population and Agriculture, 1860 and 1870.

2. U.S. Censuses of Population and Agriculture, 1850 and 1880.

3. U.S. Census of 1880, vol. 15, pp. 642–73. In 1870, less than 850 coal miners had been reported as active in Newer Appalachia at any given time. 1870 Census, vol. 3, pp. 770–89.

4. U.S. Censuses of Population and Agriculture, 1850 and 1880.

5. Weingartner, "Limits to Subsistence Agriculture," 13. Weingartner here reports the average value of 1880 Beech Creek farms in terms of 1850 dollar values, so no distortion of value is involved.

6. The extent of southern livestock depletion during the Civil War, and the limited extent of recovery achieved by 1880, are summarized for selected states by McDonald and McWhiney, "The Antebellum Southern Herdsman," 163–64.

7. U.S. Censuses of Population and Agriculture, 1860 and 1870.

8. Barns, The West Virginia State Grange, 13; and Rice, West Virginia: A History, 175.

9. Bateman, "Improvement in American Dairy Farming," 266–67; and Rice, West Virginia: A History, 175.

10. William Appleman Williams, The Roots of the Modern American Empire, 98.

11. Congressional Globe, 12 May 1852; 32d Cong., 1st sess., 1351; and Martis, The Historical Atlas, 84–85. Other details about the 1852 homestead bill are in Shannon, "The Homestead Act and the Labor Surplus," 641–43. The 1852 bill, like those of 1846, 1860, and 1862, was sponsored by Andrew Johnson of East Tennessee.

12. U.S. Census of 1860, Agriculture, clxiv–clxix. (This consists of an essay entitled "Influence of Railroads Upon Agriculture.") Alfred D. Chandler, Jr. gives only six hundred midwestern railroad miles in 1849 and eleven thousand miles in 1860. Chandler, "The Organization of Manufacturing and Transportation," 238.

13. Hine, The American West, 110, 161.

14. By the census criterion of twenty-five hundred or more inhabitants, only three Appalachian towns qualified as urban in 1860, all three of them in Virginia as of 1860. Thus Appalachia was less than 1 percent urban in 1860. By the same definition, the Midwest (Ohio, Indiana, Illinois, Michigan, and Wisconsin) was 14.1 percent urban in 1860. U.S. Census of 1970, vol. 1, pt. A, sec. 1, 65–66.

15. U.S. Census of 1870, Compendium, 694–96, 708–10.

16. Cochrane, The Development of American Agriculture, 94, 340–41 including table. U.S. population growth in the 1870s was only 26 percent, whereas farm output grew 53 percent.

17. I take this argument from Shaw, "The Progress of the World," 17. Albert Shaw dates the inauguration of American agriculture's structural unprofitability in the early

1880s, when large surpluses first manifested. This was before most Dakota homesteads had yet been established.

18. Smith and Phillips, *North America*, 236.

19. Frame, *West Virginia Agricultural and Rural Life*, pt. 1, 15; Barns, *The West Virginia State Grange*, 19–24; Mylott, *A Measure of Prosperity*, 102–6; and Simon, "The Development of Underdevelopment," 227.

20. Cummings, "Community and the Nature of Change," 73–75.

21. Of midwestern farming, Carl Sauer says that "from its beginning [it] was based on marketing products, but it also maintained a high measure of self-sufficiency." Sauer, "Homestead and Community on the Middle Border," 38. Fuller discussion on 38–39.

22. Blanche Henry Clark, *The Tennessee Yoemen*, 131.

23. U.S. Census of 1850, table 11; and 1850 Census *Compendium*, 169, 238, 244.

24. U.S. Census of 1880, *Agriculture*, 4, 117–18.

25. Atherton, *The Southern Country Store*, 129–34.

26. In West Virginia, for instance, "capital for agricultural investment was rather scarce" during the late nineteenth century. Barns, *The West Virginia State Grange*, 23.

27. U.S. Census of 1880, vol. 15, pp. 642–73. The total number of those employed at *some* time in 1880 in coal mining has been listed at 4,497 for West Virginia alone. Simon, "The Development of Underdevelopment," 229 (table 53). Of the 3,940 "average" coal-mining work force listed for Plateau counties by the 1880 census, two-thirds were listed in West Virginia, one-fifth in Kentucky, and one-seventh in Tennessee. Extrapolation from this gives a figure of about 6,745 as the total number of people employed at mining coal on the Plateau at some time in 1880. This coal work force, although small, represents an almost 800 percent increase over 1870's Plateau coal work force.

28. Otto and Anderson, "Slash and Burn Cultivation," 134, 140; and Otto, "The Decline of Forest Farming," 18–27. See 22–25 for insights into the logic but also the limits of slash-and-burn agriculture in an Appalachian topography. An economic explanation of benefits obtainable from slash-and-burn agriculture is Boserup, *The Conditions of Agricultural Growth*.

29. Rice, *The Allegheny Frontier*, 161–62.

30. McDonald and McWhiney, "The Antebellum Southern Herdsman," 157–58. Also see King, "The Closing of the Southern Range," 53–70.

31. On Georgia, see Hahn, "Hunting, Fishing, and Foraging," 55–56. On Alabama, see McDonald and McWhiney, "The South from Self-Sufficiency to Peonage," 1116.

32. Butler, "Reminiscences," 66.

33. Summers, *The Mountain State*, 30-31. See table 3 of this present book (on 27) for the criteria that the forester who made this count used to define marketable timber.

34. Thomas D. Clark, *The Greening of the South*, 24. The methods of mountain timbering are described and profusely illustrated in Clarkson, *Tumult on the Mountains*.

35. Butler, "Reminiscences," 66.

36. Thomas D. Clark, *The Greening of the South*, 47–48.

37. Ibid., 63.

38. McDonald and McWhiney, "The Antebellum Southern Herdsman," 162.

39. Hahn, *The Roots of Southern Populism*, 29–49, 170–203. Hahn emphasizes the role played by exchanges "in kind" between farmers and storekeepers.

40. Ibid. This was true *throughout* the Deep South, according to Ransom and Sutch, "Debt Peonage in the Cotton South," 641–69.

41. For the text of the 1865 act, see the 38th Cong., 2d sess., chap. 78, sec. 6, 3 March 1865, in *The Statutes at Large*, 484.

42. Hughes, *American Economic History*, 249. And see discussion on 248–49.

43. Two astute apologies for "easy money" on America's frontiers are Rockoff, "The Free Banking Era"; and Sylla, "American Banking and Growth," 214–20.

44. Russell, "The Regulation and Supervision of Banking," 17–18, 27. Also see Van Beck Hall, "The Politics of Appalachian Virginia," 180–81 (and on Hall's system of points for analyzing votes in the Virginia legislature, see 173–74).

45. Abernethy, *From Frontier to Plantation in Tennessee*, 229–31.

46. Sharp, *The Jacksonians versus the Banks*, 196; and Abernethy, "The Early Development of Commerce and Banking," 322–25.

47. Galbraith, *Money*, 75; Syndor, *The Development of Southern Sectionalism*, 104–20; Bogart and Kemmerer, *Economic History of the American People*, 363–77, 664–65; and Hammond, *Banks and Politics in America*, 453, 734.

48. Tindall and Shi, *America: A Narrative History*, 490. The exaggerated rate of population growth given there by Tindall and Shi is corrected here.

49. U.S. Census Bureau, *Historical Statistics of the United States: Colonial Times to 1970*, pt. 2, 993.; and Tindall and Shi, *America: A Narrative History*, 559.

50. John A. James, *Money and Capital Markets in Postbellum America*, 22. Yearly ratios of currency (i.e., cash) to deposits for 1867–1968 (and, after 1907, monthly ratios) appear in Friedman and Schwartz, *Monetary Statistics of the United States*, 4–57 table.

51. Perkins, "Monetary Policies," 835–36. Also see Studenski and Krooss, *Financial History of the United States*, 176–77.

52. U.S. Census Bureau, *Historical Statistics of the United States: Colonial Times to 1970*, pt. 2, 993, 1020.

53. Waller, *Feud*, 36–45.

54. Ibid., 153–54, 163–65, 195–201.

55. Ibid., 44–45.

56. Ibid., 280 note 65.

57. Ibid., 200.

58. Ibid., 43.

59. Swain, *History of Logan County, West Virginia*, 202–3.

60. John A. James, *Money and Capital Markets in Postbellum America*, 28, 90–91.

61. According to Grace Palladino, such insufficiency of cash, forcing coal operators to pay wages in other forms such as company scrips, began as early as the Civil War in Pennsylvania's anthracite fields. Palladino, "Nation Building from the Bottom Up."

62. Scott, *The Moral Economy of the Peasant*, 13. Economic principles underlying such farm-family choices are set forth on 13–15. See also Brenner, "The Social Basis of Economic Development," 28–30.

63. U.S. Census of 1870, vol. 3, pp. 770–89; and 1880 Census, vol. 15, pp. 642–73. A long ton held 2,240 pounds rather than the 2,000 pounds of the short ton, today's standard.

64. Simon, "The Development of Underdevelopment," 228 table.

65. W. Arthur Lewis, *The Evolution of the International Economic Order*, 19, 17–18. The cash-cropping of peanuts was forced on West African farmers through colonial decrees in both the British and the French colonies there. This was not a case of market forces alone inspiring producers' crop priorities.

66. U.S. Census of 1860, *Agriculture*, clxvii. More detailed prices on clxviii. These rising Cincinnati hog prices attracted considerable livestock from Appalachia as well as from the Midwest. On the western border of Newer Appalachia, the soil of the once-fertile lower valley of the Kanawha River (in Mason and Putnam counties of West Virginia) suffered severe depletion in the third quarter of the nineteenth century to achieve forced yields of corn on which to fatten hogs for the Cincinnati and eastern hog markets. Ambler and Summers, *West Virginia: The Mountain State*, 348.

67. Berry, *Western Prices Before 1861*, 124–25. Further documentation and discussion on 119–29, 183 table, 537–39, 564 tables.

68. Hughes, *American Economic History*, 185.

69. Berry, *Western Prices Before 1861*, 126, 129.

70. Earle, *Geographical Inquiry and American Historical Problems*, 312. Earle's calculations included nine farm products: wheat, corn, barley, rye, oats, flour, live hogs, dressed hogs, and cattle.

71. W. Arthur Lewis, "The Diffusion of Development," 142.

72. W. Arthur Lewis, "Economic Development," 183–84.

73. The principles involved are concisely set forth in ibid., 148–51.

74. Smith and Phillips, *North America*, 379 note 23.

75. Warren, *Bankruptcy in United States History*, 87–88, 100, 103, 110–11.

76. Krooss and Blyn, *A History of Financial Intermediaries*, 76.

77. U.S. Census of 1870, vol. 3, pp. 770–89; and 1880 Census, vol. 15, pp. 642–73.

78. In the 1870s and 1880s, says William D. Barns, "as many as twelve or even thirty families might depart in a single month" from some West Virginia counties—bound mostly for Kansas and Nebraska but many others went to Indiana, Iowa, Missouri, Arkansas, and Texas. Some went to California or Oregon. And yet, adds Barns, "West Virginia's total population continued to increase." Barns, *The West Virginia State Grange*, 21.

79. Turner, *The Frontier in American History*, 259.

80. Eller, *Miners, Millhands, and Mountaineers*, 197.

81. Brown, "The Family Behind the Migrant," 153–57. Also see Schwarzweller, Brown, and Mangalam, *Mountain Families in Transition*, 90–98.

3. Rural Appalachia's Subsistence-Barter-and-Borrow Systems

1. Rothenberg, "Markets and Massachusetts Farmers," 1.

2. Christopher Clark, *The Roots of Rural Capitalism*.

3. G. E. Carlyle, quoted in Banks, "Class and Change in a Southern Region," 18.

4. But also note that by the turn of the century, timbering and textile manufacturing were likewise growing in symbiotic relation with subsistence farming in some parts of Older Appalachia. On the symbiosis between textile labor and subsistence farming in East Tennessee's Carter County, see Jacqueline Dowd Hall, "Disorderly Women," 359–61. On subsistence farming among textile workers elsewhere, see Jacqueline Dowd Hall et al., *Like a Family*, 146–52.

5. See, for example, Crawford, "Wealth, Slaveholding and Power"; Inscoe, *Mountain Masters*, 13, 116–17; Blethen and Wood, "The Pioneer Experience to 1851," 71; Hennen, "Benign Betrayal," 54; and Waller, "Family Origins of the Hatfield-McCoy Feudists," 5–7.

6. A statement of this thesis is Philip L. White, *Beekmantown, New York*, vii–viii, 70, 114, 309–10. Its relevance to the Old Northwest is argued by William N. Parker, "From Northwest to Midwest," 17–22. For Appalachian evidence see Robert D. Mitchell, *Commercialism and Frontier*, 52–53, 131–32; Abernethy, *From Frontier to Plantation in Tennessee*, 17–19, 145–46, 159–63; Abernethy, *Three Virginia Frontiers*, 40–50, 63–69, 95; and Abernethy, *The South in the New Nation*, x–xi, 453, 457, 471.

7. Combining wage labor with part-time farming was always fairly common throughout the United States (and still remains so), but in Appalachia it was (and remains) much more common than elsewhere. For national cartographic maps of part-time farming as of 1929, see U.S. Census of Agriculture of 1935, *Part-Time Farming in the United States*, 13, 15, 17, 19, 23, 25 maps. Other maps there report as of 1934.

8. Eller, *Miners, Millhands, and Mountaineers*, 134–53, documents the predominance, in Appalachia's coal development, of northern investment funds over funds from other sources. However, Eller also shows the local origins of many early land buyers and coal operators in the region. Pp. 44–64, 201–4. A documentation of the functions that local elites usually performed for outside capitalists is Hennen, "Benign Betrayal."

9. I'm thinking here of Appalachia's well-known mine wars during the 1891–1932 period; also of trouble in the Rockies involving the Western Federation of Miners; and of similar trouble involving the International Workers of the World in the Far Northwest (which was the last timber frontier in the contiguous United States). Those were the final three major frontier regions of the contiguous United States.

10. The inaugural addresses, so to speak, of the Lemon-Henretta controversy were Henretta, "Families and Farms"; and James T. Lemon, "Early Americans and Their Social Environment."

11. Hartz, *The Liberal Tradition in America*, 89.

12. Grant, *Democracy in the Connecticut Frontier Town of Kent*.

13. Bushman, *From Puritan to Yankee*. Bushman mentions that many isolated inland farmers carted produce laboriously to market.

14. Innes, *Labor in a New Land*. See especially xv–xxi.

15. John Frederick Martin, *Profits in the Wilderness*.

16. On the "subsistence" side of the argument, see in particular Christopher Clark, "Household Economy, Market Exchange and the Rise of Capitalism"; and Pruitt, "Self-Sufficiency and the Agricultural Economy." Probably most U.S. historians are, like these

authors, anticapitalist. On why this is so, see Appleby, *Capitalism and a New Social Order: The Republican Vision of the 1790s*, 45–46.

17. A good case study from the liberals' "enterprise" school is Innes, *Labor in a New Land*, which concerns the Connecticut River valley in the seventeenth century, almost two hundred years before the period of that area's life, which was studied by Christopher Clark, who found a subsistence mentality there.

18. U.S. Censuses of Population and Agriculture, 1840, 1850, and 1880.

19. Benedict, *Farm Policies in the United States*, 356.

20. Henretta, "Families and Farms," 16, 19.

21. James T. Lemon, "The Weakness of Place and Community," 197. On this point, also see Barron, "Staying Down on the Farm," 336–37.

22. Innes, "Fulfilling John Smith's Vision," 37–38.

23. Brown, "The Family Behind the Migrant," 153–57. Also see Schwarzweller, Brown, and Mangalam, *Mountain Families in Transition*, 90–98. Those three authors liken twentieth-century Appalachian family dynamics to Frederic LePlay's concept of the *famille-souche* (which they translate as "stem-family").

24. Herbert Francis Sherwood, cited by Eller, *Miners, Millhands, and Mountaineers*, 126.

25. Potwin, *Cotton Mill People of the Piedmont*, 56–57. See also 53. Eller says that "for some mountain families the move to the mill village came only as a last resort." Eller, *Miners, Millhands, and Mountaineers*, 127. The horrendous working conditions at most southern textile mills (which Eller here details) clearly insured that most of the mountain migrants who came *and stayed* at the mills, did so only as a last resort.

26. Abraham Lincoln, "Annual Message to Congress," 3 December 1861; in Lincoln, *Complete Works of Abraham Lincoln*, vol. 7, pp. 58–59.

27. Ibid., 57.

28. The workings of such a system in the mid-nineteenth century in southwestern Virginia's Tazewell County are described by Mann, "Mountains, Land, and Kin Networks."

29. Weiman, "Families, Farms and Rural Society," 260.

30. P. M. McBride in letter to the editor of the *United Mine Workers Journal*, published in issue of 28 May 1896, 1; quoted in Corbin, *Life, Work, and Rebellion in the Coal Fields*, 34.

31. W. Arthur Lewis, *The Evolution of the International Economic Order*, 16, 19.

32. Simon, "The Development of Underdevelopment," 228 table.

33. Morris, *The Plight of the Bituminous Coal Miner*, 186–90.

34. For a summary of such a sequence over time, see Leet, "Human Fertility and Agricultural Opportunities in Ohio Counties," 145–46.

35. U.S. Census of 1880, *Agriculture*, table 8. Note that this average value of farm implements as of 1880 in eastern Kentucky represented a nominal 14.68 percent fall from the 1850 average of $27.75 worth of implements per farm. But because the dollar's value in 1880 was 13.8 percent below its value in 1850, the real fall in farm-implement value was less than 1 percent. U.S. Census Bureau, *Historical Statistics of the United States: Colonial Times to 1970*, pt. 1, 211 table.

36. In a suggestive but unclear passage, the historical geographer Carville Earle estimates that the amount of actual rural earnings "was usually higher than the cash value of rural earnings by 30 to 40 percent." Earle, *Geographical Inquiry and American Historical Problems*, 185. Earle's approach to rural analysis lends itself to quantifying barter and borrowing income, but he does not explicitly say that that is what he is quantifying here.

37. For instance, see Halperin, *The Livelihood of Kin*; Beaver, *Rural Community in the Appalachian South*, 115–17, 121; and Long, "Barter Economy Serves Cash-Poor Residents Well."

38. Polanyi, *The Great Transformation*, 56.

39. Schwarzweller, Brown, and Mangalam, *Mountain Families in Transition*, 3–70.

40. Ibid., 6–7. By comparison, some New England scholars *have* noted that barter plays an economic as well as a social role. For instance, Pruitt in Self-Sufficiency and the Agricultural Economy," 349, points out that, thanks to interfarm exchanges, "subsistence [was] possible on farms that were not sufficient." And on barter economics in early nineteenth-century Vermont, see Roth, *The Democratic Dilemma*, 20–25.

41. On this point, see Long, "Barter Economy Serves Cash-Poor Residents Well."

42. For example, see Ball, "The Southern Appalachian Folk Subculture," 72–73. To reduce the impact of "inexorable pressure . . . and absolutely overwhelming frustration," says Ball, Appalachian culture utilizes a strategy of anticipating defeat. The resultant "fatalism and apathy," Ball says, are not "sensible adaptations," but nonetheless they are "justified by religious doctrine and sustained by a social order." 73.

43. George Fowler, "Social and Industrial Conditions in the Pocahontas Coal Field," *Engineering Magazine* 27 (June 1904): 386–87; quoted in Eller, *Miners, Millhands, and Mountaineers*, 166.

44. Rochester, *Why Farmers Are Poor*, 68–69.

45. Vance, "The Region: A New Survey," 5.

46. Kirby, *Rural Worlds Lost*, 111.

47. For a summary of ethnological literature about the decline of Appalachia's traditional life, see Billings, Blee, and Swanson, "Culture, Family, and Community in Preindustrial Appalachia," 154–57, 161–67.

4. Labor-intensive Mining and the Subsistence Reproduction of Labor Power

1. Graeme Kirkham, conversation, 4 May 1985.

2. Benjamin White, "Demand for Labor and Population Growth," 227–34.

3. U.S. Dept. of Labor, Children's Bureau, *The Welfare of Children in Bituminous Coal Mining Communities in West Virginia*, by Nettie McGill, Pub. No. 117 (Washington, D.C.: Government Printing Office, 1923), 34–36; cited by Eller, *Miners, Millhands, and Mountaineers*, 237.

4. Shifflett, *Coal Towns*, 17. In the 1920s, Shifflett's father, growing up on a farm in Virginia's Blue Ridge country, was standing on a box to harness horses by about age eight.

5. Davis Coal and Coke Company, *Our Own People* 3, no. 11 (October 1918): 5. See also 3, no. 8 (August 1918): 12; and 4, no. 9 (September 1919): 6. Also see Corbin, *Life, Work, and Rebellion in the Coal Fields*, 33–35, 123–24; Rasmussen, "Monroe County, West Virginia," 18–20; Morris, *The Plight of the Bituminous Coal Miner*, 196–200; and Trotter, *Coal, Class, and Color*, 90–91. For the number of native whites, blacks, and immigrants (by country of origin) among West Virginia miners between 1880–1917, see Bailey, "A Judicious Mixture," 119 table. During those years, blacks and immigrants, counted together, outnumbered native whites in West Virginia mines only between 1907–1915.

6. Report by C. S. Richardson, in Dodge, *West Virginia*, 46–48.

7. Frame, *West Virginia Agricultural and Rural Life*, pt. 2, 41.

8. Calculated from State of West Virginia, Department of Agriculture, *Third Biennial Report, 1917–1918*, 36–39; *Fourth Biennial Report, 1917–1918*, 23; State of West Virginia, Department of Mines, *Annual Report, 1917–1918*, 237–39; *Annual Report, 1918–1919*, 249–57; and *Annual Report, 1919–1920*, 262–64. Garden value estimates for 1931–32 are given in Morris, *The Plight of the Bituminous Coal Miner*, 196–98.

9. *The Black Diamond* 60, no. 25 (22 June 1918): 554.

10. Morris, *The Plight of the Bituminous Coal Miner*, 52 table. The title of the table is "Average Number of Children Ever Born to Mothers, Listed According to Occupations of Fathers in the United States 1920." The overall U.S. average as of then (1920) was 3.3 children born per mother.

11. Rasmussen, "Monroe County, West Virginia," 3–5; and U.S. Censuses of Agriculture, 1880 and 1930.

12. Rasmussen, "Monroe County, West Virginia," 12–13, 18.

13. The concept of subsistence labor reproduction is outlined by Alavi, "Capitalism and Colonial Transformation," 3. Also see Omvedt, "Migration in Colonial India," 1–2, 11.

14. Cohen, *Women's Work, Markets, and Economic Development*, 36.

15. For a revealing 1970s interview with an eastern Kentucky woman, a mother of four, whose husband "worked out," see Shackelford and Weinberg, *Our Appalachia*, 307–12. Also see Jacqueline Dowd Hall, "Disorderly Women," 371; and Beaver, *Rural Community in the Appalachian South*, 110–12.

16. This actually does less than justice to Boeke's *social* theory, which is more convincing than his economic theory. See Boeke, *Economics and Economic Policy of Dual Societies*. On "dual economies," see 79–83. Boeke recognizes that many tradition-oriented people produce exports, but he insists that their motives are generally not "economic" in an individualistic (and thus modernizing) sense.

17. Levin, *The Export Economies*, 6–7. An application of Levin's "lack of reinvestment" argument to Appalachia appears in Simon, "The Development of Underdevelopment," 392.

18. Frank, *Crisis: In the Third World*, 160. Frank thinks that capitalism was able to achieve economic dominance within early modern Europe only because it reaped wealth from Asia, Africa, and Latin America. See Frank, *On Capitalist Underdevelopment*, 46–47. Frank's explanation for "underdevelopment" was prefigured in Gunner Myrdal's "backwash effect" suffered by less developed areas due to increasing productivity in the more

developed areas of the same country. See Myrdal, *Rich Lands and Poor,* 26–29. Useful analogies between the Third World and Appalachia are suggested by the Third World theories that are summarized in Klarén, "Lost Promise," 8–26; and in Barone, *Marxist Thought on Imperialism,* 144–87.

19. Many colonial regimes used tax demands to drive subsistence farmers into at least part-time wage labor, and several colonial regimes sponsored the creation of *new* subsistence sectors specifically to supply low-wage labor to plantations. How the British did this in Guyana is described by Mandle, *The Plantation Economy,* 35–37. Also see R. M. A. Van Zwanenberg, *Colonial Capitalism and Labour in Kenya,* 210–15.

20. U.S. Census of 1910, vol. 1, p. 310; and vols. 2 and 3, table 1; and 1920 Census, vol. 3, table 9.

21. Eller, *Miners, Millhands, and Mountaineers,* 225–26. For these particular figures, the Appalachian region was defined not as the 190-county region of the present study but rather as the 205-county region studied in the U.S. Department of Agriculture, *Economic and Social Problems and Conditions of the Southern Appalachians.* A farm is defined here by the census definition in use throughout the early twentieth century: a tract of three or more acres, or of less than three acres if its agricultural products exceeded $250 in value during the precensus year. The "rural nonfarm" category embraces all nonfarm residents outside towns of more than 2,500 population.

22. On South Africa's refinements in the deliberate exploitation of subsistence labor reproduction, see Rogerston, "Apartheid, Decentralization and Spacial Industrial Change," 62. In South Africa's coal mines, the machine loading of coal began to be economically competitive about 1958. In the 1970s, higher wages, riots, and strikes induced an increased pace of coal-mine mechanization. On that see Anthony Lemon, "Migrant Labour and Frontier Communities," 74. South Africa's coal-mine mechanization has thus apparently trailed Appalachia's by about twenty years.

23. Brown and Hillery, "The Great Migration, 1940–1960," 58–60 tables. More details and additional references in Stephen E. White, "America's Soweto."

24. Hayami and Ruttan, *Agricultural Development,* 286–88, including table 9.6. Japan's introduction of Ponlai (Japonica) rice to Taiwan in the 1920s resembled the later Green Revolution of the 1960s and 1970s throughout East and South Asia.

25. Lee, *Intersectoral Capital Flows,* 120, 30, 32; and Ho, *Economic Development of Taiwan,* chap. 6, including tables.

26. Ho, *Economic Development of Taiwan,* 60, 95–98, 149.

27. Lee, *Intersectoral Capital Flows,* 72, 77 tables. The figure of 28 percent reports the average rise in the *absolute* amount of homegrown food production that was consumed on its home farm. It does not report a rise in the *percentage* of home production that was consumed at home.

28. Ibid., 82–84.

29. Johnson and Clark, *Redesigning Rural Development,* 75.

30. Ho, *Economic Development of Taiwan,* 150–51, 156.

31. On the threatening subsistence situation that preceded and accompanied Appalachia's industrialization, see Shifflett, *Coal Towns,* xi–xiii, 13–16.

32. Johnson and Clark, *Redesigning Rural Development,* 75.

33. *Taiwan Statistical Data Book, 1987,* 214 table. Whereas in 1952 a full 91.9 percent of Taiwan's exports had been agricultural, by 1986 only 6.5 percent remained agricultural. 213 table.

34. Ho, *Economic Development of Taiwan,* 313–14.

35. *Taiwan Statistical Data Book, 1987,* 1 table.

36. Shen, *Agriculture's Place in the Strategy of Development,* 1; and Ho, *Economic Development in Taiwan,* 155.

37. Fields, *Poverty, Inequality, and Development,* 234–35; Li, *The Evolution of Policy,* 166 table; and *Taiwan Statistical Data Book, 1987,* 1, 16, 65 tables.

38. *Taiwan Statistical Data Book, 1987,* 17–18 tables.

39. Shen, *Agriculture's Place in the Strategy of Development,* 1.

40. For the Japanese part of this comparison see Ackerman, *Japan's Natural Resources.* For the Taiwanese part, see Hsieh, *Taiwan,* chaps. 7 and 20.

41. For examples of local members of the mountain elite employed by outside investors, see Hennen, "Benign Betrayal," 54–62; Gaventa, *Power and Powerlessness,* 59, 70; Eller, *Miners, Millhands, and Mountaineers,* 48, 58–63, and Pudup, "The Boundaries of Class," 142–45, 159–60. Appalachia's elite also included many families that rejected industrialization or were excluded from its rewards. The sociologist Daniel Chirot has found a pattern in the Third World around 1900 that resembles this bifurcation of Appalachia's elite. Chirot finds that Third World middle classes often "split between the 'new' element that participated in and profited from the enclave, core-dominated sector of the economy and the 'old' element that did not." Chirot, *Social Change in the Twentieth Century,* 64.

42. Large landholdings engrossed in the eighteenth century are detailed in Rasmussen, "The Absentee Legacy in Virginia's West." Large holdings transferred to absentee owners around the turn of the twentieth century are detailed in John Alexander Williams, *West Virginia and the Captains of Industry,* 154–60, 196–97.

43. This judgment appears in Simon, "The Development of Underdevelopment," 367–69, 392. For what Simon believes West Virginian coal operators could have achieved had they mustered sufficient "development-minded leadership" to overcome destructive competition among themselves, and then had they automated their mines in step with northern coal mines, see 406–7. I find this unconvincing, however, since coal-industry competition was virtually national, not merely regional.

44. For rough figures comparing coal tonnage to the far lower weight of U.S. wheat and cotton production, see Smith and Phillips, *North America,* 265 note 15.

45. See Corbin, *Life, Work, and Rebellion in the Coal Fields,* chap. 1.

46. Eller, *Miners, Millhands, and Mountaineers,* 201–4.

47. On the invention and adoption of coal-cutting machines, see Dix, *What's a Coal Miner to Do?,* 28–32.

48. U.S. Census of 1890, vol. 7, pp. 356–419.

49. Eller, *Miners, Millhands, and Mountaineers,* 165. For a summary of the 1880s Flat Top–Pocahontas coal boom, see 69–74. Also see Gillenwater, "A Cultural and Historical Geography," 21–36.

50. U.S. Census Bureau, *Special Report: Mines and Quarries, 1902,* 681–702.

51. H. G. Lewis, *Unionism and Relative Wages in the United States*, 77 table 9 (col. 6). See also 73–80.

52. Eller, *Miners, Millhands, and Mountaineers*, 162–65, 182; and Hunt, ed., *What the Coal Commission Found*, 139–42. For specific examples of company-town law enforcement, see Corbin, *Life, Work, and Rebellion in the Coal Fields*, 10–12, 78, 116–19.

53. Hotchkiss et al., *Mechanization, Employment, and Output*, vol. 1, p. xxvi; and vol. 2, p. 301 graph, 345.

54. Dix, *What's a Coal Miner to Do?*, 183 table.

55. Hotchkiss et al., *Mechanization, Employment, and Output*, vol. 1, pp. xxvi, 12.

56. Ronald L. Lewis, "From Peasant to Proletarian," 97–99, 81 including table.

57. Green, *Only a Miner*, 156–57, 159. Similarly, the successful 1893 activism of miners at Jellico, Tennessee—only thirty miles from Middlesboro—had also grown in response to long-term grievances. Jellico's large-scale coal mining went back about as long as did Coal Creek's. Ronald L. Lewis, conversation, February 1991.

58. Gaventa, *Power and Powerlessness*, 64–75, 79–83.

59. Another factor tending to slow down the growth of class antagonism was mountaineers' religious attitudes. See Corbin, *Life, Work, and Rebellion in the Coal Fields*, 146–50.

60. Stuart McGehee (archivist, Eastern Regional Coal Archives, Bluefield, West Virginia), letter, 22 December 1988.

61. State of West Virginia, "First Report . . . 1891," 10, 11, 22, 23. Note that in 1891 a national bank (the First National Bank of Bluefield) also opened for business in this coal field. The 1891 bank examiner's report does not provide figures for this national bank.

62. Calculated from the State of West Virginia, "Annual Reports . . . 1891," 77 tables. The figure given is for 1 July 1890 through 30 June 1891.

63. State of West Virginia, "First Report . . . 1891," 10, 11, 22, 23.

64. Ibid., 45; and Summers, *The Mountain State*, 20–21. Summers's source for the amount of capital invested in West Virginia coal mining is the 1890 U.S. Census.

65. Summers, *The Mountain State*, 6.

66. State of West Virginia, *Second Annual Report . . . 1902*, 22, 23, 24, 87, 110, 132.

67. State of West Virginia, Department of Mines, *Annual Report, 1901–1902*, 11, 12 tables. The outputs compared here are for 1 July 1890 through 30 June 1891, and for 1 July 1901 through 30 June 1902.

68. See table 4, above on 35.

69. The coal-wage figures used cover 1 July 1901 through 30 June 1902. State of West Virginia, Department of Mines, *Annual Report, 1901–1902*, 53, 65; and State of West Virginia, *Second Annual Report . . . 1902*, 8–9. The figure of $54.7 million represents all forms of deposits held as of 1902 in West Virginia's national as well as state banks.

70. On the presence of standard food brands in company stores as of the early 1920s, see Hunt, ed., *What the Coal Commission Found*, 152–53. This report adds that "having accustomed the mine-worker's wife to certain brands and kinds of goods," company

stores had thereby forced independent stores "to carry the same goods in order to compete with Company stores." 153.

71. McKinney, *Southern Mountain Republicans*, 10, 128–29, 143, 154. McKinney's analysis is substantiated by evidence summarized in Barnhart, "Recent Industrial Growth and Politics," 589–94. See also Barns, *The West Virginia State Grange*, 18; John Alexander Williams, *West Virginia: A Bicentennial History*, 115–20; and John Alexander Williams, *West Virginia and the Captains of Industry*, 8–9, 14, 69–79, 107, 197–98. For a scenario that could translate local political control by business interests into low wages for workers who retained ties to agriculture, see Jacqueline Dowd Hall, "Disorderly Women," 369.

72. John A. James, *Money and Capital Markets in Postbellum America*, 107–10, including tables. Also see Sylla, "The United States, 1863–1914," 250–57, including tables.

73. John A. James, *Money and Capital Markets in Postbellum America*, 108 table.

74. Ibid., 17 graph.

75. Ibid., 12–13, 189–93. Also see Sylla, "The United States, 1863–1914," 253–54, 256–57; and Krooss and Blyn, *A History of Financial Intermediaries*, chaps. 6 and 7.

76. Hughes, *American Economic History*, 357.

77. Ibid., 356.

78. Simon, "The Development of Underdevelopment," 332, 342.

79. Wright, *Old South, New South*, 167–72; and Cooper and Terrell, *The American South: A History*, 484–85. The Pittsburgh Plus system was eventually abolished in 1924 by a cease-and-desist order issued by the Federal Trade Commission to U.S. Steel Company.

80. W. Arthur Lewis, "The Diffusion of Development," 155–56.

5. The New Deal and Appalachia's Industry

1. Glen Lawhon Parker, *The Coal Industry*, 97–104; and Minton and Stuart, *Men Who Lead Labor*, 96. Also see Walls, "Central Appalachia in Advanced Capitalism," 166. Walls says that by 1927, about 38 percent of U.S. bituminous coal came from West Virginia and *eastern* Kentucky.

2. Grace Abbott, "Improvement in Rural Public Relief: The Lesson of the Coal Mining Communities," *Social Science Review* 6 (1932): 200; cited in Woodruff, *As Rare as Rain*, 176 n. 4. And Rochester, *Labor and Coal*, 118–19.

3. Rochester, *Labor and Coal*, 242 table.

4. Glen Lawhon Parker, *The Coal Industry*, 40–43.

5. Morris, *The Plight of the Bituminous Coal Miner*, 154–55.

6. Glen Lawhon Parker, *The Coal Industry*, 43–50.

7. U.S. Census of 1910, vol. 9, p. 212 table.

8. U.S. Census of 1920, vol. 11, p. 292 table.

9. Glen Lawhon Parker, *The Coal Industry*, 52–53. Machine-loaded percentages in 1940 calculated from U.S. Census of 1940, *Mineral Industries*, vol. 1, pp. 227, 263 table; and Christenson, *Economic Redevelopment in Bituminous Coal*, 144 table. On the invention and adoption of coal-loading machines, see Dix, *What's a Coal Miner to Do?*, chaps. 2 and 3.

10. Hunt, ed., *What the Coal Commission Found*, 64.

11. Rochester, *Labor and Coal*, 118–19, 242 table; and Glen Lawhon Parker, *The Coal Industry*, 56–61, 97–104.

12. Himmelberg, *The Origins of the National Recovery Administration*, 162, 188; and Dix, *What's a Coal Miner to Do?*, 187–88.

13. Himmelberg, *The Origins of the National Recovery Administration*, 189–208.

14. Hawley, *The New Deal and the Problem of Monopoly*, 20, 28–33, 81–83, 100–1, 134–36, 203–4.

15. Ibid., 205–11; and James P. Johnson, *The Politics of Soft Coal*, 13–15.

16. Bellush, *The Failure of the NRA*, 16–18.

17. James P. Johnson, *The Politics of Soft Coal*, 191. A thorough discussion of the position of John L. Lewis on coal-industry mechanization appears in Dix, *What's a Coal Miner to Do?*, 161–67, 181–84, 207–14.

18. Dubofsky and Van Tine, *John L. Lewis*, 188.

19. Duncan Kennedy (representative of the Smokeless and Appalachian Coal Association), 9 August 1933; NRA Conference on Wages and Hours, 1933, Hearing No. 49; Bituminous Coal Code of Fair Competition (NRA Code No. 24); 52.

20. Dubofsky and Van Tine, *John L. Lewis*, 190. Likewise in the *textile* code negotiations, northern interests managed to deprive southern industry of its competitive edge. The southern textile mills were coerced to pay a twelve dollars a week minimum wage, only a hair less than northern mills' thirteen dollars a week minimum wage. See Abrams, "North Carolina and the New Deal," 36–39.

21. Charles O'Neill (representative of the Northern Coal Control Association *and* the Smokeless and Appalachian Coal Association), 9 August 1933; NRA Conference on Wages and Hours, 1933, Hearing No. 49; Bituminous Coal Code of Fair Competition (NRA Code No. 24); 23, 7–8. Figures of the U.S. Bureau of Mines for 1928 show coal (including anthracite) providing 67.4 percent of U.S. energy, lignite providing 5.4 percent, oil and natural gas together providing 18.2 percent, and water power 9 percent. See Voskuil, *Minerals in Modern Industry*, 28 table.

22. Donald Richberg (NRA) and Charles O'Neill, 9 August 1933; NRA Conference on Wages and Hours, 1933, Hearing No. 49; Bituminous Coal Code of Fair Competition (NRA Code No. 24); 43, 36–37. Richberg again attacked the "open shop" on 44, 49. For the coal industry representatives' proposed clause to protect the open shop, see 18–19.

23. Gunther, *Cases and Material on Constitutional Law*, 140–57.

24. Statistical evidence for speeded-up mechanization is in James P. Johnson, *The Politics of Soft Coal*, 192 table; Glen Lawhon Parker, *The Coal Industry*, 52; and U.S. Census of 1940, *Mineral Industries*, vol. 1, p. 263 table. These three sources, when correlated with each other, reveal a late 1930s rush to mechanize coal loading in Appalachian mines. Also see Hotchkiss et al., *Mechanization, Employment, and Output*. There, Corrington Gill of the WPA reports that in West Virginia, the percentage of coal that was loaded mechanically jumped from 2 percent in 1935 to 21 percent in 1938 (vol. 1, presentation letter). See also vol. 1, pp. xxvi, 12; and vol. 2, pp. 301 graph, 345.

25. James P. Johnson, *The Politics of Soft Coal*, 190–92 tables. Johnson believes that not only in coal, but also in the U.S. economy overall, the NRA's basic premise of stim-

ulating recovery through a "cost-push" drive was chimerical. For the economy as a whole, this is borne out by Weinstein, *Recovery and Redistribution under the N.I.R.A.*

26. Harry L. Hopkins to F. W. Turner (director, West Virginia Relief Administration), 6 September 1933; NA, Federal Emergency Relief Administration (hereafter cited as FERA), State Files, West Virginia, Box 312, Folder Series 400.

27. Fisher, *After Reflation, What?*, 81 chart.

28. Lainhart et al., *Pneumoconiosis in Appalachian Bituminous Coal Miners*, 51–54, including tables and graphs. Appalachia in this instance is defined as including Pennsylvania and southeastern Ohio. A concise discussion of the link between mechanization and black lung is Dix, *What's a Coal Miner to Do?*, 104–6.

29. Cameron, "An Estimation of the Tangible Costs," 5.

30. U.S. Dept. of the Interior, Coal Mines Administration, *A Medical Survey of the Bituminous-Coal Industry.*

31. Joseph E. Martin, Jr., "Coal Miners' Pneumoconiosis."

32. Lainhart et al., *Pneumoconiosis in Appalachian Bituminous Coal Miners*, 23–27.

33. Ibid., 51–54, including tables and graphs.

34. Glen Lawhon Parker, *The Coal Industry*, 52–53.

35. As of the early 1970s, 160,000 former miners were being compensated for black lung disability, and a greater number had the disease. One estimate of the total amount of compensation paid during the 1970s was one billion dollars per year. Cameron, "An Estimation of the Tangible Costs," 96, 111.

36. Miners are now supposed to wear air filters over their mouths and noses, but many avoid using the filters. Transcribed interview conducted by author with Woodrow Mosley, 27 July 1988, Branchland, Lincoln County, West Virginia, 14–15. Transcript in Marshall University Library, Oral History of Appalachia, transcript collection, Lincoln County, West Virginia interviews.

37. Enterline, "Mortality Rates Among Coal Miners," 758–59, 765–67, including table 6. On preventive measures adopted in Britain, also see Joseph E. Martin, Jr., "Coal Miners' Pneumoconiosis," 581–83.

38. Tugwell, *Roosevelt's Revolution*, 296.

39. See Himmelberg, *The Origins of the National Recovery Administration*, 189–208.

40. Tugwell, *Roosevelt's Revolution*, 63. Documentation of economic contradictions spawned by the NRA abound in NA, NRA, State Relations Division; Correspondence: Complaints against codes, Boxes 7932–41, folders for Kentucky, Tennessee, Virginia, and West Virginia.

41. Quoted in Heilbroner, *The Making of Economic Society*, 158.

42. Weinstein, "Some Macroeconomic Impacts," 268, 272. Weinstein estimates that the NRA reduced the growth of real GNP in the U.S. at a rate of 8 percent per year.

43. Roose, *The Economics of Recession and Revival*, 144–45; and Frey, *Marketing Handbook*, 8/28 through 8/34.

6. The New Deal and Appalachia's Agriculture

1. Harvey O. Van Horn, conversation, 25 May 1991; and Berman, Conley-Spencer, and Howe, *The Monongahela National Forest*, 53–54.

2. Barnes, *A History of Roanoke*, 725.

3. Maurice Reddy (director, Kentucky Red Cross) to A. L. Schafer (director, American Red Cross Disaster Relief), 7 October 1930, quoted in Woodruff, *As Rare as Rain*, 143.

4. American Red Cross, "Kentucky Relief," 20 October 1930, cited in Woodruff, *As Rare as Rain*, 143.

5. Ann Craton, Report on Rowan County Chapter, n.d., quoted in Woodruff, *As Rare as Rain*, 143.

6. Maurice Reddy to Robert Bondy (Eastern Division, American Red Cross), 18 December 1930, quoted in Woodruff, *As Rare as Rain*, 145.

7. Dr. A. T. McCormack (Kentucky Board of Health) to Kentucky County Judges, 24 December 1930, quoted in Woodruff, *As Rare as Rain*, 145.

8. For instance, see West Virginian "Human Interest Example[s]" and county-by-county survey attached to H. D. Hatfield (senator from West Virginia) to Walter H. Newton (secretary to Herbert Hoover), 21 February 1931; in Herbert Hoover Presidential Library, West Branch, Iowa; Presidential Papers, Subject Files, Box 118, Folder "Drought Correspondence 1931, Jan.–March."

9. Mary Breckinridge, *The Quarterly Bulletin of the Frontier Nursing Service, Inc.* 6 (1931): 3–4; quoted in Woodruff, *As Rare as Rain*, 153.

10. DeWitt Smith (assistant director, Domestic Operations, American Red Cross) to Herbert Hoover, 11 February 1931; in Herbert Hoover Presidential Library, West Branch, Iowa; Presidential Papers, Subject Files, Box 118, Folder "Drought Correspondence 1931, Jan.–March." On ideological and political issues raised by the drought, see Lambert, "Hoover and Congress Debate Food Relief," 4–13.

11. Ardrey, ed., *Welcome the Traveler Home*, 146–47.

12. On West Virginia conditions: Theresa White (McDowell County Welfare Secretary and Administrator) to Loretta K. Muir (field director, West Virginia Unemployment Relief Administration), 23 and 25 September 1933; NA, FERA, State Files, West Virginia, Box 312, Folder Series 400. On East Tennessee conditions: Callahan, *TVA: Bridge Over Troubled Waters*, 45.

13. Eller, *Miners, Millhands, and Mountaineers*, 5–6, 237–38.

14. The greatest contradiction—and one that prolonged the Depression—was that between the New Deal's money-supply expansion and the NRA. As mentioned in chapter 5, the price supports written into NRA codes completely negated the growth that otherwise would have flowed during 1933–1935 from the 14 percent average annual expansion of the money supply. Weinstein estimates that the NRA retarded real GNP growth by 8 percent a year. See Weinstein, *Recovery and Redistribution under the N.I.R.A.*, 273–79.

15. Tugwell, *Roosevelt's Revolution*, 57.

16. Ibid. Harry Hopkins (to whom Tugwell refers here) ran the New Deal's Federal Emergency Relief Administration. A detailed explanation of how AAA policies displaced southern rural blacks is David R. James, "Local State Structure," 151, 164–74. Also see Johnson, Embree, and Alexander, *The Collapse of Cotton Tenancy*, 49–52; and Conrad, *The Forgotten Farmers*, 51–82, 204–9.

17. Jane Jacobs compares the New Deal's "clearance" of the South's farm-labor force to Scotland's highland clearances, which in 1792 began replacing highland tenants with sheep. Jacobs emphasizes the economic benefits entailed when workers are *pulled* to another region by jobs there—not *pushed* to places where no jobs await them. Jacobs, *Cities and the Wealth of Nations,* 79–86.

18. Rowe, *Tobacco Under the AAA,* 28, 37 maps.

19. M. L. Wilson as quoted in Hunter, "The AAA Between Neighbors," 538. Also on M. L. Wilson and the allotment idea, see Conkin, *Tomorrow a New World,* 73–84. The allotment idea went back to 1926.

20. George Sinclair Mitchell, as quoted in Hunter, "The AAA Between Neighbors," 537–38. Mitchell at the time was a colleague of Tugwell's at Columbia University. Later Mitchell worked for the U.S. Agriculture Department in North Carolina.

21. Tugwell, *Roosevelt's Revolution,* 52.

22. Later the list of farm products subject to limitation by the AAA was expanded to include rye, flax, barley, sorghum, cattle, peanuts, sugar beets, and potatoes.

23. Semple, "The Anglo-Saxons of the Kentucky Mountains," 603–4.

24. FitzGerald, *Livestock Under the AAA,* 83, 260–62; and Van L. Perkins, *Crisis in Agriculture,* 136. On corn reaching one dollar a bushel in eastern Kentucky in 1934, see Carrie Keeton (county worker), "Survey of the Rural Relief Situation in Rowan County, Kentucky," October 1935, 6; NA, BAE, Rural Relief Studies, Box 5, Folder "Rowan Co., Ky."

25. Nourse, Davis, and Black, *Three Years of the Agricultural Adjustment Administration,* 103–4, 128–30.

26. J. C. Snow (assistant Livestock Marketing Specialist, Tennessee Extension Service, Nashville) to Claude R. Wickard (chief, Corn-Hog Section, AAA, Washington), 30 March 1935; NA, Agricultural Adjustment Administration (hereafter cited as AAA), General Correspondence; 1933–35, Box 1071, Folder "Tennessee University, Snow, J. C."
When the second A A Act was passed in 1938, it authorized the continued regulation of corn (although it did not resume the regulation of hogs). The crops limited under this 1938 A A Act were to be limited whether they were grown for market or not. In a 1942 test case (Wickard v. Filburn) the Supreme Court ruled that farmers participating in AAA acreage allotments were not allowed to grow feed for their own livestock on nonallotted acres. Hughes, *American Economic History,* 459.

27. Lowitt, ed., *Journal of a Tamed Bureaucrat,* 179.

28. FitzGerald, *Livestock Under the AAA,* 83–84, 91–94.

29. Ibid., 59, 84, 129. Also an interview I conducted in January 1983 with Irwin W. Lovell, who served from 1933 to the end of the New Deal as an AAA committeeman in various programs, including the corn-hog program, in Virginia's Giles County.

30. "Regional Distribution and Description of Self-Sufficing Farms," n.d.; NA, BAE, General Correspondence, 1923–46; 1941–46, Box 664, Folder "Study—Subsistence Homesteads." This BAE study used the 1930 U.S. Census definition of a self-sufficing farm—namely, one "where the value of the [home] farm products used by the family was 50 percent or more of the total value of all products of the farm." U.S. Census

of 1930, *Agriculture,* vol. 4, p. 873. Also note that the BAE definition of Appalachia included 205 counties, whereas the definition used in the present study includes only 190 counties.

31. "Traveling Conference of the Department of Agriculture in the Southern Appalachian Region, Oct. 30–Nov. 4, 1939: Kentucky Section," Foreword, 2; NA, BAE, Appalachian Regional Office, 1934–45; Box 2, Folder "KY-030 Conferences, Southern Appalachian Traveling, Oct. 30–Nov. 4, 1939."

32. U.S. Census of Agriculture of 1935, vol. 1, county table 1; and vol. 2, county table 4. The 1930 farm population figures are for 1 April 1930, whereas the 1935 figures are for 1 January 1935.

In eastern Kentucky between 1929 and 1934, every single county saw a significant increase in the number of holdings qualifying as farms under the census definition (for which see chapter 4, note 21). In Harlan County, the number more than doubled. In Bell County, it almost doubled. And an increase of more than one-quarter took place in Carter, Floyd, Knott, Johnson, Letcher, McCreary, Perry, Pike, Whitney, and Wolfe counties.

33. H. R. Tolley (acting administrator, AAA) to Ben Kilgore (executive secretary, Kentucky Farm Bureau Federation), 26 April 1935, 2; NA, AAA, General Correspondence; 1933–35, Box 569, Folder "Ky.: Farm Bureau Federation."

34. U.S. Dept. of Agriculture, *Yearbook of Agriculture, 1935,* 702; and U.S. Dept. of Agriculture, *Agricultural Statistics, 1936,* 363.

35. Fite, "Farmer Opinion," 668–69.

36. Government intervention to hold up food prices and to support farmers' incomes continues today. These federal policies have acted to drive up the price of farmland, which, in a milieu of continuous technological innovations (itself partly caused by federal research and development), has continued forcing smaller farmers to sell out to larger farmers. Cochrane, *The Development of American Agriculture,* 390–95, 399, 416.

37. Rowe, *Tobacco Under the AAA,* 28, 37 maps.

38. John B. Hutson, transcript of 1954 interviews, Columbia University Oral History Collection, 142–43.

39. A 1927 study of 203 Laurel County, Kentucky farm families found only 22 percent of them relying entirely on farming for their income. U.S. Dept. of Agriculture, *Economic and Social Problems and Conditions of the Southern Appalachians,* 43. And Laurel was one of eastern Kentucky's least industrialized counties. In other counties, even fewer farm families relied entirely on farming.

40. John B. Hutson, transcript of 1954 interviews, Columbia University Oral History Collection, 193, 201–2. Hutson says there, "I think Alger Hiss and I were looking for some way—some new act—under which we could carry on a Triple-A program, which we could amend and would give us the authority to continue the adjustment program" (193). In this "new act we merely proposed [that] instead of taxing the commodity—which the Supreme Court had decided was unconstitutional—we would get that money from the federal treasury" (202).

41. B. A. Hensley (county agent, Putnam County, West Virginia) to C. E. Stockdale (West Virginia state executive officer, AAA), 2 November 1938; NA, AAA, General Correspondence; 1936–38, Box 997, Folder "WVU, Stockdale, C. E."

42. U.S. Census of 1940, *Agriculture*, vol. 3, pp. 784–85.

43. Cockrane, *The Development of American Agriculture*, 128 table. These figures for 1935 and 1940 each represent three-year averages centered on the year specified.

44. U.S. Census of 1940, *Agriculture*, vol. 3, pp. 784–85.

45. Fite, *American Farmers*, 71–73. Later, further chemicalization of farming occurred in the 1940s through DDT. Then in the early 1950s a range of highly toxic new chemicals came on line (p. 112). In the early 1970s most allotment programs were dropped when Soviet purchases of U.S. grain soared. Tobacco acreage, however, is still allotted in 1993.

46. U.S. Census of 1940, *Agriculture*, vol. 3, pp. 717–18.

47. U.S. Census of 1930, *Distribution*, vol. 2, pp. 113–14.

48. Fite, *American Farmers*, 72.

49. Taylor, "Depression and New Deal in Pendleton," 145.

50. On the acute lime shortage in most of West Virginia, see C. E. Stockdale (West Virginia state executive officer, AAA) to W. G. Finn (AAA), 15 December 1937; Leland Booth (West Virginia Farm Bureau) to C. E. Stockdale, 28 February 1938; and W. A. Minor (AAA) to C. E. Stockdale, 25 July 1938; NA, AAA, General Correspondence; 1936–38, Box 995, Folder "West, A. F." West Virginia's lime sources are displayed on the West Virginia Geological Survey map "Natural Resources of West Virginia," 1987.

51. On lime-access problems in eastern Kentucky, see "Traveling Conference of the Department of Agriculture in the Southern Appalachian Region, Oct. 30–Nov. 4, 1939," sheet attached to "Statement," and also 30; NA, BAE, Appalachian Regional Office, 1934–45; Box 2, Folder "KY-030 Conferences, Southern Appalachian Traveling, Oct. 30–Nov. 4, 1939."

52. As of 1936 in West Virginia, a federal subsidy of up to $2.50 per year was allowed per acre limed. The federal subsidy had extensive influence in popularizing liming in Appalachia. This is obvious from the U.S. Census of 1940, *Agriculture*, vol. 1, pts. 3 and 4, county table 10, lines 46–51; as compared with the 1930 Census, *Agriculture*, vol. 2, pt. 2, county table 12, lines 8–11.

53. L. C. Gray (Division of Land Economics, BAE) to Helen M. Dingham (executive secretary, Conference of Southern Mountain Workers), 19 December 1930; NA, BAE, General Correspondence, 1923–46; 1923–35, Box 253, Folder "Conference of Southern Mountain Workers (Temporary Folder)."

54. Gray and Clayton, "Introduction," in U.S. Dept. of Agriculture, *Economic and Social Problems and Conditions of the Southern Appalachians*, 6. See also 2–5.

55. J. Russell Smith, "Farming Appalachia," 333.

56. Ibid., 334–35. Also see J. Russell Smith, *North America*, 209 including note, 326–27; and J. Russell Smith, *Tree Crops*.

57. J. Russell Smith, *North America*, 209 note 9.

58. Arthur E. Morgan, speech to Technical Club, Engineering Club and other groups, Madison, Wisconsin, 1 October 1934, quoted in Morgan, *The Making of the TVA*, 62. Arthur Morgan served as TVA chairman 1933–1938. A fuller account of the TVA "tree crop" episode appears in Arthur E. Morgan, "Vagaries: Number Four: A Forest Policy and Culture Which Might Have Been," typed MS in the archives of Community Service, Inc. of Yellow Springs, Ohio.

59. Morgan, *The Making of the TVA*, 63. Also see Richards, "The Future of TVA Forestry," 648–52. On the division of power among the three TVA directors, see Selznick, *TVA and the Grass Roots*, 147–51; and Whisnant, *Modernizing the Mountaineer*, 58–61.

60. Ruttan, "The TVA and Regional Development," 152–53, 155–56; and Selznick, *TVA and the Grass Roots*, 98–99.

61. Ruttan, "The TVA and Regional Development," 157.

62. Smith and Phillips, *North America*, 258.

63. Figures for 1929 from Charles S. Johnson et al., *Statistical Atlas of Southern Counties*, 43–54, 87–137, 177–93, 207–22, 245–61. This volume omits West Virginia, whose figures are thus taken from the U.S. Census of 1930, *Agriculture*, vol. 2, pt. 2, 319–23.

64. U.S. Census of Agriculture of 1959, Final Report, vol. 1, pts. 24, 25, 26, 28, 30, 31, and 32: Counties. County table 11, pts. 1 and 2.

65. U.S. Census of Agriculture of 1982, vol. 1, pts. 1, 10, 17, 33, 42, and 48. County Data, table 15. This census, like others in recent years, includes grass for silage and green crop with its harvested-hay acreage. With its harvested-corn acreage, this census includes corn for silage where it is of a significant amount.

7. The Welfare of Rural Appalachia

1. Quoted in Mertz, *New Deal Policy and Southern Rural Poverty*, 253. See also 226–27, 229–30, 235.

2. U.S. Dept. of Agriculture, *Economic and Social Problems and Conditions of the Southern Appalachians*.

3. Regarding an early 1935 rather than early 1936 beginning of phase two in agricultural adjustment policy, see Kirkendall, *Social Scientists and Farm Politics*, 136–40; and John B. Hutson, transcript of 1954 interviews, Columbia University Oral History Collection, 201–2, 209.

4. U.S. Dept. of Agriculture, AAA, Program Planning Division, *Regional Problems in Agricultural Adjustment*, frontispiece map.

5. Two cogent critical summaries of the diagnosis and policies of the Appalachian Regional Commission are Walls, "Central Appalachia in Advanced Capitalism," 47–61; and Whisnant, *Modernizing the Mountaineer*, chaps. 5 and 6.

6. See Glen Lawhon Parker, *The Coal Industry*, 42 chart.

7. Lainhart et al., *Pneumoconiosis in Appalachian Bituminous Coal Miners*, 23–28, 47–54, including tables and graphs.

8. Conkin, *Tomorrow a New World*, 35–36.

9. Frame, *West Virginia Agricultural and Rural Life*, pt. 2, 42. Also see 62–63.

10. Morgan, *The Small Community*, xii, 55–61, 105–6.

11. Ibid., 75.

12. Morgan and his wife spent many years planning a private school in Massachusetts, but before that plan reached fruition he was appointed president of Antioch College in Yellow Springs, Ohio, a post he held 1920–1936.

13. David Lilienthal, "Some Observations on the TVA," address to TVA employees, Knoxville, 12 June 1936, quoted in McCraw, *Morgan vs. Lilienthal*, 65.

14. Arthur E. Morgan, "Some Suggestions for a Program to Promote Better Opportunities for Rural Young People Especially in the Southern Highlands," n.d., 2; in Arthur E. Morgan Papers, Antioch College Library, Box III B3, Folder by title of paper.

15. Arthur E. Morgan, "Group Industries' Problems and Their Solution," speech delivered at the University of Tennessee, Knoxville, 9 November 1933, p. 10; copy at the TVA Technical Library, Knoxville, in Arthur E. Morgan, "Speeches and Writings," vol. 1 (of 2), section 4. A copy is also located in the Arthur E. Morgan Papers, Antioch College Library, Yellow Springs, Ohio.

16. Ibid., 14. For further details on Morgan's local-money proposal and the controversy that followed, see Arthur E. Morgan, "Vagaries: Number Two: Local Economy in the TVA," typed MS, copy in the archives of Community Service, Inc. of Yellow Springs, Ohio. A slightly revised account appears in Morgan, *The Making of the TVA,* 58–59. Beyond company-store scrips, other local monies have circulated in various parts of Appalachia at various times. In North Carolina's Watauga County during the 1910s, for instance, a store at Valle Crucis "issued its own money of account, a metal scrip called 'lightweights,' to local farmers who traded at the store." To earn "lightweights," farmers brought in mainly apples and dairy products. John Alexander Williams, letter, 17 December 1992.

17. Fisher, *Stamp Scrip,* 38–39.

18. Davidson and Leonard, "Cumberland Homesteads," 83. On the significant decline of West Virginia coal production in 1933 (while Pennsylvania, Indiana, and Illinois were all gaining slightly), see Glen Lawhon Parker, *The Coal Industry,* 42 chart. Kentucky and Ohio lost coal tonnage also, but only slightly.

19. For a detailed account, see Conkin, *Tomorrow a New World.*

20. Howell, "The New Deal for Tenant Farmers." See especially 8–17 on a self-organized group of displaced farmers who achieved success in Grundy County, Tennessee with the help of rural rehabilitation loans.

21. "Progress Report of the West Virginia Land-Use Planning Advisory Committee and its Subcommittees in the Development of a Unified State Program . . ." (mimeograph), 1 June 1941; NA, BAE, Appalachian Regional Office, 1934–45; Box 5C, Folder "WV-184-041 Reports."

22. C. R. Draper "A Study of the People and Conditions in a Low-Income Farming Area in the Southern Tip of Lewis County, West Virginia" (hectograph), Weston, West Virginia, 1941, 5, 7, 14, 16, 20, including tables; NA, BAE, Appalachian Regional Office, 1934–45; Box 5C, Folder "WV-184-041 Reports." U.S. and West Virginia population age data from the U.S. Census of 1950, *Population,* vol. 2, pt. 1, p. 93; and pt. 48, p. 30. My figures for southern Lewis County exclude two affluent families in the district who combined commercial farming with part-time wage work, each earning about three thousand dollars in money a year. No other family in any category earned more than eight hundred dollars in money a year.

23. Salstrom, "Subsistence Farming, Capitalism, and the Depression," 386.

24. C. R. Draper, "A Study of the People and Conditions in a Low-Income Farming Area in the Southern Tip of Lewis County, West Virginia" (hectograph), Weston, West Virginia, 1941, 7; NA, BAE, Appalachian Regional Office, 1934–45; Box 5C, Folder "WV-184-041 Reports."

25. Ibid., 7–8.

26. Ibid.

27. Figures from the papers of Matthew M. Neely, West Virginia University Library, West Virginia and Regional History Collection, A. & M. No. 1414, Box 9, Folder "Stock Material." CWA input drawn from Carl Riggs, "Final Report of the Work Projects Administration in West Virginia," 16 April 1943, 27; NA, WPA, Final State Reports, Box 7.

28. Carl Riggs, "Final State Report of the Work Projects Administration in West Virginia," 16 April 1943, 83; NA, WPA, Final State Reports, Box 7. Another 3 percent of the WPA's 1937 West Virginia workers are identifiable as young farm residents whom the Depression had prevented from entering the work force.

29. The U.S. Census of 1940, *Agriculture*, vol. 3, p. 37 gives the West Virginia farm population as 27 percent of that state's total population. Among West Virginia's WPA workers in 1938, besides the 23 percent "displaced from agriculture" we must count here the 3 percent of WPA workers who lived on farms but who had not yet officially entered the work force due to the Depression. This gives 26 percent of the WPA's West Virginia workers as farm residents, only 1 percent less than farm residents represented in West Virginia's total population.

30. "Progress Report of the West Virginia Land-Use Planning Advisory Committee and its Subcommittee in the Development of a Unified State Program . . ." (mimeograph), 1 June 1941, 36; NA, BAE, Appalachian Regional Office, 1934–45; Box 5C, Folder "WV-184-041 Reports." The thirty-five-dollar-an-acre financial incentive for tree planting as of June 1941 marked an advance over earlier incentives. In 1936 the rate had been only five dollars per acre, even for planting trees on crop land. West Virginia Extension, Agricultural News Service, press release, "Soil Practises [*sic*] Approved by Sec'y Agriculture," 11–16 May 1936, West Virginia University Library, West Virginia and Regional History Collection, Papers of the West Virginia Country Life Movement, A. & M. No. 3050, Box 2, Folder "Miscellaneous."

31. Not all of these species were AAA-approved for all of West Virginia. Only yellow poplar and black locust were approved for the entire state. For details see C. E. Stockdale to W. G. Finn, 26 August 1936, with attached "Recommended Practices for Planting of Forest Trees in West Virginia," and W. G. Finn to C. E. Stockdale, 16 September 1936, granting approval for those practices; NA, AAA, General Correspondence; 1936–38, Box 995, Folder "West, A–F."

32. "Land-Use Planning Circular for Lewis County, West Virginia (Physical, Economical and Sociological Reference Information)" (mimeographed), June 1939, 2. Prepared cooperatively by the Extension Economist, West Virginia Agricultural Extension Service, and the Associated Land-Use Planning Specialist for West Virginia, Northeast Region, BAE. Copy in NA, BAE, Appalachian Regional Office, 1934–45; Box 5C, Folder "WV-104-04 Land Use Planning Research or Studies."

In addition, a booklet for use throughout West Virginia recommended slopes of up to forty degrees as "suitable for pastures provided a good sod can be maintained." G. G. Pohlman, *Land Classification in West Virginia based on Use and Agricultural Value* (printed booklet), Agricultural Experiment Station, College of Agriculture, West Virginia University, Morgantown.

33. Thomas D. Clark, *The Greening of the South*, 80.

34. West Virginia Department of Agriculture, *Market Bulletin* 74, no. 2 (February 1990): 1–2; data cited from U.S. Department of Agriculture, *National Resources Inventory*, 1977, 1982, and 1987.

35. Remarks by J. C. McAmis (University of Tennessee Extension Division) at a "Round Table on Agriculture," quoted in Maggard, "From Farmers to Miners," 53. Later, in the 1930s, McAmis directed the TVA's Agricultural Relations Department, working closely with Harcourt A. Morgan.

36. Davidson and Leonard, "Cumberland Homesteads," 89–90.

37. D. T. Painter (TVA supervisor) to Dr. T. B. Hutcheson (Virginia Polytechnic Institute), n.d.; as quoted in "Poor Land—A Handicap to Our People" (mimeographed), County Agricultural Program Planning Group Discussion Leaflet #1, Agricultural Extension Div., V.P.I., January 1939, 12–13; NA, BAE, Appalachian Regional Office, 1934–45; Folder "Virginia 1939, County Planning Program." This research by D. T. Painter took place on Dunmore soil slopes at 15 to 37 percent inclines in Wythe and Washington Counties, Virginia. The amount of precipitation in that locale averaged about forty-four inches annually. Painter made his follow-up vegetative counts in June 1938 but he does not specify the dates on which his fifteen-month soil erosion and water run-off measurements began and ended. Also unspecified is whether 16 or 20 percent phosphate was used.

38. West Virginia Extension, Agricultural News Service, press release, "Soil Practises [*sic*] Approved by Sec'y Agriculture," 11–16 May 1936; West Virginia University Library, West Virginia and Regional History Collection, Papers of the West Virginia Country Life Movement, A. & M. No. 3050, Box 2, Folder "Miscellaneous."

39. J. Russell Smith, "Farming Appalachia," 333; and J. Russell Smith, *North America*, 209 including note, 326–27. Also see J. Russell Smith, *Tree Crops*, where Smith explores general principles for mountain and hill agriculture.

40. C. E. Stockdale to W. G. Finn, 26 August 1936, and W. G. Finn to C. E. Stockdale, 16 September 1936; NA, AAA, General Correspondence; 1936–38, Box 995, Folder "West, A–F."

41. J. Russell Smith, "Farming Appalachia," 334–35. Also of interest is a more recent work, Douglas and Hart, *Forest Farming*.

Conclusion

1. Turner, *The Significance of Sections in American History*, 38.

2. U.S. Censuses of Population, 1840 and 1880.

3. U.S. Censuses of Population and Agriculture, 1840, 1850, and 1880.

4. U.S. Censuses of Agriculture, 1850 and 1880.

5. Ronald L. Lewis, conversation, November 1990.

6. Stuart McGehee (Eastern Regional Coal Archives, Bluefield, West Virginia), letter, 22 December 1988.

7. John A. James, *Money and Capital Markets in Postbellum America*, 22. For the data outlined above, see 22–39. Also see Studenski and Krooss, *Financial History of the United States*, 176–91; and Chapman and Westerfield, *Branch Banking*, 58–64.

8. U.S. Bureau of the Census, *Historical Statistics of the United States: Colonial Times to 1970*, pt. 2, pp. 993, 1020.

9. Hughes, *American Economic History*, 71–79, 194–213. Also see Lester, *Monetary Experiments*, 17–33, 56–160, 287–89.

10. Otto and Anderson, "Slash and Burn Cultivation in the Highlands South," 139–140.

11. Ibid., 135 map; and U.S. Census of 1880, vol. 3, table 7.

12. A summary of Gramsci's concept of "historical blocs" is in Lears, "The Concept of Cultural Hegemony," 571.

13. Simon, "The Development of Underdevelopment."

14. Gunnar Myrdal calls this an automatic "backwash effect" suffered by less developed areas as a result of increasing productivity in the more developed areas of the same country. Myrdal, *Rich Lands and Poor*, 26–29.

15. Transcribed interview by author with Mabel Elkins at Myra, Lincoln County, West Virginia, 26 July 1988, 17–18. Transcript in Marshall University Library; Oral History of Appalachia, transcript collection; Lincoln County, West Virginia interviews.

16. Galpin et al., *A Study of the People of West Virginia*, 29.

17. See, for example, Morris, *The Plight of the Bituminous Coal Miner*, 198.

18. "Southern Appalachian Economic and Social Problems Discussed in Government Report," U.S. Agriculture Dept. press release, 25 March 1935, 4–5; copy in NA, BAE, Southern Appalachian Study, 1929–35; Box 140, Folder "1932–35." And Eller, *Miners, Millhands, and Mountaineers*, 225. The 1929–1935 study defined Appalachia as 205 counties, fifteen more than the present book. That study assumed that "with improved standards of living, increased accessibility, more external contacts, and better educational preparation for various types of economic pursuits, increasing numbers of the population will seek their livelihood outside of the region." Gray and Clayton, "Introduction," in U.S. Dept. of Agriculture, *Economic and Social Problems and Conditions of the Southern Appalachians*, 5.

19. Eller, *Miners, Millhands, and Mountaineers*, 226 note 8.

20. A convincing argument against the economic usefulness of the concept of "economic exploitation" is Roemer, "Should Marxists Be Interested in Exploitation?"

21. Examples of Appalachian people migrating elsewhere with reluctance are given by Jones, *The Dispossessed*, 99–101, 217, 229; and by Coles, *The South Goes North*, chap. 6.

22. *U.S. Census of Agriculture: 1959, Final Report—Vol. 1—Part 25—Counties: West Virginia*, 138–39, 148–49.

23. Lozier and Althouse, "Social Enforcement of Behavior Toward Elders in an Appalachian Mountain Settlement," 79. More details on 76–77.

24. Heilbroner, *The Making of Economic Society*, 147 including note.

25. Tugwell, *Roosevelt's Revolution*, 61.

26. Ibid., 61–63.

27. Poling, ed., *West Virginia: Economic-Statistical Profile, 1987*, 502 map; and *Taiwan Statistical Data Book, 1987*, 17–18 tables.

28. Moulton, *Income and Economic Progress*, 125–26.

29. Willis, *The Theory and Practice of Central Banking*, 456–62, 467–68.

30. Sperling, "West German Foreign Economic Policy during the Reagan Administration," 94.

31. McKay, Hill, and Buckler, *A History of World Societies,* second edition, Vol. C, 1271 graph.

32. Van Goethem, *The Americanization of World Business,* 75.

33. DeFrank and Duval, "West Virginia in a Global Economy: The Impact of Foreign Trade and Investment," 1.

Bibliography

Unpublished Primary Sources Cited

Antioch College Library, Yellow Springs, Ohio. Papers of Arthur E. Morgan.

Columbia University Oral History Collection. Transcript of John B. Hutson interviews, conducted in 1954. (Hutson was chief of the Tobacco Section of the AAA.)

Community Service, Inc., Yellow Springs, Ohio. Archives.

Herbert Hoover Presidential Library, West Branch, Iowa. Presidential Papers, Subject Files.

Interview Notes Held by the Author. Irwin W. Lovell of Giles County, Virginia. Interviewed in January 1983.

Marshall University Library, Special Collections, Huntington, West Virginia. Oral History of Appalachia, Transcript Collection. Lincoln County, West Virginia, interviews. Two interviews with Ray and Mabel Elkins, 18 and 26 July 1988, Myra, West Virginia (interviewed by Paul Salstrom); Interview with Woodrow Mosley, 27 July 1988, Branchland, West Virginia (interviewed by Paul Salstrom).

Tennessee Valley Authority Technical Library, Knoxville, Tennessee. Arthur E. Morgan holdings.

United States National Archives.
    Records of the Agricultural Adjustment Administration. Record Group 145.
        General Correspondence (entry 1).
    Records of the Bureau of Agricultural Economics. Record Group 83.
        General Correspondence (entry 19).
        Rural Relief Studies (entry 156).
        Southern Appalachian Study, 1929–1935 (entry 180).
        Appalachian Regional Office, 1934–1945 (entry 266).
    Records of the Federal Emergency Relief Administration and Works Progress Administration. Record Group 69.
        State Files.
    Records of the National Recovery Administration. Record Group 9.
        Code Record Section. Conference on Wages and Hours, 1933. Hearings.
        State Relations Division (entry 101).
    Records of the Works Progress Administration. Record Group 69.
        Final State Reports.

West Virginia Public Radio, Charleston, West Virginia. Commentary transcripts.

West Virginia University Library, West Virginia and Regional History Collection, Morgantown, West Virginia.

Papers of Matthew M. Neely (U.S. senator from West Virginia, 1923–1929, 1931–1941), A. & M. No. 1414.

Papers of the West Virginia Country Life Movement, 1913–1963. A. & M. No. 3050.

Secondary Sources and Published Primary Sources

Abernethy, Thomas Perkins. "The Early Development of Commerce and Banking in Tennessee." *Mississippi Valley Historical Review* 14 (1927): 311–25.

———. *From Frontier to Plantation in Tennessee: A Study in Frontier Democracy.* Chapel Hill: University of North Carolina Press, 1932.

———. *The South in the New Nation, 1789–1819.* Baton Rouge: Louisiana State University Press, 1961.

———. *Three Virginia Frontiers.* Baton Rouge: Louisiana State University Press, 1940. Reprint. Gloucester, Mass.: Peter Smith, 1962.

Abrams, Douglas Carl. "North Carolina and the New Deal, 1932–1940." Ph.D. diss., University of Maryland, 1981.

Ackerman, Edward A. *Japan's National Resources and Their Relation to Japan's Economic Future.* Chicago: University of Chicago Press, 1953.

Alavi, Hamza. "Capitalism and Colonial Transformation." Paper presented at the Seminar on Underdevelopment and Subsistence Reproduction in Southeast Asia, April 1978, University of Bielefeld, Germany.

Ambler, Charles E. *West Virginia: Stories and Biographies.* Chicago: Rand McNally, 1942.

Ambler, Charles E., and Festus P. Summers. *West Virginia: The Mountain State.* 2d ed. Englewood Cliffs, N.J.: Prentice-Hall, 1958.

Appleby, Joyce. *Capitalism and a New Social Order: The Republican Vision of the 1790s.* New York: New York University Press, 1984.

Ardery, Julia S., ed. *Welcome the Traveler Home: Jim Garland's Story of the Kentucky Mountains.* Lexington: University Press of Kentucky, 1983.

Atherton, Lewis E. *The Southern Country Store, 1800–1860.* Baton Rouge: Louisiana State University Press, 1949.

Bailey, Kenneth R. "A Judicious Mixture: Negroes and Immigrants in the West Virginia Mines, 1880–1917." In *Blacks in Appalachia,* edited by William H. Turner and Edward J. Cabbell. Lexington: University Press of Kentucky, 1985.

Ball, Richard A. "The Southern Appalachian Folk Subculture as a Tension-Reducing Way of Life." In *Change in Rural Appalachia: Implications for Action Programs*, edited by John D. Photiadis and Harry K. Schwarzweller. Philadelphia: University of Pennsylvania Press, 1970.

Banks, Alan J. "Class and Change in a Southern Region: Eastern Kentucky, 1870–1930." Unpublished paper.

Barnhart, John D. "Recent Industrial Growth and Politics in the Southern Appalachian Region." *Mississippi Valley Historical Review* 17 (1931): 581–94.

Barnes, Raymond P. *A History of Roanoke*. Radford, Va.: Commonwealth Press, 1968.

Barns, William D. *The West Virginia State Grange: The First Century, 1873–1973*. Morgantown, W.Va.: Privately published, 1973.

Barone, Charles A. *Marxist Thought on Imperialism: Survey and Critique*. Armonk, N.Y.: M. E. Sharpe, 1985.

Barron, Hal S. "Staying Down on the Farm: Social Processes of Settled Rural Life in the Nineteenth-Century North." In *The Countryside in the Age of Capitalist Transformation: Essays in the Social History of Rural America*, edited by Steven Hahn and Jonathan Prude. Chapel Hill: University of North Carolina Press, 1985.

Bateman, Fred. "Improvement in American Dairy Farming, 1850–1910: A Quantitative Analysis." *Journal of Economic History* 28 (1968): 255–73.

Bauzon, Kenneth E., and Charles Frederick Abel. "Dependency: History, Theory, and a Reappraisal." In *Dependency Theory and the Return of High Politics*, edited by Mary Ann Tetreault and Charles Frederick Abel. Westport, Conn.: Greenwood Press, 1986.

Beaver, Patricia Duane. *Rural Community in the Appalachian South*. Lexington: University Press of Kentucky, 1986.

Bellush, Bernard. *The Failure of the NRA*. New York: Norton, 1975.

Benedict, Murray R. *Farm Policies in the United States, 1790–1950: A Study of their Origins and Development*. New York: Twentieth Century Fund, 1953.

Berman, Gillian Mace, Melissa Conley-Spencer, and Barbara Howe. *The Monongahela National Forest, 1915–1990*. Morgantown: West Virginia University, Public History Program, March 1992.

Berry, Thomas Senior. *Western Prices Before 1861: A Study of the Cincinnati Market*. Cambridge: Harvard University Press, 1943.

Billings, Dwight, Kathleen Blee, and Louis Swanson. "Culture, Family, and Community in Preindustrial Appalachia." *Appalachian Journal* 13 (1986): 154–70.

The Black Diamond 60, no. 25 (22 June 1918). (Coal industry journal.)

Blethen, H. Tyler, and Curtis W. Wood, Jr. "The Pioneer Experience to 1851." In *The History of Jackson County,* edited by Max R. Williams. Sylva, N.C.: Jackson County Historical Society, 1987.

————. "Scotch-Irish Society in Southwestern Carolina, 1780–1840." Unpublished paper. N.d.

————. "A Trader on the Western Carolina Frontier." In *Appalachian Frontiers: Settlement, Society, and Development in the Preindustrial Era,* edited by Robert D. Mitchell. Lexington: University Press of Kentucky, 1991.

Boeke, J. H. *Economics and Economic Policy of Dual Societies as Exemplified by Indonesia.* New York: Institute of Pacific Relations, 1953.

Bogart, Ernest L, and Donald L. Kemmerer. *Economic History of the American People.* New York: Longmans, Green, 1942.

Bogue, Donald J. "Economic Areas as a Tool for Research and Planning." *American Sociological Review* 15 (1950): 409–16.

Bogue, Donald J., and Calvin L. Beale. *Economic Areas of the United States.* New York: Free Press of Glencoe, 1961.

Boserup, Ester. *The Conditions of Agricultural Growth.* Chicago: Aldine, 1965.

Bowman, Mary Jean, and W. Warren Haynes, *Resources and People in East Kentucky.* Baltimore: Johns Hopkins Press, 1963.

Brenner, Robert. "The Social Basis of Economic Development." In *Analytical Marxism,* edited by John Roemer. Cambridge: Cambridge University Press, 1986.

Brown, James S. "The Family Behind the Migrant." *In Appalachia in the Sixties: Decade of Reawakening,* edited by David S. Walls and John B. Stephenson. Lexington: University Press of Kentucky, 1972.

Brown, James S., and George A. Hillery, Jr. "The Great Migration, 1940–1960." In *The Southern Appalachian Region: A Survey,* edited by Thomas R. Ford. Lexington: University of Kentucky Press, 1962.

Bush, Florence Cope. *Dorie: Woman of the Mountains.* Sevierville, Tenn.: Nandel Publishing, 1988.

Bushman, Richard L. *From Puritan to Yankee: Character and the Social Order in Connecticut, 1690–1765.* Cambridge: Harvard University Press, 1967.

Butler, P. H. "Reminiscences." *Hickory & Lady Slippers* 4, bk. 2 (1979): 14–69. (Reprinted from the *Widen (W.Va.) News,* Jan. 1936–Dec. 1938.)

Callahan, North. *TVA: Bridge Over Troubled Waters.* South Brunswick, N.J.: A. S. Barnes, 1980.

Cameron, Robert B. "An Estimation of the Tangible Costs of Black Lung Disease Related Disability to the Bituminous Coal Mine Operators of Appalachia." Appalachian Resources Project, University of Tennessee, Publication 47, 15 June 1976.

Caudill, Harry M., *Night Comes to the Cumberlands: A Biography of a Depressed Area.* Boston: Little, Brown, 1963.

Chandler, Alfred D., Jr. "The Organization of Manufacturing and Transportation." In *Economic Change During the Civil War Era,* edited by David T. Gilchrist and W. David Lewis. Greenville, Del.: Eleutherian Mills and Hagley Foundation, 1965.

Chapman, John M., and Ray B. Westerfield. *Branch Banking: Its Historical and Theoretical Position in America and Abroad.* New York: Harper & Brothers, 1942.

Chirot, Daniel. *Social Change in the Twentieth Century.* New York: Harcourt Brace Jovanovich, 1977.

Christenson, C. L. *Economic Redevelopment in Bituminous Coal: The Special Case of Technological Advance in United States Coal Mines, 1930–1960.* Cambridge: Harvard University Press, 1962.

Clark, Blanche Henry. *The Tennessee Yeomen, 1840–1860.* Nashville: Vanderbilt University Press, 1942. Reprint. New York: Octagon, 1971.

Clark, Christopher. "Household Economy, Market Exchange and the Rise of Capitalism in the Connecticut Valley, 1800–1860." *Journal of Social History* 13 (1979): 169–89.

———. *The Roots of Rural Capitalism: Western Massachusetts, 1780–1860.* Ithaca: Cornell University Press, 1990.

Clark, Thomas D. *The Greening of the South: The Recovery of Land and Forest.* Lexington: University Press of Kentucky, 1984.

Clarkson, Roy B. *Tumult on the Mountains: Lumbering in West Virginia, 1770–1920.* Parsons, W.Va.: McClain Printing, 1964.

Cochrane, Willard W. *The Development of American Agriculture: A Historical Analysis.* Minneapolis: University of Minnesota Press, 1979.

Cohen, Marjorie Griffin. *Women's Work, Markets, and Economic Development in Nineteenth-Century Ontario.* Toronto: University of Toronto Press, 1988.

Coles, Robert. *The South Goes North.* Vol. 3 of *The Children of Crisis.* Boston: Little, Brown, 1970.

Congressional Globe. 46 vols. Washington, D.C., 1834–73. 32d Cong. 1st Session.

Conkin, Paul K. *Tomorrow a New World: The New Deal Community Program.* Ithaca: Cornell University Press, 1959.

Conrad, David Eugene. *The Forgotten Farmers: The Story of Sharecroppers in the New Deal.* Urbana: University of Illinois Press, 1965.

Cooper, William J., Jr., and Thomas E. Terrell. *The American South: A History.* New York: McGraw-Hill, 1991.

Corbin, David Alan. *Life, Work, and Rebellion in the Coal Fields: The Southern West Virginia Miners, 1880–1922.* Urbana: University of Illinois Press, 1981.

Crawford, Martin. "Wealth, Slaveholding and Power in the Southern Mountains: Ashe County, North Carolina in 1860–1861." Paper presented at the Ninth Annual Appalachian Studies Conference, March 1986, Appalachian State University.

Cummings, Joe. "Community and the Nature of Change: Sevier County, Tennessee, in the 1890s." *East Tennessee Historical Society Publications* 58–59 (1986–87): 66–88.

Cuppett, Rearden S. "Harrison Hagans and His Times." Master's thesis, West Virginia University, 1933.

Davidson, Dwight M., Jr., and Olen E. Leonard. "Cumberland Homesteads." In *A Place on Earth: A Critical Appraisal of Subsistence Homesteads,* edited by Russell Lord and Paul H. Johnstone. Washington, D.C.: Bureau of Agricultural Economics, 1942.

Davis Coal and Coke Company. *Our Own People: The Monthly Magazine of the Employes of the Davis Coal and Coke Company* 3 and 4 (1918 and 1919).

DeFrank, Anthony, and Robert D. Duval. "West Virginia in a Global Economy: The Impact of Foreign Trade and Investment." *West Virginia Public Affairs Reporter* 6, no. 2 (Spring 1989). Issued by the Institute for Public Affairs, West Virginia University, Morgantown.

DiMarco, Luis Eugenio, ed. *International Economics and Development: Essays in Honor of Raúl Prebisch.* New York: Academic Press, 1972. (Contains bibliography of writings by Raúl Prebisch.)

Dix, Keith. *What's a Coal Miner to Do?: The Mechanization of Coal Mining.* Pittsburgh: University of Pittsburgh Press, 1988.

Dodge, J. R. *West Virginia: Its Farms, Forests, Mines and Oil-Wells.* Philadelphia: J. B. Lippincott, 1865.

Douglas, J. Sholto, and Robert A. de J. Hart. *Forest Farming: Towards a Solution to Problems of World Hunger and Conservation.* London: Watkins, 1976.

Dubofsky, Melvyn, and Warren Van Tine. *John L. Lewis: A Biography.* New York: Quadrangle/New York Times Book, 1977.

Earle, Carville. *Geographical Inquiry and American Historical Problems.* Stanford: Stanford University Press, 1992.

———. "Regional Economic Development West of the Appalachians, 1815–1860." In *North America: The Historical Geography of a Changing Continent,* edited by Robert D. Mitchell and Paul A. Groves. Totowa, N.J.: Rowman and Littlefield, 1987.

Eller, Ronald D. *Miners, Millhands, and Mountaineers: Industrialization of the Appalachian South, 1880–1930.* Knoxville: University of Tennessee Press, 1982.

Enterline, Philip E. "Mortality Rates Among Coal Miners." *American Journal of Public Health* 54 (1964): 758–68.

Faragher, John Mack. *Sugar Creek: Life on the Illinois Prairie.* New Haven: Yale University Press, 1986.

Fields, Gary. *Poverty, Inequality, and Development.* Cambridge: Cambridge University Press, 1980.

Fisher, Irving. *After Reflation, What?* New York: Adelphi, 1933.

———. *Stamp Scrip.* New York: Adelphi, 1933.

Fite, Gilbert C. *American Farmers: The New Minority.* Bloomington: University of Indiana Press, 1981.

———. "Farmer Opinion and the Agricultural Adjustment Act, 1933." *Mississippi Valley Historical Review* 48 (1962): 656–73.

FitzGerald, D. A. *Livestock Under the AAA.* Washington, D.C.: Brookings Institution, 1935.

Ford, Thomas R., ed. *The Southern Appalachian Region: A Survey.* Lexington: University of Kentucky Press, 1962.

Frame, Nat T. *West Virginia Agricultural and Rural Life.* 2 pts. in 1 vol. Bound copy in stacks of West Virginia University Library, West Virginia and Regional History Collection.

Frank, Andre Gunder. *Crisis: In the Third World.* New York: Holmes and Meier, 1981.

———. *On Capitalist Underdevelopment.* Bombay: Oxford University Press, 1975.

Friedman, Milton, and Anna Jacobson Schwartz. *Monetary Statistics of the United States: Estimates, Sources, Methods.* New York: National Bureau of Economic Research, 1970.

Frey, Albert Wesley. *Marketing Handbook.* New York: Ronald Press, 1965.

Galbraith, John Kenneth. *Money: Whence It Came, Where It Went.* Boston: Houghton, Mifflin, 1975.

Gallman, Robert E. "Changes in Total U.S. Agricultural Productivity in the Nineteenth Century." *Agricultural History* 46 (1972): 191–210.

———. "Self-Sufficiency in the Cotton Economy of the Antebellum South." *Agricultural History* 44 (1970): 5–23.

Galpin, S. L., et al. *A Study of the People of West Virginia.* Charleston: State Planning Board of West Virginia, 1937.

Garland, Jim. *See* Ardrey, Julia S., ed.

Gaventa, John. *Power and Powerlessness: Quiescence and Rebellion in an Appalachian Valley.* Urbana: University of Illinois Press, 1980.

Gibson, Thomas. *Sacrifice and Sharing in the Philippine Highlands: Religion and Society among the Buid of Mindoro.* London: Athlone Press, 1986.

Gillenwater, Mack Henry. "A Cultural and Historical Geography of Mining Settlements in the Pocahontas Coal Field of Southern West Virginia." Ph.D. diss., University of Tennessee, 1972.

Grant, Charles S. *Democracy in the Connecticut Frontier Town of Kent.* New York: Columbia University Press, 1961.

Gray, Lewis Cecil. *History of Agriculture in the Southern United States to 1860.* Vol. 2. Washington, D.C.: Carnegie Institution, 1933. Reprint. New York: Peter Smith, 1941.

Gray, L. C., and C. F. Clayton. "Introduction." In U.S. Department of Agriculture, *Economic and Social Problems and Conditions of the Southern Appalachians.* U.S. Department of Agriculture Miscellaneous Publication No. 205. Washington, D.C.: Government Printing Office, 1935. Reprint. N.p.: Johnson Reprint, 1970.

Green, Archie. *Only a Miner: Studies in Recorded Coal-Mine Songs.* Urbana: University of Illinois Press, 1972.

Gump, Lucy K. "Half Pints to Horse Shoes: Meeting the Needs of a Growing Eighteenth Century Appalachian Frontier." Paper presented at the Sixteenth Annual Appalachian Studies Conference, March 1993, East Tennessee State University.

Gunther, Gerald. *Cases and Materials on Constitutional Law.* 10th ed. Mineola, N.Y.: Foundation Press, 1980.

Hahn, Steven. "Hunting, Fishing, and Foraging: Common Rights and Class Relations in the Postbellum South." *Radical History Review* 26 (1982): 37–64.

———. *The Roots of Southern Populism: Yeoman Farmers and the Transformation of the Georgia Upcountry, 1850–1890.* New York: Oxford University Press, 1983.

Hall, Jacqueline Dowd. "Disorderly Women: Gender and Labor Militancy in the Appalachian South." *Journal of American History* 73 (1986): 354–82.

Hall, Jacqueline Dowd, et al. *Like a Family: The Making of a Southern Cotton Mill World.* Chapel Hill: University of North Carolina Press, 1987.

Hall, Van Beck. "The Politics of Appalachian Virginia, 1790–1830." In *Appalachian Frontiers: Settlement, Society, and Development in Preindustrial Appalachia,* edited by Robert D. Mitchell. Lexington: University Press of Kentucky, 1991.

Halperin, Rhoda H. *The Livelihood of Kin: Making Ends Meet "The Kentucky Way."* Austin: University of Texas Press, 1990.

Hammond, Bray. *Banks and Politics in America: From the Revolution to the Civil War.* Princeton: Princeton University Press, 1957.

Hartz, Louis. *The Liberal Tradition in America: An Interpretation of American Political Thought Since the Revolution.* New York: Harcourt, Brace, 1955.

Hawley, Ellis W. *The New Deal and the Problem of Monopoly: A Study in Economic Ambivalence.* Princeton: Princeton University Press, 1966.

Hayami, Yujiro, and Vernon W. Ruttan. *Agricultural Development: An International Perspective.* Rev. and expanded ed. Baltimore: Johns Hopkins University Press, 1985.

Heilbroner, Robert L. *The Making of Economic Society.* Englewood Cliffs, N.J.: Prentice-Hall, 1962.

Heinemann, Ronald L. *Depression and New Deal in Virginia: The Enduring Dominion.* Charlottesville: University Press of Virginia, 1983.

Hennen, John. "Benign Betrayal: Capitalist Intervention in Pocahontas County, West Virginia, 1890–1910." *West Virginia History* 50 (1991): 46–62.

Henretta, James A. "Families and Farms: *Mentalité* in Pre-Industrial America." *William and Mary Quarterly,* 3d ser. 35 (1978): 3–32.

Hilliard, Sam Bowers. *Atlas of Antebellum Southern Agriculture.* Baton Rouge: Louisiana State University Press, 1984.

———. *Hog Meat and Hoecake: Food Supply in the Old South, 1840–1860.* Carbondale: Southern Illinois University Press, 1972.

Himmelberg, Robert F. *The Origins of the National Recovery Administration: Business, Government, and the Trade Association Issue.* New York: Fordham University Press, 1976.

Hine, Robert V. *The American West: An Interpretive History.* Boston: Little, Brown, 1973.

Ho, Samuel P. S. *The Economic Development of Taiwan, 1860–1970.* New Haven: Yale University Press, 1978.

Hofstra, Warren S. "Land Policy and Settlement in the Northern Shenandoah Valley." In *Appalachian Frontiers: Settlement, Society, and Development in the Preindustrial Era,* edited by Robert D. Mitchell. Lexington: University Press of Kentucky, 1991.

Hotchkiss, Willard E., et al. *Mechanization, Employment, and Output Per Man in Bituminous-Coal Mining.* 2 vols. in 1. WPA National Research Project, Report No. E-9. Philadelphia, August 1939.

Howell, Benita J. "The New Deal for Tenant Farmers: Government Planning and Indigenous Community Development on the Cumberland Plateau." *Journal of the Appalachian Studies Association* 3 (1991).

Hsich, Chiao-min. *Taiwan—ilha Formosa: A Geography in Perspective.* London: Butterworths, 1964.

Hsiung, David C. "How Isolated Was Appalachia? Upper East Tennessee, 1780–1835." *Appalachian Journal* 16 (1989): 336–49.

———. "Isolation and Integration in Upper East Tennessee, 1780-1960: The Historical Origins of Appalachian Characterizations." Ph.D. diss., University of Michigan, 1991.

Hughes, Jonathan. *American Economic History.* Expanded ed. Glenview, Ill.: Scott, Foresman, 1987.

Hunt, Edward Eyre, ed. *What the Coal Commission Found: An Authoritative Summary by the Staff.* Baltimore: Williams & Wilkins, 1925.

Hunter, Robert F. "The AAA Between Neighbors: Virginia, North Carolina, and the New Deal Program." *Journal of Southern History* 44 (1978): 537–70.

Hutchinson, William K., and Samuel H. Williamson. "The Self- Sufficiency of the Antebellum South: Estimates of the Food Supply." *Journal of Economic History* 31 (1971): 591–612.

Innes, Stephen. "Fulfilling John Smith's Vision: Work and Labor in Early America." In *Work and Labor in Early America,* edited by Stephen Innes. Chapel Hill: University of North Carolina Press, 1988.

————. *Labor in a New Land: Economy and Society in Seventeenth Century Springfield.* Princeton: Princeton University Press, 1983.

Inscoe, John C. *Mountain Masters, Slavery, and the Sectional Crisis in Western North Carolina.* Knoxville: University of Tennessee Press, 1989.

Issawi, Charles. "Middle East Economic Development, 1815–1914: The General and the Specific." In *Studies in the Economic History of the Middle East,* edited by M. A. Cook. London: Oxford University Press, 1970.

Jacobs, Jane. *Cities and the Wealth of Nations: Principles of Economic Life.* New York: Random House, 1984.

James, David R. "Local State Structure and the Transformation of Southern Agriculture." In *Studies in the Transformation of Southern Agriculture,* edited by A. Eugene Havens. Boulder, Colo.: Westview, 1986.

James, John A. *Money and Capital Markets in Postbellum America.* Princeton: Princeton University Press, 1978.

Johnson, Bruce F., and William C. Clark. *Redesigning Rural Development: A Strategic Perspective.* Baltimore: Johns Hopkins University Press, 1982.

Johnson, Charles S., et al. *Statistical Atlas of Southern Counties: Listing and Analysis of Socio-Economic Indices of 1104 Southern Counties.* Chapel Hill: University of North Carolina Press, 1941.

Johnson, Charles S., Edwin R. Embree, and Will W. Alexander. *The Collapse of Cotton Tenancy.* Chapel Hill: University of North Carolina Press, 1935.

Johnson, Hugh. *The Blue Eagle from Egg to Earth.* Garden City, N.Y.: Doubleday, Doran, 1935.

Johnson, James P. *The Politics of Soft Coal.* Urbana: University of Illinois Press, 1979.

Jones, Jacqueline. *The Dispossessed: America's Underclasses from the Civil War to the Present.* New York: Basic Books, 1992.

Jussaume, Raymond Adelard, Jr. *Japanese Part-Time Farming: Evolution and Impacts.* Ames: Iowa State University Press, 1991.

Kada, Rychei. *Part-Time Farming: Off-Farm Employment and Farm Adjustment in the United States and Japan.* Tokyo: Center for Academic Publications Japan, 1980.

Kemp, Tom. *Industrialization in the Non-Western World.* London: Longman, 1983.

King, J. Crawford, Jr. "The Closing of the Southern Range: An Exploratory Study." *Journal of Southern History* 48 (1982): 53–70.

Kirby, Jack Temple. *Rural Worlds Lost: The American South, 1920–1960.* Baton Rouge: Louisiana State University Press, 1987.

Kirkendall, Richard S. *Social Scientists and Farm Politics in the Age of Roosevelt.* Columbia: University of Missouri Press, 1966.

Klarén, Peter F. "Lost Promise: Explaining Latin American Underdevelopment." In *Promise of Development: Theories of Change in Latin America,* edited by Peter F. Klarén and Thomas J. Bossert. Boulder, Colo.: Westview, 1986.

Krooss, Herman E., and Martin R. Blyn. *A History of Financial Intermediaries.* New York: Random House, 1971.

Kump, H. G. *State Papers and Public Addresses.* Charleston, W.Va.: Jarrett Printing, 1937.

Lainhart, W. S., et al. *Pneumoconiosis in Appalachian Bituminous Coal Miners.* Cincinnati: U.S. Public Health Service, 1969.

Lambert, Roger. "Hoover and Congress Debate Food Relief: 1930–1931." *Red River Valley Historical Review* 7, no. 4 (1982): 4–13.

Lears, T. J. Jackson. "The Concept of Cultural Hegemony: Problems and Possibilities." *American Historical Review* 90 (1985): 567–93.

Lee, Teng-hui. *Intersectoral Capital Flows in the Economic Development of Taiwan, 1895–1960.* Ithaca: Cornell University Press, 1971.

Leet, Don R. "Human Fertility and Agricultural Opportunities in Ohio Counties: From Frontier to Maturity, 1810–1860." In *Essays in Nineteenth Century Economic History: The Old Northwest,* edited by David C. Klingaman and Richard K. Vedder. Athens: Ohio University Press, 1975.

Lemon, Anthony. "Migrant Labour and Frontier Commuters: Reorganizing South Africa's Black Labour Supply." In *Living Under Apartheid: Aspects of Urbanization and Social Change in South Africa,* edited by David M. Smith. London: George Allen & Unwin, 1982.

Lemon, James T. "Early Americans and Their Social Environment." *Journal of Historical Geography* 6 (1980): 115–131.

————. "The Weakness of Place and Community in Early Pennsylvania." In *European Settlement and Development in North America,* edited by James R. Gibson. Toronto: University of Toronto Press, 1978.

Lester, Richard A. *Monetary Experiments: Early American and Recent Scandinavian.* Princeton: Princeton University Press, 1939. Reprint. New York: Augustus M. Kelley, 1970.

Levin, Jonathan V. *The Export Economies: Their Pattern of Development in Historical Perspective.* Cambridge: Harvard University Press, 1960.

Lewis, H. G. *Unionism and Relative Wages in the United States: An Empirical Inquiry.* Chicago: University of Chicago Press, 1963.

Lewis, Ronald L. "From Peasant to Proletarian: The Migration of Southern Blacks to the Central Appalachian Coalfields." *Journal of Southern History* 55 (1989): 77–102.

Lewis, W. Arthur. "The Diffusion of Development." In *The Market and the State: Essays in Honour of Adam Smith,* edited by Thomas Wilson and Andrew S. Skinner. Oxford: Clarendon Press, 1976.

———. "Economic Development with Unlimited Supplies of Labour." *Manchester School of Economic and Social Studies* 22, no. 2 (1954): 139–91.

———. *The Evolution of the International Economic Order.* Princeton: Princeton University Press, 1978.

———. "Reflections on Unlimited Labor." In *International Economics and Development: Essays in Honor of Raúl Prebisch,* edited by Luis Eugenio DiMarco. New York: Academic Press, 1972.

Li, K. T. *The Evolution of Policy Behind Taiwan's Development Success.* New Haven: Yale University Press, 1988.

Lincoln, Abraham. *Complete Works of Abraham Lincoln.* Edited by John G. Nicolay and John Hay. Vol. 7. New and enlarged ed. Harrowgate, Tenn.: Lincoln Memorial University, 1894.

Long, Kate. "Barter Economy Serves Cash-Poor Residents Well." *Charleston (W.Va.) Gazette,* 21 Oct. 1989, p. 1.

Love, Joseph L. "Raúl Prebisch and the Origins of the Doctrine of Unequal Exchange." *Latin American Research Review* 15, no. 3 (1980): 45–72.

Lowitt, Richard, ed. *Journal of a Tamed Bureaucrat: Nils A. Olsen and the BAE.* Ames: Iowa State University Press, 1980.

Lozier, John, and Ronald Althouse. "Social Enforcement of Behavior Toward Elders in an Appalachian Mountain Settlement." *Gerontologist* 14 (1974): 69–80.

Maggard, Sally. "From Farmers to Miners: The Decline of Agriculture in Eastern Kentucky." In *Science and Agricultural Development,* edited by Lawrence Busch. Totowa, N.J.: Allanheld, Osmun, 1981.

Mandle, Jay R. *The Plantation Economy: Population and Economic Change in Guyana, 1838–1960.* Philadelphia: Temple University Press, 1973.

Mann, Ralph. "Mountains, Land, and Kin Networks: Burkes Garden, Virginia in the 1840s and 1850s." *Journal of Southern History* 58 (1992): 411–34.

Martin, John Frederick. *Profits in the Wilderness: Entrepreneurship and the Founding of New England Towns in the Seventeenth Century.* Chapel Hill: University of North Carolina Press, 1991.

Martin, Joseph E., Jr., M.D. "Coal Miners' Pneumoconiosis." *American Journal of Public Health* 44 (1954): 581–91.

Martis, Kenneth C. *The Historical Atlas of the United States Congressional Districts, 1789–1983.* New York: Free Press, 1982.

Matthews, Ralph. *The Creation of Regional Dependency.* Toronto: University of Toronton Press, 1983.

McCraw, Thomas K. *Morgan vs. Lilienthal: The Feud within the TVA.* Chicago: Loyola University Press, 1970.

McDonald, Forrest, and Grady McWhiney. "The Antebellum Southern Herdsman: A Reinterpretation." *Journal of Southern History* 41 (1975): 147–66.

———. "The South from Self-Sufficiency to Peonage: An Interpretation." *American Historical Review* 85 (1980): 1095–18.

McKay, John P., Bennett D. Hill, and John Buckner. *A History of World Societies.* Vol. C. 2d ed. Boston: Houghton, Mifflin, 1988.

McKinney, Gordon B. *Southern Mountain Republicans, 1865–1900: Politics and the Appalachian Community.* Chapel Hill: University of North Carolina Press, 1978.

McMaster, Richard K. "The Cattle Trade in Western Virginia, 1760–1830." In *Appalachian Frontiers: Settlement, Society, and Development in the Preindustrial Era,* edited by Robert D. Mitchell. Lexington: University Press of Kentucky, 1991.

Merrens, Harry Roy. *Colonial North Carolina in the Eighteenth Century: A Study in Historical Geography.* Chapel Hill: University of North Carolina Press, 1964.

Merrill, Michael. "A Survey of the Debate over the Nature of Exchange in Early America." Paper presented to the Social Science History Association, 1987.

Mertz, Paul E. *New Deal Policy and Southern Rural Poverty.* Baton Rouge: Louisiana State University Press, 1978.

Minton, Bruce, and John Stuart. *Men Who Lead Labor.* New York: Modern Age Books, 1937.

Mitchell, B. R. *International Historical Statistics: Africa and Asia.* New York: New York University Press, 1982.

Mitchell, Robert D. *Commercialism and Frontier: Perspectives on the Early Shenandoah Valley.* Charlottesville: University Press of Virginia, 1977.

Moore, Tyrel Gilce, Jr. "An Historical Geography of Economic Development in Appalachian Kentucky, 1800–1930: Coal Mining, Agriculture, Regional Development." Ph.D. diss., University of Tennessee, 1984.

Morgan, Arthur E. *The Making of the TVA*. Buffalo, N.Y.: Prometheus Books, 1974.

————. *The Small Community: Foundation of Democratic Life: What It Is and How to Achieve It*. New York: Harper & Brothers, 1942.

Morris, Homer Lawrence. *The Plight of the Bituminous Coal Miner*. Philadelphia: University of Pennsylvania Press, 1934.

Moulton, Harold G. *Income and Economic Progress*. Washington, D.C.: Brookings Institution, 1935.

Mylott, James P. *A Measure of Prosperity: A History of Roane County, West Virginia*. Charleston, W.Va.: Mountain State Press, 1984.

Myrdal, Gunnar. *Rich Lands and Poor: The Road to World Prosperity*. New York: Harper & Row, 1957.

Nakamura, James I. *Agricultural Production and the Economic Development of Japan, 1873–1922*. Princeton: Princeton University Press, 1966.

Nakamura, Takafusa. *Economic Growth in Prewar Japan*. New Haven: Yale University Press, 1971.

Noe, Kenneth William. "Southwest Virginia, the Virginia and Tennessee Railroad, and the Union, 1816–1865." Ph.D. diss., University of Illinois, 1990.

North, Douglass C. *Growth and Welfare in the American Past: A New Economic History*. Englewood Cliffs, N.J.: Prentice-Hall, 1966.

Nourse, Edwin G., Joseph S. Davis, and John D. Black. *Three Years of the Agricultural Adjustment Administration*. Washington, D.C.: Brookings Institution, 1937.

Olsen, Nils A. *See* Lowitt, Richard, ed.

Omvedt, Gail. "Migration in Colonial India." Paper presented at the Seminar on Underdevelopment and Subsistence Reproduction in Southeast Asia, April 1978, University of Bielefeld, Germany.

Osako, Masako M. "Forest Preservation in Tokugawa Japan." In *Global Deforestation and the Nineteenth Century World Economy*, edited by Richard P. Tucker and John F. Richards. Durham, N.C.: Duke University Press, 1983.

Otto, John Solomon. "The Decline of Forest Farming in Southern Appalachia." *Journal of Forest History* 27 (1983): 18–27.

————. "The Migration of Southern Plain Folk: An Interdisciplinary Synthesis." *Journal of Southern History* 51 (1985): 183–200.

Otto, J. S., and N. E. Anderson. "Slash and Burn Agriculture in the Highlands South: A Problem in Comparative Agricultural History." *Comparative Studies in Society and History* 24 (1982): 131–47.

Palladino, Grace. "Nation Building from the Bottom Up: Homefront Strategies in Civil War Pennsylvania." Paper presented at the Southern Historical Association, November 1992, Atlanta.

————. "The Poor Man's Fight: Draft Resistance and Labor Organization in Schuylkill County, Pennsylvania, 1860–1865." Ph.D. diss., University of Pittsburgh, 1983.

Parker, Glen Lawhon. *The Coal Industry: A Study in Social Control.* Washington, D.C.: American Council on Public Affairs, 1940.

Parker, William N. "From Northwest to Midwest: Social Bases of a Regional Economy." In *Essays in Nineteenth Century Economic History: The Old Northwest,* edited by David C. Klingamen and Richard K. Vedder. Athens: Ohio University Press, 1975.

Perkins, Edwin J. "Monetary Policies." In *Encyclopedia of American Political History,* edited by Jack P. Greene. New York: Charles Scribner's Sons, 1984.

Perkins, Van L. *Crisis in Agriculture: The Agricultural Adjustment Administration and the New Deal, 1933.* Berkeley: University of California Press, 1969.

Pillsbury, Richard. "The Europeanization of the Cherokee Settlement Landscape Prior to Removal: A Georgia Case Study." *Geoscience and Man* 23 (29 April 1983): 59–69.

Pohlman, G. G. *Land Classification in West Virginia Based on Use and Agricultural Value.* Booklet. Agricultural Experiment Station, College of Agriculture, West Virginia University, Morgantown, n.d.

Polanyi, Karl. *The Great Transformation.* Boston: Beacon Press, 1957.

Poling, Maggie A., ed. *West Virginia: Economic-Statistical Profile, 1987.* Charleston: West Virginia Chamber of Commerce, 1987.

Potwin, Marjorie A. *Cotton Mill People of the Piedmont: A Study in Social Change.* New York: Columbia University Press, 1927.

Prebisch, Raúl. *The Economic Development of Latin America and its Principal Problems.* Lake Success, N.Y.: United Nations, Department of Economic Affairs, Doc. No. E/CN.12/89/Rev.1, 27 April 1950.

Pruitt, Bettye Hobbs. "Self-Sufficiency and the Agricultural Economy of Eighteenth-Century Massachusetts." *William and Mary Quarterly,* 3d ser. 41 (1984): 333–64.

Pudup, Mary Beth. "The Boundaries of Class in Preindustrial Appalachia." *Journal of Historical Geography* 15 (1989): 139–62.

————. "The Limits of Subsistence: Agriculture and Industry in Central Appalachia." *Agricultural History* 64 (1990): 61–89.

Rankin, John. *Abolitionist: The Life of Rev. John Rankin, written by himself in his 80th year.* Huntington, W.Va.: Appalachian Movement Press, 1978.

Ransom, Roger L., and Sutch, Richard. "Debt Peonage in the Cotton South After the Civil War." *Journal of Economic History* 32 (1972): 641–69.

————. *One Kind of Freedom: The Economic Consequences of Emancipation.* Cambridge: Cambridge University Press, 1977.

Rasmussen, Barbara. "The Absentee Legacy in Virginia's West, 1781–1915." Ph.D. diss., West Virginia University, 1992.

———. "Monroe County, W. Va.: Life and Work Where There Is No Coal." Paper presented at the Twelfth Annual Appalachian Studies Conference, March 1989, West Virginia University.

Rice, Otis K. *The Allegheny Frontier: West Virginia Beginnings, 1730–1830*. Lexington: University Press of Kentucky, 1970.

———. *West Virginia: A History*. Lexington: University Press of Kentucky, 1985.

Richards, Edward C.M. "The Future of TVA Forestry." *Journal of Forestry* 36 (1938): 643-52.

Rochester, Anna. *Labor and Coal*. New York: International Publishers, 1931.

———. *Why Farmers Are Poor: The Agricultural Crisis in the United States*. New York: International Publishers, 1940.

Rockoff, Hugh. "The Free Banking Era: A Reexamination." *Journal of Money, Credit, and Banking* 4 (1974): 141-67.

———. *The Free Banking Era: A Re-Examination*. New York: Arno Press, 1975.

Roemer, John. "Should Marxists Be Interested in Exploitation?" In *Analytical Marxism*, edited by John Roemer. Cambridge: Cambridge University Press, 1986.

Rogerston, Christian M. "Apartheid, Decentralization and Spatial Industrial Change." In *Living Under Apartheid: Aspects of Urbanization and Social Change in South Africa*, edited by David M. Smith. London: George Allen & Unwin, 1982.

Rohrbough, Malcolm J. *The Land Office Business: The Settlement and Administration of American Public Lands, 1789–1837*. New York: Oxford University Press, 1968.

Roose, Kenneth D. *The Economics of Recession and Revival: An Interpretation of 1937–1938*. New Haven: Yale University Press, 1954.

Rostow, W. W. *The Stages of Economic Growth: A Non-Communist Manifesto*. Cambridge: Cambridge University Press, 1961.

Roth, Randolph A. *The Democratic Dilemma: Religion, Reform, and the Social Order in the Connecticut River Valley of Vermont, 1791–1850*. Cambridge: Cambridge University Press, 1987.

Rothenberg, Winifred Barr. "Markets and Massachusetts Farmers: A Paradigm of Economic Growth in Rural New England, 1750–1855." Ph.D. diss., Brandeis University, 1984.

Rowe, Harold B. *Tobacco Under the AAA*. Washington, D.C.: Brookings Institution, 1935.

Russell, Robert M. "The Regulation and Supervision of Banking in West Virginia." Master's thesis, Marshall University, 1965.

Ruttan, Vernon W. "The TVA and Regional Development." In *TVA: Fifty Years of Grassroots Bureaucracy,* edited by Edwin C. Hargrove and Paul K. Conkin. Urbana: University of Illinois Press, 1983.

Salstrom, Paul. "Subsistence Farming, Capitalism, and the Depression in West Virginia." *Appalachian Journal* 11 (1984): 384–94.

Sauer, Carl. "Homestead and Community on the Middle Border." In *Carl Sauer, Land and Labor.* Berkeley and Los Angeles: University of California Press, 1969.

Schrecker, John E. *The Chinese Revolution in Historical Perspective.* New York: Praeger, 1991.

Schwarzweller, Harry K., James S. Brown, and J. J. Mangalam. *Mountain Families in Transition: A Case Study of Appalachian Migration.* University Park: Pennsylvania State University Press, 1971.

Scott, James C. *The Moral Economy of the Peasant: Rebellion and Subsistence in Southeast Asia.* New Haven: Yale University Press, 1976.

Selznick, Philip. *TVA and the Grass Roots: A Study in the Sociology of Formal Organization.* Paperback ed. New York: Harper & Row, 1966.

Semple, Ellen Campbell. "The Anglo-Saxons of the Kentucky Mountains: A Study in Anthropogeography." *Geographical Journal* 17 (1901): 588–623.

Shackelford, Laurel, and Bill Weinberg, eds. *Our Appalachia.* New York: Hill and Wang, 1977.

Shannon, Fred A. "The Homestead Act and the Labor Surplus." *American Historical Review* 41 (1936): 637–51.

Sharkey, Robert P. "Commercial Banking." In *Economic Change in the Civil War Era,* edited by David T. Gilchrist and W. David Lewis. Greenville, Del.: Eleutherian Mills and Hagley Foundation, 1965.

Sharp, James Roger. *The Jacksonians versus the Banks: Politics after the Panic of 1837.* New York: Columbia University Press, 1970.

Shaw, Albert. "The Progress of the World." *Review of Reviews* (New York) 92, no. 4 (October 1935): 11–18.

Shen, T. H., ed. *Agriculture's Place in the Strategy of Development: The Taiwan Experience.* Taipei: Joint Commission on Rural Reconstruction, July 1974.

Shifflett, Crandall A. *Coal Towns: Life, Work, and Culture in Company Towns of Southern Appalachia, 1880–1960.* Knoxville; University of Tennessee Press, 1991.

Silver, Timothy H. "Vanishing Indians, Vanishing Animals: Trade and Ecology in the English Colonial Southeast." Paper presented at the Conference on Forests, Habitats, and Resources, May 1987, Duke University.

Simon, Richard Mark. "The Development of Underdevelopment: The Coal Industry and Its Effect on the West Virginia Economy, 1880–1930." Ph.D. diss., University of Pittsburgh, 1978.

Smith, J. Russell. "Farming Appalachia." *American Review of Reviews* 53 (1916): 329–36.

———. *North America*. New York: Harcourt, Brace, 1925.

———. *Tree Crops: A Permanent Agriculture*. New York: Harcourt, Brace, 1929.

Smith, J. Russell, and M. Ogden Phillips. *North America*. New York: Harcourt, Brace, 1942.

Smith, Thomas C. *The Agrarian Origins of Modern Japan*. Stanford: Stanford University Press, 1959.

———. *Nakahara: Family Farming and Population in a Japanese Village*. Stanford: Stanford University Press, 1977.

Sperling, James C. "West German Foreign Economic Policy during the Reagan Administration." *German Studies Review* 12 (1990): 85–109.

The Statutes at Large, Treaties, and Proclamations of the United States of America: From December 1863 to December 1865. Boston: Little, Brown, 1866.

Stealey, John Edmund, III. "Notes on the Ante-Bellum Cattle Industry from the McNeill Family Papers." *Ohio History* 75 (Winter 1966): 38–47, with notes at 70–72.

Stephenson, John B. *Shiloh: A Mountain Community*. Lexington: University of Kentucky Press, 1968.

Studenski, Paul, and Herman E. Krooss. *Financial History of the United States*. 2d ed. New York: McGraw-Hill, 1963.

Summers, George W. *The Mountain State: A Description of the Natural Resources of West Virginia*. Charleston, W.Va.: Moses W. Donnally, 1893.

Swain, G. T. *History of Logan County, West Virginia*. Logan: G. T. Swain, 1927.

Sydnor, Charles S. *The Development of Southern Sectionalism, 1819–1848*. Baton Rouge: Louisiana State University Press, 1948.

Sylla, Richard. "American Banking and Growth in the Nineteenth Century: A Partial View of the Terrain." *Explorations in Economic History* 9 (1971–72): 197–227.

———. "The United States, 1863–1913." In *Banking and Economic Development: Some Lessons of History*, edited by Rondo Cameron. New York: Oxford University Press, 1972.

Taiwan Statistical Data Book, 1987. Taipei: Republic of China, Council for Economic Planning and Development, June 1987.

Taylor, John Craft. "Depression and New Deal in Pendleton: A History of a West Virginia County from the Great Crash to Pearl Harbor." Ph.D. diss., Pennsylvania State University, 1980.

Thorndale, William, and William Dollarhide. *Map Guide to the U.S. Federal Censuses, 1790–1920*. Baltimore: Genealogical Publishing, 1987.

Thorp, Daniel B. "Doing Business in the Backcountry: Retail Trade in Colonial Rowan County, North Carolina." *William and Mary Quarterly,* 3d ser. 48 (1991): 387–408.

Tindall, George B., and David E. Shi. *America: A Narrative History.* Brief 2d ed. New York: Norton, 1989.

Tippett, Tom. *When Southern Labor Stirs.* New York: Jonathan Cape and Harrison Smith, 1931.

Trotter, Joe William, Jr. *Coal, Class, and Color: Blacks in Southern West Virginia, 1915–32.* Urbana: University of Illinois Press, 1990.

Tugwell, Rexford G. *Roosevelt's Revolution: The First Year—A Personal Perspective.* New York : Macmillan, 1977.

Turner, Frederick Jackson. *The Frontier in American History.* New York: Henry Holt, 1920.

―――. *The Significance of Sections in American History.* New York: Henry Holt, 1932. Reprint. New York: Peter Smith, 1950.

United States. Dept. of Agriculture. *Agricultural Statistics, 1936.* Washington, D.C.: Government Printing Office, 1936.

―――. Dept. of Agriculture. *Economic and Social Problems and Conditions of the Southern Appalachians.* Miscellaneous Publication No. 205. Washington, D.C.: Government Printing Office, 1935. Reprint. Johnson Reprint, 1970.

―――. Dept. of Agriculture. Agricultural Adjustment Administration. Program Planning Division. *Regional Problems in Agricultural Adjustment.* Washington, D.C.: Government Printing Office, March 1935.

―――. Dept. of Agriculture. *Yearbook of Agriculture, 1935.* Washington, D.C.: Government Printing Office, 1935.

―――. Dept. of Commerce. Bureau of Economic Analysis. Regional Economic Information System. Data series released April 1992.

―――. Dept. of Commerce. Bureau of the Census. Censuses of the United States. 1790–1982.

―――. Dept. of Commerce. Bureau of the Census. *Historical Statistics of the United States: Colonial Times to 1970.* Bicentennial ed. 2 pts. Washington, D.C.: Government Printing Office, 1975.

―――. Dept. of the Interior. Coal Mines Administration. *A Medical Survey of the Bituminous-Coal Industry.* Washington, D.C.: Government Printing Office, 1947.

Vance, Rupert B. "The Region: A New Survey." In *The Southern Appalachian Region: A Survey,* edited by Thomas R. Ford. Lexington: University of Kentucky Press, 1962.

Van Goethem, Pierre. *The Americanization of World Business: Wall Street and Superiority of American Business.* New York: Herder and Herder, 1972.

Van Zwanenberg, R. M. A. *Colonial Capitalism and Labour in Kenya, 1919–1939.* Nairobi: East African Literature Bureau, 1975.

Vickers, Daniel. "Competency and Competition: Economic Culture in Early America." *William and Mary Quarterly,* 3d ser. 47 (1990): 3–29.

Voskuil, Walter H. *Minerals in Modern Industry.* 1930. Reprint. Port Washington, N.Y.: Kennikat Press, 1970.

Waller, Altina L. "Family Origins of the Hatfield-McCoy Feudists." Paper presented at the Conference on the Appalachian Frontier, May 1985, James Madison University.

————. *Feud: Hatfields, McCoys, and Social Change in Appalachia, 1860–1900.* Chapel Hill: University of North Carolina Press, 1988.

Walls, David Stuart. "Central Appalachia in Advanced Capitalism: Its Coal Industry Structure and Coal Operator Associations." Ph.D. diss., University of Kentucky, 1978.

Warren, Charles. *Bankruptcy in United States History.* Cambridge: Harvard University Press, 1935.

Weiman, David F. "Families, Farms and Rural Society in Preindustrial America." *Research in Economic History,* supp. 5, pt. B (1989): 255–77.

Weingartner, Paul J. "Limits to Subsistence Agriculture: Farming in Beech Creek, 1850–1880." Paper presented at the Twelfth Annual Appalachian Studies Conference, March 1989, West Virginia University.

Weinstein, Michael M. *Recovery and Redistribution Under the N.I.R.A.* Amsterdam: North-Holland, 1980.

————. "Some Macroeconomic Impacts of the National Industrial Recovery Act, 1933–1935." In *The Great Depression Revisited,* edited by Karl Brunner. The Hague: Martinus Nijhoff, 1981.

Weller, Jack E. *Yesterday's People: Life in Contemporary Appalachia.* Lexington: University of Kentucky Press, 1965.

West Virginia, State of. "Annual Reports of the State Inspectors of Mines in the First and Second Districts of the State of West Virginia, for the Year Ending June 30, 1891." In *Messages and Accompanying Documents, West Virginia Governor, 1893.* Charleston, W.Va.: Moses W. Donnally, 1893.

————. Department of Agriculture. *Biennial Reports.* 1917–1918 and 1919–1920.

————. Department of Agriculture. *Market Bulletin* 74, no. 2 (February 1990).

————. Department of Mines. *Annual Reports.* 1901–1902, 1917–1918, 1918–1919, and 1919–1920.

————. "First Report of the State Bank Examiner of the State of West Virginia, for the Year Ending September 30, 1891." In *Biennial Report of the*

Auditor of the State of West Virginia for the Years 1891 and 1892. Charleston, W.Va.: Moses W. Donnally, 1893.

——. *Second Annual Report of the Commissioner of Banking, State of West Virginia, 1902.* Charleston, W.Va.: Tribune, 1902.

——. State Geological Survey. "Natural Resources of West Virginia." 1987. Map.

Whisnant, David E. *Modernizing the Mountaineer: People, Power, and Planning in Appalachia.* New York: Burt Franklin, 1980.

White, Benjamin. "Demand for Labor and Population Growth in Colonial Java." *Human Ecology* 1 (1973): 217–36.

White, Philip L. *Beekmantown, New York: Forest Frontier to Farm Community.* Austin: University of Texas Press, 1970.

White, Richard. *The Roots of Dependency: Subsistence, Environment, and Social Change Among the Choctaws, Pawnees, and Navajos.* Lincoln: University of Nebraska Press, 1983.

White, Stephen E. "America's Soweto: Population Redistribution in Appalachian Kentucky, 1940–1986." *Appalachian Journal* 16 (1989): 350–60.

Wilhelm, Gene, Jr. "Animal Drives: A Case Study in Historical Geography." *Journal of Geography* 66 (1967): 327–34.

Wilkinson, Richard G. *Poverty and Progress: An Ecological Perspective on Economic Development.* New York: Praeger, 1973.

Williams, H. David. "Gold Fever: The Gold Rush in Georgia." Paper presented at the Thirteenth Annual Appalachian Studies Conference, March 1990, Helen, Georgia.

Williams, John Alexander. *West Virginia: A Bicentennial History.* New York: W. W. Norton, 1976. (Reprinted in 1984 as *West Virginia: A History* with unchanged pagination.)

——. *West Virginia and the Captains of Industry.* Morgantown: West Virginia University Library, 1976.

Williams, William Appleman. *The Roots of the Modern American Empire.* New York: Random House, 1969.

Willis, Henry Parker. *The Theory and Practice of Central Banking—With Special Reference to the American Experience.* New York: Harper & Brothers, 1936.

Woodruff, Nan Elizabeth. *As Rare as Rain: Federal Relief in the Great Southern Drought of 1930–31.* Urbana: University of Illinois Press, 1985.

Woodside, Jane Harris. "Creating the Path as You Go: John Gaventa and Highlander." *Now and Then* 17, no. 3 (Fall 1990): 17–21.

Wright, Gavin. *Old South, New South: Revolutions in the Southern Economy Since the Civil War.* New York: Basic Books, 1986.

Index